The Unbelievable Power of Suggestion

The Unbelievable Power of Suggestion

Dr. Joseph Murphy

Copyright © 2009 by Dr. Joseph Murphy.

ISBN: Hardcover 978-1-4500-0422-0
       Softcover 978-1-4500-0421-3

All rights reserved. No part of this book may be reproduced or transmitted in any form or by any means, electronic or mechanical, including photocopying, recording, or by any information storage and retrieval system, without permission in writing from the copyright owner.

Edited by: Dr. Herminia Boyer
Cover Design and Photography by: International Designer, W. Patrick Brooks
Authorized by: The Jean L. Murphy Revocable Trust
3156 Toopal Drive
Oceanside, California 92058-7490

This book was printed in the United States of America.

To order additional copies of this book, contact:
Xlibris Corporation
1-888-795-4274
www.Xlibris.com
Orders@Xlibris.com

Contents

Chapter 1	Rise, Take Up Thy Bed, and Walk	7
Chapter 2	Suggestions for the Jealous Heart	12
Chapter 3	Your Subconscious Mind is Amenable to Suggestion	20
Chapter 4	Your Emotions are a Subject to Suggestions and Commands	33
Chapter 5	Suggestions for Some Simple Facts of Life	43
Chapter 6	The Wonderful Will of God	53
Chapter 7	Life Plays No Favorites	62
Chapter 8	You Have the Power to Control Suggestions	68
Chapter 9	Man's Greatest Enemy and The Power of Suggestion	72
Chapter 10	Suggested Ways to Get Results	85
Chapter 11	The Power is in You and Not in Others	102
Chapter 12	Suggestions for Wealth and Prosperity	107
Chapter 13	Affirmation is a Form of Suggestion	112
Chapter 14	Suggested Prayer Techniques to Achieve Your Goals in Life	127
Chapter 15	The Suggested Way is Spiritual	141
Chapter 16	Auto Suggestion and the Wonders of Sleep	156
Chapter 17	Suggesting a Quiet Mind to Achieve the Right Decisions	169
Chapter 18	Suggestions For Harmonious Relationships	178
Chapter 19	The Law of Life is the Law of Belief	185
Chapter 20	The Power of Suggestion to Success	190
Chapter 21	The Power of Suggestion Towards Wholeness	202
Chapter 22	How Dominant Suggestions Control Lesser Thoughts	211
Chapter 23	Experience Good Fortune and Peace of Mind Through The Power Of Suggestion	217

Chapter 1

RISE, TAKE UP THY BED, AND WALK

"After this there was a feast of the Jews; and Jesus went out to Jerusalem.

"Now there is at Jerusalem by the sheep market a pool, which is called in the Hebrew tongue Bethesda, having five porches.

"In these lay a great multitude of impotent folk, of blind, halt, withered, waiting for the moving of the water.

"For an angel went down at a certain season into the pool, and troubled the water; whosoever then first after the troubling of the water stepped in was made whole of whatsoever disease he had.

"And a certain man was there, which had an infirmity thirty and eight years.

"When Jesus saw him lie, and knew that he had been now a long time in that case, he saith unto him, Wilt thou be made whole?

"The impotent man answered him, Sir, I have no man, when the water is troubled, to put me into the pool: but while I am coming, another stepped down before me.

"Jesus saith unto him, Rise, take up thy bed, and walk.

"And immediately the man was made whole, and took up his bed, and walked: and on the same day was the Sabbath."

John 5:1-9

The pool with the five porches represents your own mind and your five senses. The blind, halt, withered, and lame represent the ideals, dreams, and aspirations of your heart which lie frozen in the bed of your mind due to negative race mind suggestions which you have accepted consciously and unconsciously.

The angel which troubles the water is your desire for health, guidance, true place, and accomplishment. As long as you have the desire, your mind is troubled; and the moment you realize your desire, your mind is one piece or made whole.

"Whosoever then first after the troubling of the water stepped in was made whole of whatsoever disease he had."?

The account says that Jesus asked the man, who had an infirmity for thirty and eight years, "Wilt thou be made whole?" He answered by saying, "I have no man, when the water is troubled, . . . but while I am coming another stepped down before me."

In other words, this man was giving power to others and establishing all kinds of alibis and excuses. He probably was blaming the weather, the past, conditions, circumstances, heredity, etc. He was giving priority to externals rather than the Healing Power of God which is omnipotent.

He had a multitude of impotent folk in his mind, such as false imagery, thoughts of incurability, and false concepts of God and His love.

The blind, the halt, the withered, and the lame represent the idiotic and barbaric beliefs of some that you must suffer, that God is punishing you, that sickness is visited upon you by an angry God. One of these impotent ideas creeps into the healing pool of the omnipresent God before you.

Jesus said, "Rise, take up thy bed and walk." In other words, cease lying down in the bed of your mind and listening to all these false suggestions about other powers. Take up the power of God in your mind, and call upon His Healing Presence, and the Holy Spirit of God will flow through you vitalizing, energizing, and transforming you, making you every whit whole.

Dr. Evelyn Fleet, Director of the Psychological Truth Forum in London, and an associate there of the author, told me about a friend of hers who had been crippled with arthritis for many years. He had taken all kinds of drugs and received the best forms of medical therapy without results. Dr. Fleet said that this man got up in his club in London one evening and demonstrated to all the men there how he could flex his fingers, bend his legs, and do all the things he could not do when he was immobilized with arthritis, due to the fact that joints were full of calcareous deposits resulting in the deformity of his hands and legs.

His story went somewhat like this: After many years of therapy, in desperation he said to his doctor on Harley Street: "Can't something be done," I must be healed!"

His doctor said, "Yes, if you get all that bitterness, ill will, and hostility out of your soul, I believe you can be healed."

This was the turning point in his life. Suddenly he had an intense desire to get well and came to a decision in his mind to cleanse his mind once and for all. He realized that he had been holding on to some old grudges and pet peeves and that he had been seething with resentment and vindictiveness toward a number of people. Moreover, he had been condemning himself for years because at some time previously he had embezzled a large sum of money from a relative of his for whom he worked. He had never made amends, and he felt that he was being punished for this "sin," as he called it. He said that his physical disorder undoubtedly was coming to him, that he deserved it, and that God was punishing him.

He came to Dr. Fleet, and she told him that Jesus said to the man sick with palsy: *"Son, be of good cheer; thy sins be forgiven thee."* (Matthew 9:2) *"For whether it is easier to say, Thy sins be forgiven thee; or to stay, Arise, and walk?"* (Matthew 9:5) Dr. Fleet told her friend that he should forgive himself and make amends to his relative. He restored the money by sending it anonymously and felt a tremendous sense of relief. At her suggestion, he made a list of all those men and women whom he hated and resented and began to bombard each one several times daily with loving, kind, harmonious thoughts. He forgave himself for harboring all these negative and vengeful thoughts for many years. He filled his mind daily with the thoughts of the 23rd Psalm and 91st Psalm, and he affirmed constantly, "God's love cleanses my mind and heart, and I am made whole."

Dr. Fleet introduced me to this man in early August of 1963; he was vital, strong, alert, and full of life and love.

He believed that he had the right to be well. As long as he believed he should be punished, he held on to his crippled condition. When he realized all he had to do was to forgive himself, forgive others, and make amends where possible, and believe in his right to perfect health, his subconscious mind responded. This man saw the mighty benefits in health, peace of mind, and vitality in forgiveness of himself and others. *"Thy sins are forgiven thee; Arise and walk."* (Matthew 9:5)

In February 1963, I spoke before a group of businessmen in Hong Kong, and one of the men present told me all the reasons why he could not be healed of his condition. He had all kinds of alibis and excuses. He was blaming the weather, the past, conditions, circumstances, heredity, and other things. He was giving priority to externals rather than to the Infinite Healing Presence within him. His friends told him that he would never be healed, that God was punishing him, that he had offended God, and that he should resign himself to his condition.

He had an ulcerated leg for five or six years which caused excruciating pain and lameness, necessitating the use of crutches from time to time. It would heal for a while and then break out again. He said his father had the same thing and that he supposed it was hereditary. He said that he had resigned himself to it.

I explained to him the meaning of the following biblical quotation: *"Rise, take up thy bed, and walk."* (John 5:8) In other words, cease lying down in the bed of your mind and listening to all these false suggestions about other powers. Take up the power of God in your mind and call upon His Healing Presence, and the Healing Presence will flow through you vitalizing, energizing, and transforming you, making you whole.

This man stopped fearing and expecting a relapse. For about five or ten minutes in the morning and evening he affirmed with deep understanding: "I have a Silent Partner, a Healing Presence which knows how to heal, and His Healing Presence is bringing about the beauty of wholeness now. I believe now that my Silent Partner is saturating my whole being with its love, beauty, and perfection."

This slight alteration in his approach led him out of lameness and pain into radiant health. I received a letter from him in June 1963, in which he stated that he had burned up his crutches, and he walks the earth a free man and a happy man. He decided to rise and walk through the power of God.

Take Up Your Bed and Walk Triumphantly

All the qualities and powers of God are within you. Rise, take up your bed and walk means to take up the truth of God and walk free in the light and glory of God. Walk like the polio victim in a new vision. A new place in your mind. Your body will follow your mental vision or image. You go where your vision is. Your vision, when sustained by faith and intensively repeated, will be objectified on the screen of space. You must constantly watch over the patterns presented to your conscious mind. If you are negligent, indolent, lazy, and apathetic, you will allow the thoughts and imagery of the race mind to enter in, and your mind will become contaminated with the distorted morbid pictures of the world mass mind.

The race mind believes in limitation, disaster, misfortune, accident, death, and disease as independent of the mind of man. Thus, the necessity for prayer, for having regular communion with God, and for filling your mind with the eternal verities and truths of God which change not. Thereby, counter-convictions are established against all the false beliefs of the race mind.

You are a child of God and destined some day to be what God intended you to be-a happy man, a joyous man, a peaceful man who enters, as Paul says, into the glorious liberty of the sons of God. All the power and wisdom of God are in you, enabling you to rise over all problems and endowing you with complete mastery over your own life. Your life is God's life, and your mind is God's mind. This is why you are eternal and will live forever. You, together with all men, will some day awaken to the transcendent glory of your God-Self, and you will see yourself as God sees you now—the perfect man.

Clothe yourself mentally with majesty and might and realize your oneness with God. Imagine your health, happiness, and freedom. Walk in the light of God, knowing He is a lamp unto your feet at all times. Become an open channel through which God plays these truths on your heart strings.

"Son, thou art ever with me, and all that I have is thine." (Luke 15:31)

Chapter 2

SUGGESTIONS FOR THE JEALOUS HEART

For jealousy is the rage of a man: therefore he will not spare in the day of vengeance (Proverbs 6:34).

Set me as a seal upon thine heart, as a seal upon thine arm: for love is strong as death; jealousy is cruel as the grave: the coals thereof are coals of fire, which hath a most vehement flame (Song of Solomon 8:6).

"*Trifles light as air, are to the jealous confirmation strong as proof of holy writ*" (Shakespeare).

"*Jealousy sees things always with magnifying glasses which make little things large, of dwarfs giants, of suspicions truths*" (Cervantes).

"*Jealousy is the injured lover's hell*" (Milton).

"*The jealous man poisons his own banquet and then eats it.*

"*Oh, beware of jealousy; it is the green-eyed monster, which doth mock the meat it feeds on*" (Shakespeare).

"Jealousy," says Rochefoucauld, "is in some sort rational and just; it aims at the preservation of a good which we think belongs to us." It is in this sense that God is said to be a jealous God, because he is earnestly and, as it were, passionately desirous of our supreme love, reverence and service.

In our modern, everyday language, we speak of a jealous person as one who feels resentment against another because of his success, worldly achievements or monetary advantages. A jealous person is inclined to be troubled by suspicions or fears of rivalry, unfaithfulness, etc., as in love or aims.

The Bible, in Exodus 20:5, says: . . . *For I the Lord thy God am a jealous God* . . . This means that you must recognize the Living Spirit Almighty as supreme and omnipotent and refuse to give power to any created thing. In other words, you should not worship a created thing; you must give all allegiance, loyalty and devotion to the One Presence and Power within you, called I AM, or Spirit.

For example, if you are looking for promotion or advancement and you say to yourself: "The boss is blocking my good; but for him I would be promoted and receive greater emoluments," at that moment you have exalted him, a false god. Actually, you are making the boss a god and denying the One Source from whom all blessings flow. Your subconscious mind knows that your loyalty is divided and consequently does not respond.

You are like the double-minded man, unstable in all your ways. On the one hand he is affirming that God is the Source of his supply, meeting all his needs, and then in the next breath he is resenting his employer for not promoting him and increasing his salary. You must never give power to any person, place or thing, for actually you are transferring the power within you to externals. You must give exclusive devotion and loyalty to the One Power within you, which responds according to the nature of your thoughts and belief.

Forgive Yourself for Harboring Negative and Jealous Thoughts

A man who had ulcers refused to take any medication from his doctor. His faith was in Vitamin C; but he had ulcerated thoughts of jealousy and resentment toward a partner. He was also envious and resentful of his wife, who was making more money than he was.

I explained to him that his faith and confidence should be in the One Supreme Power—the Source of all life. Food is important, vitamins are important, but not preeminently so. You don't put food, diet or vitamins before the Infinite Healing Presence—the only Healing Power there is.

His healing prayer was: "I forgive myself for harboring negative, jealous thoughts, and I radiate love, peace and goodwill to my wife and partner. God's healing love saturates my whole being. God's river of peace saturates my mind and heart. Whenever a jealous or envious thought comes to me, I will affirm: 'God's love fills my soul.'"

He practiced this discipline, and in a few weeks' time his ulcers disappeared. He realized that ulcerated thoughts of jealousy, envy, ill will and fear caused his ulcers. By reversing the process, and by contemplating harmony, love, wholeness, goodwill and peace, a healing took place. He had to give recognition to the Creator alone, and not to His manifestations. Always look to the Primary Cause, the Source of life itself, not the secondary cause. A doctor can prescribe a good diet for you, but then realize that whatever you eat or drink is transmuted into beauty, order, symmetry and proportion.

He Had Been the Victim of Hypnotic Suggestion

A fledgling writer had his manuscript rejected by six organizations, and he said to me that a reader told him the reason was due to a malefic configuration of Saturn and other planets in his chart. I said to him that he would be far better off if he had never heard of Saturn.

God is immutable law, and whatever we impress on our subconscious mind is expressed on the screen of space. He began to understand that he had been the victim of hypnotic suggestion which he accepted. He was giving power to a planet instead of to the God Who made it as well as the whole universe. There is only One Being, One Power; and a spiritual minded thinker does not give power to the phenomenalistic world. He gives all allegiance and worship to the One Power. *I am the Lord, that is my name and my glory will I not give to another, neither my praise to graven images* (Isaiah 42:8).

I read his manuscript. It was very good, and his writing was worthy of acceptance and approval. I suggested that he get in touch with the president of a book publishing company, a friend of the author, and I added: "I'm sure he will see the value of it."

I suggested that he pray as follows: "Infinite Intelligence opens up the perfect way for the acceptance, manufacture and sale of my manuscript; and this man I am going to see is God's man. The Spirit in me speaks to the Spirit in him, and there are harmony, peace and understanding between us. I release the manuscript to him, and it is God in action, which is all around harmony and peace."

The president of the publishing company accepted his manuscript. This man predicated his success upon remembrance of the One Power and not on the created thing. He realized he was not a victim of a malefic configuration of planets in the sky, but that he was a victim of a negative suggestion. The planets have no power, but if you believe they have power over you, it is done unto you as you believe. The law of life is the law of belief . . . *As thou hast believed, so be it done unto thee* . . . (Matthew 8:13).

There is a mass mind or race mind belief that a person born under a certain sign will have certain characteristics, proclivities and talents. It isn't because a man is born under the sign of Taurus that he has certain traits and tendencies; but, rather, it is the mass mind belief about that date or season of the year.

God indwells every person, and any person can contact the Divine Presence within and transform his life. You mould and fashion your own destiny, and it is written: . . . *Whatsoever a man soweth, that shall he also reap* (Galatians 6:7). *For as he thinketh in his heart, so is he* . . . (Proverbs 23:7).

Your thought and feeling represent the Father within, which doeth the works. Your heart in the Bible represents your subconscious mind; and whatever you impregnate in your subconscious comes forth as expression, condition and event. Phineas Parkhurst Quimby in 1847 said, "Man is belief expressed."

What do you believe? Your habitual thinking, or your regular train of thoughts will cause you to arrive, like a train, at a certain destination.

Programming Your Subconscious Mind

Today we read a lot about programming of computers. The computer responds according to whatever is fed into it. When you were young, there is the possibility that you were told a great number of things which were false. Perhaps one of your parents said to you: "Your brother is much smarter than you. Why don't you be like him? He is an angel." This probably gave rise to jealousy and competition as well as resentment.

You were born with only two fears: fear of falling and fear of noise. These represent nature's protective mechanism. Quimby said that every child is like a white tablet upon which everyone who comes along scribbles something. Modern day educators term this a tabula rasa, or blank tablet. Remember, you were born with the Infinite Spirit, or God, within you—the very life of you.

Always ask yourself this simple question: "What did I inherit from God?" If your subconscious has been programmed negatively, you can reverse it by filling your subconscious with life-giving patterns, such as: "God's love fills my soul. God's peace saturates my whole being. The harmony, light, and glory of the Infinite saturate my whole being, and I am illumined from On High."

Do this regularly at least three or four times a day. When a negative thought comes to you, chop off its head by affirming: "Divine love fills my soul." Prayer is a habit, but it is a very good habit. Suppose you have been trained in the wrong way to play the piano or drive a car. You can, by practice, unlearn the old way and play or drive the right way. Many dogs in the First and Second World Wars were trained to kill, but after the war they were retrained to become lovers of mankind again.

Suggested Mantras

Many men and women, at my suggestion, use this mantra every morning for about 15 minutes and also at night for about 15 minutes. They close their eyes, relax on a coach, and talk to their bodies as follows: "My toes are relaxed, my feet are relaxed, my ankles are relaxed, the cables of my legs are relaxed, my knees and thighs are relaxed, my abdominal muscles are relaxed, my hands and arms are relaxed, my neck is relaxed, my brain is relaxed, and I am at peace

After relaxing their bodies in the above manner, they silently whisper to themselves for about 15 minutes: "God's love fills my soul." They repeat this over and over again like a lullaby in the morning and for about 15 minutes prior to sleep. They have told me that it is a wonderful way to recharge their mental and spiritual batteries. They accomplish more. Many have told me that their blood pressure became normal; they experienced far less tension during the day. Their health improved, jealousy and envy disappeared, and they became more affable, amiable, cordial and genial. The simple mantra, "God's love fills my soul," has worked wonders in their lives.

He that loved not knoweth not God; for God is love (I John 4:8). The practice of this mantra dissolves all jealousy and envy.

Another Wonderful Mantra

Many use this wonderful, healing and vitalizing mantra: "God's peace fills my soul." They use it the same way as the preceding one, 15 minutes morning and evening prior to sleep. They sleep in peace and wake in joy. Moreover, they find peace in their home, office, and in their relations with others. They also find peace in their pocket books, because when you tune in with the God of peace within you, all things are added to you.

Thou wilt keeps him in perfect peace, whose mind is stayed on thee: because he trusted in thee (Isaiah 26:3). Peace *I leave with you, my peace I give unto you . . .* (John 14:27). *For God is not the author of confusion, but of peace, as in all churches of the saints* (I Corinthians 14:33). *Let the peace of God rule in your hearts . . . .* (Colossians 3:15).

The practice of the above mantra, "God's peace fills my soul," brings peace into your home, your heart, your business and all phases of your life. The ancients said that peace is the power at the heart of God. When you are presented with any difficulty, challenge or problem, during the day, silently affirm, "God's peace fills my soul." You will be amazed how quickly the solution or the creative idea will present itself, which reveals the answer. New, original, creative ideas will come to you during each day, and you will find yourself vivified, recharged and God intoxicated.

The above-mentioned mantra is the Divine antibody. The habitual use of this mantra does away with all resentment, hostility, anger, etc. Equanimity, serenity and tranquility become a living part of you, as the apple becomes a part of your blood stream.

He Said, "I am Not Jealous"

Your emotions govern you. Emotion follows thought. You can't visualize an emotion, but you can look back at an old scene, an old lawsuit or some old hurt and grievance and imagine the particular scene again. Of course, you will generate a destructive emotion and reinfecting yourself all over again. When the old hurt comes to your mind, practice the law of substitution and affirm: "God's peace fills my soul." You will neutralize it immediately. Your emotions are compulsive.

A man said to me, "I'm not jealous. I don't have a jealous bone in my body." But actually the opposite was true. He had employed detectives, checking up every day on his fiancée. She discovered it and broke off the engagement and would have nothing more to do with him. Oftentimes I say to women, "Don't pay too much attention to what a man says. Watch what he does. What he does is what he means."

His actions belied his statement that there was not a jealous bone in his body. I explained to him that jealousy cripples him emotionally and blocks all his good, holding him back in all phases of his life. Jealousy is the green-eyed monster. He began to see that his jealousy was abnormal and was really based on a sense of inferiority and inadequacy within himself. Jealousy is a child of fear. Love casts out fear, for fear is a torment; and jealousy burns up the tissues like a consuming fire.

If a man loves a woman, he does not do anything unloving. He trusts her in the same manner as, when a child, he looked into his mother's eyes and saw love there. If a man loves a woman, he loves to see her as she ought to be: happy, joyous, free, and expressing herself at her highest level. Love is not jealousy. Love is not possessiveness. Love is not suspicion, neither is it emotional blackmail, such as, "If you loved me you would give up smoking or eating ham" or some other similar foolish, asinine statement. Love has nothing to do with smoking, eating ham or taking a cocktail. Love frees; it gives; it is the Spirit of God in action.

This man learned to pray for a wife, realizing that he marries character and that he doesn't get what he wants in life; he gets what he has established in his mentality. In other words, he must establish the mental equivalent in his subconscious in order to demonstrate what he wants.

Accordingly, he affirmed night and morning: "Infinite Spirit attracts to me a spiritually minded woman who harmonizes with me perfectly. This takes place in Divine order through Divine love. There are mutual love, freedom and respect between us."

He attracted a wonderful legal secretary, and they harmonize perfectly. Every time he thinks of her, he affirms: "God loves you and cares for you." There is no occasion for jealousy where love dwells. He realizes that it is impossible to think of two things at the same time. He can't think of two things at the same time. He can't think of jealousy and love at the same time; no more so than he could laugh and cry at the same time. Two unlike things repel each other. Love and jealousy cannot dwell together.

Jealousy is a Mental Poison

A jealous person usually blames others as if they were responsible for his inferiority or inadequacy. A jealous person generates mental poisons which bring on all manner of disease. Actually, he is destroying himself from the inside. Remember, you are unique. There is no one in the world like you. Others do not have the same toe print or thumbprint; neither do they have the same digestive or glandular systems. They don't think, speak or act like you.

You are an individualized expression of God, and you are here to express yourself in a new and wonderful way. There is no misfit in the universe. You are needed. There is no unwanted note in the symphony; all notes are necessary. "We are all parts of one stupendous whole, whose body nature is and God the soul."

To be envious of others is to demean you. It means you are rejecting your own Divinity, which is the Source of all blessings. When jealous of another, you are placing that person on a pedestal and demoting yourself, thereby attracting lack, loss, limitation and impoverishment to you. It makes no sense. You have heard the expression, "She is green with envy." This is why jealousy is called the green-eyed monster. The eyes are the windows of the soul. It is true the eyes reveal jealousy, which is a mental sickness. Remember also, a jealous person is an angry person.

Though while he lived he blessed his soul: and men will praise thee, when thou doest well to thyself (Psalms 49:18). Do the very best you can, radiating love and goodwill to all. Love is cordiality, geniality, kindness, good feeling toward all, wishing for everyone all the blessings of life. Love is the fulfilling of the law of health, wealth, peace and prosperity. Cooperate with others. Become enthusiastic. Claim that you are always expressing yourself at the highest level. As you continue in this attitude of mind, you will receive approbation, promotion and recognition.

Rejoice in the Affluence of Others

You can always sell faith, confidence, laughter, goodwill, zeal and enthusiasm; furthermore, these qualities are translatable to abundance, security, true expression and a full life. Rejoice in the affluence of others. As you do, you will attract more wealth to yourself. To be jealous or envious of the wealth of others is to impoverish you all the more. Actually, you are denying your own Divinity and saying to yourself: "They can have all that good and I can't," thereby depriving yourself of the very things you seek. Envy and jealousy represent gross ignorance. Ignorance is the only sin, and all the suffering in the world is the consequence.

Sons of God

For as many are led by the Spirit of God, they are the sons of God (Romans 8:14). You are a son, or expression of God when you begin to express health, vitality, beauty, love and success in your life. What governs you now? Are you governed by wisdom, truth and beauty, or by ignorance, fear and superstition? The dominant mood governs you. Let the Spirit of light, love, truth and joy rule and govern you, and you will begin to express more and more of the attributes and qualities of God.

Learn to Lead a Full and Happy Life

Saturate your mind with these truths: "At the center of my being is peace. God's river of peace saturates my whole being. I am Divinely guided in all ways. Divine love dissolves everything unlike itself in my subconscious mind. I salute the Divinity in every person I meet, and I make it a habit to call forth the Divinity in every person by silently affirming, 'God's love fills your soul.' I realize that God is personified in all men and women. God flows through me now, filling up all the empty vessels in my life. God's riches—spiritual, mental and material—flow through me now, and I am immersed in the Holy Omnipresence. Wonders happen as I pray."

CHAPTER 3

YOUR SUBCONSCIOUS MIND IS AMENABLE TO SUGGESTION

And he saith unto me, Seal not the sayings of the prophecy of this book: for the time is at hand. He that is unjust, let him be unjust still: and he which is filthy, let him be filthy still: and he that is righteous, let him be righteous still: and he that is holy, let him be holy still (Revelation 22:10-11).

You are your own prophet, because according to your belief is it done unto you. Your own inner feeling, your faith, your inner mood and expectancy determine that which is to come. The future is always your present thoughts made visible. Whatever you unite with mentally and emotionally is a prophecy of that which is to come.

Be a true prophet, be a good prophet. Expect only good fortune and good fortune shall be yours. The children of misfortune are those who ascribe power to externals, other people and the mass mind. These are the illegitimate children of your world. You must first change yourself; then your world will change. Unfortunately, man is always trying to change the other person.

Grant your relatives, friends and all other people the right to be different. Grant them their peculiarities, idiosyncrasies and religious viewpoints. Permit them to worship differently from yourself. Be glad there are Catholics, Jews, Protestants and Buddhists, as well as followers of other religions. If the other person is mean and nasty, that is no reason why you should be, also. You are here to let your light so shine before men that they will see your good works and recognize you as being a good example to all.

Spend some time every day radiating the glory, beauty and love of God, and never mind whether the other fellow does it or not. You are not responsible if some friend of yours shoot his or her spouse. All you are responsible for is the way you think about him or her. Since your thought is creative, you will therefore bless both, realizing that the journey of the deceased person is ever onward, upward and God ward and that the light of God shines in the person who committed the act.

You have a mind, and you should learn how to use it. There are two levels of your mind—the conscious or rational level, and the subconscious or irrational level. You think with your conscious mind, and whatever you habitually think sinks down into your subconscious mind, which creates according to the nature of your thoughts. Your subconscious mind is the seat of your emotions and is the creative mind. If you think good, good will follow; if you think evil, evil will follow. This is the way your mind works.

The Subconscious Mind Works for Good and Bad Ideas Alike

The main point to remember is once the subconscious mind accepts an idea, it begins to execute it. It is an interesting and subtle truth that the law of the subconscious mind works for good and bad ideas alike. This law, when applied in a negative way, is the cause of failure, frustration, and unhappiness. However, when your habitual thinking is harmonious and constructive, you experience perfect health, success, and prosperity.

Peace of mind and a healthy body are inevitable when you begin to think and feel in the right way. Whatever you claim mentally and feel as true, your subconscious mind will accept and bring forth into your experience. The only thing necessary for you to do is to get your subconscious mind to accept your idea, and the law of your own subconscious mind will bring forth the health, peace, or the position you desire. You give the command or decree, and your subconscious will faithfully reproduce the idea impressed upon it. The law of your mind is this: You will get a reaction or response from your subconscious mind according to the nature of the thought or idea you hold in your conscious mind.

Psychologists and psychiatrists point out that when thoughts are conveyed to your subconscious mind, impressions are made in the brain cells. As soon as your subconscious accepts any idea, it proceeds to put it into effect immediately. It works by association of ideas and uses every bit of knowledge that you have gathered in your lifetime to bring about its purpose. It draws on the infinite power, energy, and wisdom within you. It lines up all the laws of nature to get its way. Sometimes it seems to bring about an immediate solution to your difficulties, but at other times it may take days, weeks, or longer.... *Its ways are past finding out.*

Conscious and Subconscious Terms Differentiated

You must remember that these are not two minds. They are merely two spheres of activity within one mind. Your conscious mind is the reasoning mind. It is that phase of mind which chooses. For example, you choose your books, your home, and your partner in life. You make all your decisions with your conscious mind. On the other hand, without any conscious choice on your part, your heart is kept functioning automatically, and the process of digestion, circulation, and breathing are carried on by your subconscious mind through processes independent of your conscious control.

Your subconscious mind accepts what is impressed upon it or what you consciously believe. It does not reason things out like your conscious mind, and it does not argue with you controversially. Your subconscious mind is like the soil which accepts any kind of seed, good or bad. Your thoughts are active and might be likened unto seeds. Negative, destructive thoughts continue to work negatively in your subconscious mind, and in due time will come forth into outer experience which corresponds with them.

Remember, your subconscious mind does not engage in proving whether your thoughts are good or bad, true or false, but it responds according to the nature of your thoughts or suggestions. For example, if you consciously assume something as true, even though it may be false, your subconscious mind will accept it as true and proceed to bring about results which must necessarily follow, because you consciously assumed it to be true.

Suggestions and Your Subconscious

Innumerable experiments by psychologists and others on persons in the hypnotic state have shown that the subconscious mind is incapable of making selections and comparisons which are necessary for a reasoning process. They have shown repeatedly that your subconscious mind will accept any suggestions, however false. Having once accepted any suggestion, it responds according to the nature of the suggestion given.

Your subconscious mind is amenable to suggestions and it is controlled by suggestion. One of the corollaries of the law of suggestion is that your subconscious mind does not engage in inductive reasoning, which means that it does not institute a line of research by collecting facts, classifying them and estimating their relative evidential values.

Its method of reasoning is purely deductive. This is true whether the premise is true or false. In other words, its deductions from a false premise are as logically correct as from a true one. Thus, if it is suggested to a hypnotized subject that he is a dog, he will immediately play that role and perform the acts of a dog, so far as it is physically possible to do so, while at the same time believing himself to be a dog.

In all probability, you have seen subjects play the role of the type of character suggested to them by the operator or hypnotist, for the subject believes himself to be the actual personality suggested. For instance, you could suggest to a hypnotized subject that he is President Roosevelt; and if at some time in the past he had heard President Roosevelt speak or address the nation, his own personality would be completely submerged under the influence of the suggestion. He would believe himself to be the late President Roosevelt.

A skilled hypnotist may suggest to one of his students in the hypnotic state that his back itches, to another that his nose is bleeding, to another that he is a marble statue, to another that he is freezing and the temperature is below zero. Each one will follow out the line of his particular suggestion, totally oblivious to all his surroundings which do not pertain to his idea.

This simple illustration portray clearly the difference between your conscious reasoning mind and your subconscious mind which is impersonal, non-selective, and accepts as true whatever your conscious mind believes to be true. Hence, the importance of selecting thoughts, ideas, and premises which bless, heal, inspire, and fill your soul with joy.

Objective and Subjective Mind Clarified

Your conscious mind is sometimes referred to as your objective mind because it deals with outward objects. The objective mind takes cognizance of the objective world. Its media of observation are your five physical senses. Your objective mind is your guide and director in your contact with your environment. You gain knowledge through your five senses. Your objective mind learns through observation, experience, and education. As previously pointed out, the greatest function of the objective mind is that of reasoning.

Suppose you are one of the thousands of tourists who come to Los Angeles annually. You would come to the conclusion that it is a beautiful city based upon your observation of the parks, pretty gardens, majestic buildings, and lovely homes. This is the working of your objective mind.

Your subconscious mind is oftentimes referred to as your subjective mind. Your subjective mind takes cognizance of its environment by means independent of the five senses. Your subjective mind perceives by intuition. It is the seat of your emotion and the storehouse of memory. Your subjective mind performs its highest functions when your objective senses are in abeyance. In a word, it is that intelligence which makes itself manifest when the objective mind is suspended or in a sleepy, drowsy state.

Your subjective mind sees without the use of natural organs of vision. It has the capacity of clairvoyance and Clair-audience. Your subjective mind can leave your body, travel to distant lands, and bring back information oftentimes of the most exact and truthful character. Through your subjective mind you can read the thoughts of others, read the contents of sealed envelopes and closed safes. Your subjective mind has the ability to apprehend the thoughts of others without the use of the ordinary objective means of communication. It is of the greatest importance that we understand the interaction of the objective and subjective mind in order to learn the true art of prayer.

The Subconscious Cannot Reason Like Your Conscious Mind

Your subconscious mind cannot argue controversially. Hence, if you give it wrong suggestions, it will accept them as true and will proceed to bring them to pass as conditions, experiences, and events. All things that have happened to you are based on thoughts impressed on your subconscious mind through belief. If you have conveyed erroneous concepts to your subconscious mind, the sure method of overcoming them is by the repetition of constructive, harmonious thoughts frequently repeated which your subconscious mind accepts, thus forming new and healthy habits of thought and life, for your subconscious mind is the seat of habit.

The habitual thinking of your conscious mind establishes deep grooves in your subconscious mind. This is very favorable for you if your habitual thoughts are harmonious, peaceful, and constructive.

If you have indulged in fear, worry, and other destructive forms of thinking, the remedy is to recognize the omnipotence of your subconscious mind and decree freedom, happiness, and perfect health. Your subconscious mind, being creative and one with your divine source, will proceed to create the freedom and happiness which you have earnestly decreed.

The Tremendous Power of Suggestion

You must realize by now that your conscious mind is the "watchman at the gate," and its chief function is to protect your subconscious mind from false impressions. You are now aware of one of the basic laws of mind: Your subconscious mind is amenable to suggestion. As you know, your subconscious mind does not make comparisons, or contrasts, neither does it reason and think things out for itself. This latter function belongs to your conscious mind. It simply reacts to the impressions given to it by your conscious mind. It does not show a preference for one course of action over another.

The Unbelievable Power of Suggestion

The following is a classic example of the tremendous power of suggestion. Suppose your approach a timid-looking passenger on board ship and say to him something like this: "You look very ill. How pale you are! I feel certain you are going to be seasick. Let me help you to your cabin." The passenger turns pale. Your suggestion of seasickness associates itself with his own fears and forebodings. He accepts your aid down to the berth, and there your negative suggestion, which was accepted by him, is realized.

Different Reactions to the Same Suggestion

It is true that different people will react in different ways to the same suggestion because of their subconscious conditioning or belief. For example, if you go to a sailor on the ship and say to him sympathetically, "My dear fellow, you're looking very ill. Aren't you feeling sick? You look to me as if you were going to be seasick."

According to his temperament he either laughs at your "joke," or express a mild irritation. Your suggestion fell on deaf ears in this instance because your suggestion of seasickness was associated in his mind with his own immunity from it. Therefore, it called up not fear or worry, but self-confidence.

The dictionary says that a suggestion is the act or instance of putting something into one's mind, the mental process by which the thought or idea suggested is entertained, accepted, or put into effect. You must remember that a suggestion cannot impose something on the subconscious mind against the will of the conscious mind. In other words, your conscious mind has the power to reject the suggestion given. In the case of the sailor, he had no fear of seasickness. He had convinced himself of his immunity, and the negative suggestion had absolutely no power to evoke fear.

The suggestion of seasickness to the other passenger called forth his indwelling fear of seasickness. Each of us has his own inner fears, beliefs, opinions, and these inner assumptions rule and govern our lives. A suggestion has no power in and of itself except it is accepted mentally by you. This causes your subconscious powers to flow in a limited and restricted way according to the nature of the suggestion.

How He Lost His Arm

Every two or three years I give a series of lectures at the London Truth Forum in Caxton Hall. This is a Forum I founded a number of years ago. Dr. Evelyn Fleet, the director, told me about an article which appeared in the English newspapers dealing with the power of suggestion. This is the suggestion a man gave to his subconscious mind over a period of about two years: "I would give my right arm to see my daughter cured." It appeared that his daughter had a crippling form of arthritis together with a so-called incurable form of skin disease. Medical treatment had failed to alleviate the condition, and the father had an intense longing for his daughters healing, and expressed his desire in the words just quoted.

Dr. Evelyn Fleet said that the newspaper article pointed out that one day the family was out riding when their car collided with another. The father's right arm was torn off at the shoulder, and immediately the daughter's arthritis and skin condition vanished.

You must make certain to give your subconscious only suggestions which heal, bless, elevate, and inspire you in all your ways. Remember that your subconscious mind cannot take a joke. It takes you at your word.

How She Restored Her Memory

A woman, aged seventy-five, was in the habit of saying to her, "I am losing my memory." She reversed the procedure and practiced induced auto-suggestion several times a day as follows: "My memory from today on is improving in every department. I shall always remember whatever I need to know at every moment of time and point of space. The impressions received will be clearer and more definite. I shall retain them automatically and with ease. Whatever I wish to recall will immediately present itself in the correct form in my mind. I am improving rapidly every day, and very soon my memory will be better than it has ever been before." At the end of three weeks, her memory as back to normal, and she was delighted.

How He Overcame a Nasty Temper

Many men who complained of irritability and bad temper proved to be very susceptible to autosuggestion and obtained marvelous results by using the following statements three or four times a day—morning, noon, and at night prior to sleep for about a month. "Henceforth, I shall grow more good-humored. Joy, happiness, and cheerfulness are now becoming my normal states of mind. Every day I am becoming more and more lovable and understanding. I am now becoming the center of cheer and good will to all those about me, infecting them with good humor. This happy, joyous, and cheerful mood is now becoming my normal, natural state of mind. I am grateful."

The Constructive and Destructive Power of Suggestion

Some illustrations and comments on Heterosuggestion: Heterosuggestion means suggestions from another person. In all ages the power of suggestion has played a part in the life and thought of man in every period of time and in each country of the earth. In many parts of the world it is the controlling power in religion.

Suggestion may be used to discipline and control ourselves, but it can also be used to take control and command over others who do not know the laws of mind. In its constructive form it is wonderful and magnificent. In its negative aspects it is one of the most destructive of all the response patterns of the mind, resulting in patterns of misery, failure, suffering, sickness, and disaster.

Have You Accepted Any of These?

From infancy on the majority of us have been given many negative suggestions. Not knowing how to thwart them, we unconsciously accepted them. Here are some of the negative suggestions: "You can't." "You'll never amount to anything." "You mustn't.": "You'll fail." "You haven't got a chance." "You're all wrong." "It's o use." "It's no use." "It's not what you know, but who you know." "The world is going to the dogs." "What's the use, nobody cares." "It's no use trying so hard." "You're too old now." "Things are getting worse and worse." "Life is an endless grind." "Love is for the birds." "You just can't win." "Pretty soon you'll be bankrupt." "Watch out, you'll get the virus." "You can't trust a soul," etc.

Unless, as an adult, you use constructive autosuggestion, which is a reconditioning therapy, the impressions made on you in the past can cause behavior patterns that cause failure in your personal and social life. Autosuggestion is a means releasing you from the mass of negative verbal conditioning that might otherwise distort your life pattern, making the development of good habits difficult.

You can Counteract Negative Suggestions

Pick up the paper any day, and you can read dozens of items that could sow the seeds of futility, fear, worry, anxiety, and impending doom. If accepted by you, these thoughts of fear could cause you to lose the will for life. Knowing that you can reject all these negative suggestions by giving your subconscious mind constructive autosuggestions, you counteract all these destructive ideas.

Check regularly on the negative suggestions that people make of you. You do not have to be influenced by destructive Heterosuggestion. All of us have suffered from it in our childhood and in our teens. If you look back, you can easily recall how parents, friends, relatives, teachers, and associates contributed in a campaign of negative suggestions. Study the things said to you, and you will discover much of it was in the form of propaganda. The purpose of much of what was said was to control you or instill fear into you.

This Heterosuggestion process goes on in every home, office, factory, and club. You will find that many of these suggestions are for the purpose of making you think, feel, and act as others want you to and in ways that are to their advantage.

How Suggestion Killed a Man

Here is an illustration of Heterosuggestion: A relative of mine went to a crystal gazer in India who told him that he had a bad heart and predicted that he would die at the next new moon. He began to tell all members of his family about this prediction, and he arranged his will.

This powerful suggestion entered into his subconscious mind because he accepted it completely. My relative also told me that this crystal gazer was believed to have some strange occult powers, and he could do harm or good to a person. He died as predicted not knowing that he was the cause of his own death. I suppose many of us have heard similar stupid, ridiculous, superstitious stories.

Let us look at what happened in the light of our knowledge of the way the subconscious mind works. Whatever the conscious, reasoning mind of man believes, the subconscious mind will accept and act upon. My relative was happy, healthy, vigorous, and robust when he went to see the fortuneteller. She gave him a very negative suggestion which he accepted. He became terrified, and constantly dwelt upon the fact that he was going to die at the next new moon. He proceeded to tell everyone about it, and he prepared for the end. The activity took place in his own mind, and his own thought was the cause. He brought about his own so-called death, or rather destruction of the physical body, by his fear and expectation of the end.

The woman who predicted his death had no more power than the stones and sticks in the field. Her suggestion had no power to create or bring about the end she suggested. If he had known the laws of the mind, he would have completely rejected the negative suggestion and refused to give her words any attention, knowing in his heart that he was governed and controlled by his own thought and feeling. Like tin arrows aimed at a battleship, her prophecy could have been completely neutralized and dissipated without hurting him.

The suggestions of others in themselves have absolutely no power whatever over you accepts the power that you give them through your own thoughts. You have to give your mental consent; you have to entertain the thought. Then, it becomes your thought, and you do the thinking. Remember, you have the capacity to choose. Choose life! Choose love! Choose health!

Do not Decree Your Own Demise

The late Dr. Frederick Bailes, one of the great teachers in Los Angeles for many years, told me of a friend of his who used to say to him, "Bailes, all members of my family passed on when they reached seventy-two. I will be seventy-two next year, and that's it."

Dr. Bailes told his friend of the dangers of making such a statement, as his subconscious would accept it. He paid no attention, though, and on his seventy-second birthday he dropped dead in the street. He had decreed his own demise. The Bible says: *For by thy words thou shalt be justified, and by thy words thou shalt be condemned* (Matthew 12:37).

Others say, "I'm too old now. I won't last much longer. You know, I am sixty-five." These suggestions of weakness, decrepitude and old age enter into the subconscious mind and come forth after their kind. Let your words heal, bless and inspire yourself and everybody else.

The Power of an Assumed Major Premise

Your mind works like a syllogism. This means that whatever major premise your conscious mind assumes to be true determines the conclusion your subconscious mind comes to in regard to any particular question or problem in your mind. If your premise is true, the conclusion must be true as in the following example:

> Every virtue is laudable;
> Kindness is a virtue;
> Therefore, kindness is laudable.

Another example is as follows:

> All formed things change and pass away;
> The Pyramids of Egypt are formed things;
> Therefore, some day the Pyramids will pass away.

The first statement is referred to as the major premise, and the right conclusion must necessarily follow the right promise.

A college professor, who attended some of my science of mind lectures in May, 1962, at Town Hall, New York, said to me, "Everything in my life is topsy-turvy, and I have lost health, wealth, and friends. Everything I touch turns out wrong."

I explained to him that he should establish a major premise in his thinking, that the infinite intelligence of his subconscious mind was guiding, directing, and prospering him spiritually, mentally, and materially. Then his subconscious mind would automatically direct him wisely in his investments, decisions, and also heal his body and restore his mind to peace and tranquility.

This professor formulated an over-all picture of the way he wanted his life to be, and this was his major premise:

"Infinite intelligence leads and guides me in all my ways, Perfect health is mine, and the Law of Harmony operates in my mind and body. Beauty, love, peace and abundance are mine. The principle of right action and divine order govern my entire life. I know my major premise is based on the eternal truths of life, and I know, feel, and believe that my subconscious mind responds according to the nature of my conscious mind thinking."

He wrote me as follows: "I repeated the above statements slowly, quietly, and lovingly several times a day knowing that they were sinking deep down into my subconscious mind, and that results must follow. I am deeply grateful for the interview you gave me, and I would like to add that all departments of my life are changing for the better. It works!"

The Subconscious Does Not Argue

Your subconscious mind is all-wise and knows the answers to all questions. It does not argue with you or talk back to you. It does not say, "You must not impress me with that." For example, when you say, "I can't do this." "I am too old now." "I can't meet this obligation." "I was born on the wrong side of the tracks." "I don't know the right politician," you are impregnating your subconscious with these negative thoughts, and it responds accordingly. You are actually blocking your own good, thereby bringing lack, limitation, and frustration into your life.

Do Not Congest Your Subconscious Mind

When you set up obstacles, impediments, and delays in your conscious mind, you are denying the wisdom and intelligence resident in your subconscious mind. You are actually saying in effect that your subconscious mind cannot solve your problem. This leads to mental and emotional congestion, followed by sickness and neurotic tendencies.

To realize your desire and overcome your frustration, affirm boldly several times a day: "The infinite intelligence which gave me this desire leads, guides, and reveals to me the perfect plan for the unfolding of my desire. I know the deeper wisdom of my subconscious is now responding, and what I feel and claim within is expressed I the without. There is a balance, equilibrium, and equanimity."

If you say, "There is no way out, I am lost; there is no way out of this dilemma; I am stymied and blocked," you will get no answer or response from your subconscious mind. If you want the subconscious to work for you, give it the right request, and attain its co-operation. It is always working for you. It is controlling your heartbeat this minute and also your breathing. It heals a cut on your finger, and its tendency is life ward, forever seeking to take care of you and preserve you. Your subconscious has a mind of its own but it accepts your patterns of thought and imagery.

Suggested Thinking

1. Think good, and good follows. Think evil, and evil follows. You are what you think all day long.
2. Your subconscious mind does not argue with you. It accepts what your conscious mind decrees. If you say, "I can't afford it," it may be true, but do not say it. Select a better thought, decree, "I'll buy it. I accept it in my mind."
3. You have the power to choose. Choose health and happiness. You can choose to be friendly, or you can choose to be unfriendly. Choose to be co-operative, joyous, friendly, lovable and the whole world will respond. This is the best way to develop a wonderful personality.
4. Your conscious mind is the "watchman at the gate." Its chief function is to protect your subconscious mind from false impressions. Choose to believe that something good can happen and is happening now. Your greatest power is your capacity to choose. Choose happiness and abundance.
5. The suggestions and statements of others have no power to hurt you. The only power is the movement of your own thought. You can choose to reject the thoughts or statements of others and affirm the good. You have the power to choose how you will react.
6. Watch what you say. You have to account for every idle word. Never say, "I will fail; I will lose my job; I can't pay the rent." Your subconscious cannot take a joke. It brings all these things to pass.
7. Your mind is not evil. No force of nature is evil. It depends how you use the powers of nature. Use your mind to bless, heal and inspire all people everywhere.
8. Never say, "I can't." Overcome that fear by substituting the following, "I can do all things through the power of my own subconscious mind."

9. Begin to think from the standpoint of the eternal truths and principles of life and not from the standpoint of fear, ignorance, and superstition. Do not let others do your thinking for you. You choose your own thoughts and make your own decisions.
10. You are the captain of your soul (subconscious mind) and the master of your fate. Remember, you have the capacity to choose. Choose life! Choose love! Choose health! Choose happiness!
11. Whatever your conscious mind assumes and believes to be true, your subconscious mind will accept and bring to pass. Believe in good fortune, divine guidance, right action, and all the blessings of life.

CHAPTER 4

YOUR EMOTIONS ARE A SUBJECT TO SUGGESTIONS AND COMMANDS

The ancient Greeks said: As you study yourself, you seem to be made up of four parts: Your physical body, emotional nature, intellect, and the Spiritual Essence which is called the Presence of God. The I AM within you, the Divine Presence, is your Real Identity Which is Eternal.

You are here to discipline yourself, so that your intellectual, emotional, and physical nature are completely spiritualized. These four phases of your nature are called the four beasts of *The Book of Revelation*. (*The Revelation of St. John* means God revealing himself as man.

The real way for you to discipline and bridle your intellectual and emotional nature is by the Practice of the Presence of God all day long.

You have a body; it is a shadow or reflection of the mind. It has no power of itself, any initiative, or volition. It has no intelligence of itself; it is completely subject to your suggestions and decrees. Look upon your body as a great disc upon which you play your emotions and beliefs. Being a disc, it will faithfully record all your emotionalized concepts and never deviate from them; therefore, you can register a melody of love and beauty, or one of grief and sorrow upon it. Resentment, jealousy, hatred, anger, and melancholia are all expressed in the body as various diseases. As you learn to control your mental and emotional nature, you will become a channel for the Divine, and release the imprisoned splendor that is within you.

Think over this for a moment: You cannot buy a healthy body with all the money in the world, but you can have health through riches of the mind, such as thoughts of peace, harmony, and perfect health.

Let us dwell now on the emotional nature of man. It is absolutely essential for you to control your emotions if you want to grow spiritually. You are considered grown up or emotionally mature when you control your feelings. If you cannot discipline or bridle your emotions, you are a child even though you are fifty years old.

He Became a Constructive Thinker

I had a most interesting session with a man whom we shall call Mr. X, who has been phoning and corresponding with me for some time. I gave him spiritual advice over the phone, and the following is the history of the case. He is the son of a very wealthy father in the East, who had been very cruel and autocratic, insisting that the son come up to his standards in the business. This young man had a neurotic hatred for his father and began to strike back by writing vitriolic articles about big business; moreover, he went back East and lectured on the values of a communistic society to a club to which his father belonged, knowing that this would infuriate his father. His desire, as he said, was to strike back at his father. In the meantime, because of this emotional hostility and suppressed rage, plus his sense of guilt, he began to drink excessively, becoming an inebriate, or compulsive drinker. He also developed ulcers and high blood pressure; and, as if that were not enough, he was on the verge of bankruptcy.

My explanation (over the phone) of the reason for his actions supplied 75 percent of his cure. He realized that he was being emotionally immature and was consuming alcohol to assuage his sense of guilt just as someone else would take aspirin for a headache. Actually, it suddenly dawned on him that he was literally destroying himself by attempting to hit back at his father's ideals and policies. He decided to reverse his attitude by following the technique of scientific prayer.

He affirmed out loud frequently during the day: "I surrender my father to God. I release him completely and wish for him health, peace, success, and all the blessings of life. Whenever I think of him, I will affirm at once, 'I have released you. God's peace fills your soul.' I am divinely guided. Divine law and order govern me. Divine love and Divine peace saturate my soul. My food and drink are God's ideas, which constantly unfold within me, bringing me harmony, health, and peace. God thinks, speaks and acts through me, and I am Divinely expressed and fulfilled in all ways."

He repeated these truths frequently out loud, which prevented his mind from wandering. Whenever any negative thoughts came to his mind, he would affirm: "God loves me and cares for me." After a few weeks, he became a constructive thinker.

His "Movie" Technique

Every night for about ten minutes in a perfectly relaxed state, he imagined I was in front of him congratulating him on his freedom from alcohol, and whenever the shakes and the jitters seized him with the craving for another drink, he would cause to flash in his mind the mental movie, knowing there was an Almighty Power backing him up. It was only a matter of a few weeks until he was completely free from the curse of compulsive drinking. His new attitude changed everything. Today, three months later, at dinner with me in Las Vegas, he told me his business has prospered so well that his assets are worth over $200.000. His psychic perception had enabled him to make the correct and shrewd decisions necessary in accumulating a fortune.

You must remember that the greatest tyrant is a false idea which controls a man's mind holding him in bondage. The idea you hold about yourself or others induces definite emotions in you.

Psychologically speaking, emotions compel you for good or evil. If you are full of resentment toward someone or possessed by a grudge, this emotion will have an evil influence over you, and govern your actions in a manner which has nothing to do with what you say is the original cause. When you want to be friendly and cordial, you will be ugly, cynical, and sour. When you want to be healthy, successful, and prosperous in life, you will find everything going wrong. Those of you reading this book are aware of your capacity to choose a concept of peace and good will. Accept the idea of peace in your mind, and let it govern, control, and guide you.

Within you are a designer, an architect, and a weaver. They take the image of your mind and mold it into a pattern of life which brings you peace, joy, and victory. The greatest and richest galleries are the galleries of the mind devoted to wisdom, truth, and beauty.

Picture Your Ideal in Life

Live mentally with this ideal. Let the ideal captivate your perceptive imagination. You will move in the direction of the mental image which governs your mind. The ideals of life are like the dew of heaven, which moves over the arid areas of your mind, refreshing and invigorating you. With your disciplined imagination, you can soar above all appearances, discord, and sense evidence, and imagine the way things ought to be while realizing the sublime principle of harmony operating through, in, and behind all things. Reject the evidence of your senses and realize that the inside controls the outside. Your mental image is the reality, or the inside, and its external manifestation, or form, is the outside.

Quimby pointed out that ideas are our masters, and that we are slaves to the ideas we entertain. The concept of peace with which you now live will induce the feeling of peace and harmony. Your feeling is the spirit of God operating at the human level; this feeling of peace and good will compel you to right action. You are now governed by Divine Ideas which are mothered by the Holy Spirit.

Uncontrolled or undisciplined emotion is destructive. For example, if you have a powerful automobile, it will take you through the roughest country, or to the top of a high hill; however, you must control the automobile. If you do not know how to drive, you may hit a telegraph pole or another car. Should you step on the gas instead of the brake, the car may be destroyed.

It is wonderful to posses a strong, emotional nature provided you are the master. Your emotions are controlling you if you permit yourself to get angry over trifles or agitated over practically nothing. If you get upset over what you read in the newspapers, you are not controlling your emotions. You must learn to blend your intellect and emotions together harmoniously. The intellect of man is all right in its place, but it should be anointed or illumined with the Wisdom of God.

A man recently asked me: "How do I know when I am truly thinking?" That is a good question, and the answer I gave him is simply this: You are thinking when you are activating your mind from the standpoint of eternal verities and the Cosmic truths of God, which are the same yesterday, today, and forever. You are not thinking in the true sense of the term when you are reacting to the headlines in the newspapers, radio propaganda, or from the standpoint of tradition, dogma, creeds, or environmental conditions or circumstances.

This man who asked the question had been, as a matter of course, merely swallowing the thoughts of the columnists in the *Los Angeles Times*, and he was full of the ideas of local and state politicians. These were not his thoughts: rather, they were thoughts of others and were mostly of a negative nature.

He immediately saw the light and began to think for himself, taking as his spiritual yardstick:

> *Whatsoever things are true, whatsoever things are honest,*
> *Whatsoever things are just, whatsoever things are pure, whatsoever?*
> *things are lovely, whatsoever things are of good report; if there be any virtue,*
> *and if there be any praise, think on these things* (Philippians 4:8).

Whenever any thoughts or ideas were propounded to him, he would reason between the two opposing ideas or thoughts and come to a conclusion in his mind as to what was true from the standpoint of spiritual principles.

When the thought of failure came to him from time to time, he was always affirmed boldly: *The Cosmic Infinite can't fail. I was born to succeed. Success is mine now, and the Infinite Intelligence in my subconscious mind responds and gives me the power, the strength, and the answer I need.*

He is now thinking from the standpoint of what is true of God, which is true cosmic thinking. There is no longer any fear or worry in his thinking, and his mind is serene.

There are many people who are always trying to intellectualize God. You cannot define the Infinite. Spinoza said that to define God is to deny him. You have met the highly intellectual man who says that man cannot survive death, because he does not take his brain with him. Somehow he is so clever he really believes the brain thinks by itself. Such a man is looking at everything from a three-dimensional standpoint; that is where the intellect ceases.

The intellect, as I said previously, is all right in its place—for example, in our everyday work, and in all kinds of science, art, and industry. However as we approach the Living Spirit almighty within, we are compelled to leave the world of the intellect and go beyond into the realm of spiritual values which are perfection, and where dimension is infinity.

When man's intellect is blended with the emotions of love, peace, and goodwill, he will not use explosives and knowledge of chemistry for the destruction of mankind. The reason man uses the atomic bomb, submarine, and other implements of warfare to destroy his fellow creature are because his spiritual awareness and knowledge lag so far behind his intellectual achievements.

This was another question propounded at one of my lectures. One woman said, "If God is love and if He is All-God and All-Wise, why doesn't He stop war, crime, murder, and rapine? Why does He permit thousands and millions of children to die of hunger and countless other thousands to become crippled and maimed by the ravages of war?" She seemed to be angry at God.

The answer is very simple. God is the Universal Being, the Cosmic Power, the Supreme and Infinite Intelligence working on a cosmic scale or from the standpoint of the Universal. The law, simply stated, is that the Universal can only act on the plane of the particular or individual by becoming the individual. In other words, God rules the world and acts solely on the Cosmic plan, moving as unity, harmony, rhythm, order, beauty, and proportion. The only way God can work through you is through your thought, feeling and mental imagery.

You have volition, choice, and initiative. You have freedom to become a murderer or a holy man; otherwise, you would not be an individual. You are not compelled to be good or holy; you have freedom to choose harmony, peace, joy, love, abundance, and all the blessings of life.

You were not compelled to love your husband or wife. You said, "I choose him (or her) from all the others in the world." . . . *Choose you this day that ye will serve* . . . (Joshua 24:15).

As long as man remains emotionally immature, and while he harbors resentment, ill will, jealousy, hate, and anger, he is at war with himself and with others; multiply the one man and you have a nation.

The law of God governs the individual, the nation, and the world. God can't stop wars, crime, disease, discord, and accidents. All judgment is given to the son, which means your mind. You judge yourself by the way you think.

You are the one to initiate peace in your own mind and heart, and then *your* world will be at peace. There is no one to change but yourself. Start now. As you do this, your whole world will magically melt into the image and likeness of your concept of yourself, and your desert will rejoice and blossom as the rose. This indeed is letting Cosmic Power work wonders for you.

You Can Control Your Emotions

Let us see how emotions are generated. Suppose you observe a cripple; perhaps you are moved to pity. On the other hand you may look at your young, beautiful child, and you feel an emotion of love welling up within you. You know that you cannot imagine an emotion, but if you imagine an unpleasant episode or event of the past, you induce the corresponding emotion. Remember it is essential to entertain the thought first before you induce an emotion.

An emotion is always the working out of an idea in the mind. Have you noticed the effect of fear upon the face, eyes, heart, and other organs? You know the effect of bad news or grief on the digestive tract. Observe the change that takes place when it is found the fear is groundless.

All negative emotions are destructive and depress the vital forces of the body. A chronic worrier usually has trouble with digestion. If something very pleasant occurs in his experience, the digestion becomes normal, because normal circulation is restored, and the necessary gastric secretions are no longer interfered with.

The way to overcome and discipline the emotions is not through repression or suppression. When you repress an emotion, the energy accumulates in the subconscious and remains snarled there. In the same manner as the pressure increases in the boiler, if all the valves are closed, and you increase the heat of the fire, finally there will be an explosion.

The Positive Emotion of Faith and Confidence

Today in the field of psychosomatics we are discovering that many cases of ill health, as arthritis, asthma, cardiac troubles, and failure in life, etc., may be due to suppressed or repressed emotions, perhaps occurring during early life or childhood.

These repressed or suppressed emotions rise like ghosts to haunt you later on. There is a spiritual and psychological way to banish these ghosts which walk in the gloomy gallery of your mind. The ideal way is the law of substitution. Through the law of mental substitution, you substitute a positive, constructive thought for the negative. When negative thoughts enter your mind, do not fight them; just think of God and His Love; you will find the negative thoughts disappear. *"I say unto you, that ye resist no evil."* (Math. 5:39) If a person is fearful, the positive emotion of faith and confidence will completely destroy it.

If you sincerely wish to govern your emotions, you must maintain control over your thoughts. By taking charge of your thoughts, you can substitute love for fear. The instant you receive the stimulus of a negative emotion supplant it with the mood of love and good will. Instead of giving way to fear, say, "One with God is a majority." Fill your mind with concepts of peace, love, and faith in God; then the negative thoughts cannot enter.

You mold, fashion, and create your own future by your present thoughts made manifest, because, as Emerson said, "You are what you think all day long." Change your present thoughts and you change your whole life. You can direct the Cosmic Power within you and thereby control your life experiences; you can actually bring to pass the cherished desires of your heart.

Your mind is constantly in motion as thoughts, images, ideas, dreams, and aspirations come and go. Your world is constantly changing in harmony with your habitual thinking. You create for yourself success or failure, affluence or poverty, health or sickness, and peace or pain by your conscious and subconscious thought. *For as a man thinketh in his heart* (subconscious mind), *so is he . . .* (Proverbs 23:7). Any thought of yours—good or bad—if consciously accepted, is implanted in your subconscious mind, and it comes forth after its kind. This is why you create your own future.

It is far easier to cremate, burn up, and destroy negative thoughts at the moment they enter the mind, rather than try to dislodge them when they have taken possession of your mind. Refuse to be a victim of negative emotions through controlling your thought and thinking of God and His Attributes. You can be master of all emotions and conditions. *"He that is slow to anger is better than the mighty; and he that rules his spirit than he that takes a city."*

The Book of Revelation deals with the control of the intellectual and emotional life of man. It says in Chapter 4, verses 6, 7, and 8: "And before the throne *there was* a sea of glass like unto crystal: and in the midst of the throne, and round about the throne, *were* four beasts full of eyes before and behind.

"And the first beast was like a lion, and the second beast like a calf, and the third beast had a face as a man, and the fourth beast was like a flying eagle.

"And the four beasts had each of them six wings about him; and they were full of eyes within: and they rest not day and night, saying, Holy, holy, holy, Lord God Almighty, which was, and is, and is to come."

The sea of glass before the throne means the inner peace of God, for God is peace. Deep in the centre of your being, the Infinite One lies stretched in smiling repose. It is the Living Presence of God within you. You stand before this throne. The throne is a symbol of authority. Your emotional conviction of a deep, abiding faith in the God-Power is your authority in consciousness. To say it simply: Your inner conviction is your throne in heaven, because therein lies your power. "According to your faith is it done unto you."? Faith is a positive, emotional attitude knowing that the good I seek is mine now.

The four beasts forever before the throne are the four phases of your being: spiritual, mental, emotional, and physical. In order to get your emotional nature on a spiritual basis, it is necessary to understand these four beasts; in doing so you learn the gentle art of scientific prayer which in the final analysis is the answer to all problems. Study these four potencies of consciousness.

The lion is the king of the jungle; it means God, your I AMNESS.

Taurus means the bull or beast of burden. Your burden is your desire. You labor in your imagination to make your desire a part of your consciousness.

Aquarius means the water bearer; it means meditation. The word *meditation* means to eat of God or your good, to feast upon your ideal. You pour water on your ideal, meaning you dwell upon and pour love on it which is the water of life. Something happens as you mentally feast upon your ideal; you generate an emotion; the latter is the spirit of God moving on your behalf. Your emotion is the Holy Spirit moving at human levels. God is a reactive, reciprocal Power within you. Your emotion responds according to the nature of the idea. As you emotionalize your idea, it sinks into the subconscious mind as an impression; this is called the *Eagle or Scorpio*, meaning the Divine impregnation. These are the four stages of the unfoldment or manifestation of an ideal or desire. Whatever is impressed is expressed.

The four beasts had each of them six wings. *The six wings* refer to the mental, creative act. When idea and feeling blend together in harmony and faith, there has taken place a wedding ceremony in the mind. Knowledge of this mental, creative act gives you wings; enables you to soar aloft above the storms and struggles of the world, and find peace and strength in your own mind.

Let us take an illustration explaining the story of spiritual and mental creation: In the name *Jehovah* is concealed the perfect way to pray scientifically; thereby bringing all discordant emotions under scientific control. Sheba, Yod-He-Vau-He, is composed of four letters. *Yod* means God, I AM; *He* means desire or idea; *Vau* is feeling or conviction; the final *He* is the manifestation of what you felt as true inside. The third letter *Vau is* considered the most important of all. It enables you to feel you are that which you desire to be. Walk in the mental atmosphere that you now are what you want to be; this mood will jell within you, and you will experience the joy of the answered prayer. The word *Vau also* means nail. *To nail your* desire is to fix it in consciousness, so that you are at peace about it.

Remember you do not have to live in a world of sickness and confusion created by your own errors or ignorance. You have the power and the capacity to imagine and feel you are what you desire to be. As you completely accept your desire mentally, that you now are what you wish to be, through mental absorption, you have completed the name or the creative way of God as portrayed in the name: *Yod-He-Vau-He*. In other words you have completed the creative process in your own mind as outlined by Troward in his *Bible Mystery and Bible Meaning*. To know how to pray scientifically is to be able to control your emotions. "More things are wrought by prayer than this world dreams of."

The Right Answer

When your motivation is right and based on love and goodwill to all men, and when your mind is free from self-condemnation and self-criticism and you have no desire whatever to take advantage of any person in any way, you will gradually be able to recognize that intuitive feeling which gives you the right answer to your question. The answer may come in many ways, but one of the most frequent is that inner hunch that tells you either to go ahead or to hold back. Your conscious, reasoning mind may try to get in the way, but after you have reasoned the matter out pro and con and then turned the matter over to your deeper mind, full of wisdom and intelligence, you must be alert for the intuitive flash which often wells up spontaneously from your deeper mind. Remember, the impulses, urges, and monitions of your subconscious are always life ward, as your subconscious mind seeks to heal, protect, and save you from financial loss, accidents, and foolish expenditures of energy and talents. Self-preservation is the first law of life, and this is the law of your subjective mind.

The Tabernacle

Feel that you are now what you desire to be; then Infinite Intelligence takes charge, and acts on the thoughts, ideas, and actions of others, so that they aid us in the realization of our desire. (In the same manner a seed attracts to it all things, such as chemicals, water, sunshine, air, etc., necessary for its growth.)

We are always using this Principle, Power, Intelligence, and Wisdom all the days of our life. When we lift our hand to write, we use this Power and Energy. In the same manner when we breathe, we are using the same air.

For example, I am writing now. The ideas expressed come from the One Mind, common to all individual men. There is only Once Source, and that is God. We do not originate anything; for all ideas live, move, and have their being in God. This Infinite Being, Consciousness, Awareness, or whatever we choose to call it is the only Originator—the Fountain of all. All men drink from this One Source or spring. You will understand from these truths that when we look at the sun or a tree, we all see a sun and a tree, which shows that all of us are using the One Mind.

There is, therefore, no such thing as an atheist; there could not be, because he is using the Mind, the Power, and the Intelligence which is of God. He is alive, and the very Life of him is God, for God is Life. When he says, "I do not believe in God," you can see how absurd it is. He knows, and he believes, he is alive. Aliveness, Awareness is God.

As a teacher I wish to point out that there is no teacher who could give you anything new; he could not; neither can he give you truth. All any teacher can do is to awaken that which is already within you. You house God. As the Book of Revelation says, "The tabernacle of God is with man." A teacher causes you to see the truth which was always there; he kindles a fire if he is a good teacher; then you warm yourself by its glow. But the fire, the glow, and the warmth, thereof, were always within you. The real teacher, if he has a good knowledge of truth, will teach you freedom, and tell you frankly that you do not owe him any personal allegiance, since your heart belongs to God or the Truth. "To thine own self be true, as the night the day, thou canst then be false to no man." The teacher of truth will tell you if you do not get anything from him, to go elsewhere where you will be blessed. We call our own; there is no competition in truth.

You do not have to strive toward a goal; for the goal you seek already is, and through your treatment work you appropriate it by accepting the state desired in consciousness. All states coexist in the Greater Now, or other dimensions of your mind. It is like the keyboard of a piano; the music you wish to play is already in the piano; all you do is strike the proper keys and chords to bring it forth, but the tune or the sonata was always there; you do not create it. All you did was to recognize a certain composition and to bring it forth. You can play on the piano *Pop Goes the Weasel* or *a Beethoven Sonata*; the piano does not care.

Similarly look at the English alphabet; you did not create it; it always existed in Infinite Mind. With this alphabet you can write a beautiful, magnificent drama of life, or you may write a gossip column that may cause some misguided person to commit suicide.

We must strike the key to bring forth our music also; our music is: harmony, health, peace, true place, or expression in life. We strike the proper key by contemplating the reality of the state sought now, feeling, and believing ourselves to possess it.

CHAPTER 5

SUGGESTIONS FOR SOME SIMPLE FACTS OF LIFE

To think implies comparison of one thing with another, of one proposition with another. If the mental instrument of man can only say, "Yes," comparison is obviously impossible. To think is to choose. *Choose ye this day that ye shall serve.* You have a choice between two things; to one of them you say, "Yes," to the other, "No."

For example, when you ask, "Why," you are seeking a reason. All reasoning involves selecting one thing and rejecting another. It would be impossible to select or reject unless your mind had the power of affirmation and rejecting. You are truly thinking when your thoughts are positive, constructive, harmonious, and when you reject all fears and contemplate the reality of your desire, knowing that there is an Almighty Power lodged in your subconscious depths which responds to your thought, and this Power will bring your thoughts to fruition. You are truly thinking when you reason things out in your mind, rejecting all concepts unfit for a mind dedicated to peace and harmony. You are truly thinking when you realize that there is a solution, a way out, knowing that a subjective wisdom will respond to your creative thoughts when you are free from fear. If you are worried, fearful, or anxious, you are not thinking in the true sense of the word; it is the race mind thinking in you. Think on whatsoever things are lovely and of good report.

Recently a woman asked me if it was a sign of insanity to talk to oneself. Apparently, her husband engages in this act occasionally. I explained to her that talking to oneself is not unusual and is not necessarily a sign of insanity. Her husband was merely reacting to the pressures of his business.

Basically, the reaction is caused by the sensing of the two selves in each of the spiritual; namely, the human, or five-sense man and us. Children often chatter with invisible playmates, which are explained by some psychologists as a keener sense of the subjective self. In many circles the psychic explanation of the reaction is put forth and accepted.

It Is Wise to Tell No man

It is foolish to talk about your dreams, aspirations, plans and secret desires with others. Your prayer is with the Father within. Whatever you claim and feel to be true in the silence of your soul, the Spirit in you will validate and honor and bring to pass. It is foolish to pluck a flower before it blooms and blossoms. This does not mean that when you go to a doctor, psychologist or attorney you do not tell him your problem, because he is there to help you and cooperate with you. What you convey to a clergyman or doctor is a secret, and he or she keeps that information in confidence.

A girl in a local office was telling everybody recently that she was going to marry the boss and that she had an engagement ring, yet it was another girl in the office who actually married the boss. Keep your own counsel and stop talking about something that has not yet happened. There is the man who is always talking about the home he is going to build, the book he is going to write, and the vast amount of money he is going to make. You can rest assured he never accomplishes any of these things he is bragging and boasting about. The man who writes a book sits down and writes it, has it published and then tells you about it. Withhold your speech until results speak for themselves.

A great number of people dissipate the force of excellent resolutions by talking too much about them. A young man in a local bank was promised a promotion to executive vice president. He told his wife about it, but forgot to tell her to keep it confidential until it had happened. She told all her friends as well as his friends in the bank, and the wives of the other men in the bank created such uproar, claiming their husbands had seniority, etc., that he never did receive the promotion.

Make it a point to mind your own business. It is called "MYOB." You will find it very profitable. Be sure you do not tell your relatives or your so-called best friend your secret prayer. Your best friend is God. A college teacher told me that she told her immediate family that she was going around the world on a guided cruise costing seven thousand dollars. They immediately poured ice cold water on the idea. A brother wanted to borrow money for his family business and said she should lend him the money. Others claimed they needed money for an operation, etc. Instead of rejoicing in her good fortune and wishing her a *bon voyage*, they resented the trip and tried to prevent it. Nevertheless, she went on the cruise and is much wiser now. Go, and tell no man.

A Divine Harmonious Solution

While talking with her husband, I found that he was quite rational. His reason for talking to himself was that he was experiencing a serious legal problem, and the inner spiritual side of him criticized his outer words and actions. This quarrel set up a state of imbalance, which was resolved when he began to claim, "There is a Divine harmonious solution through the wisdom of the Infinite within me." As he adhered to this simple truth, he found in a short time that his prayer paid dividends. There was an amicable settlement out of court.

Talking with a man who had very high blood pressure, and who was on medication, the author learned that his complaint was that he would like to find inner peace, but that the articles in the morning newspaper vexed, annoyed and irritated him beyond measure. He even allowed the headlines to disturb him.

I pointed out to him that it is true that the world goes from one crisis to another, but that it need not affect him personally. He began to perceive and understand that he as an individual could not prevent crime, mass murder, social upheavals, war and disease, but that he could take charge of his own reactions and modify his attitude toward these happenings. There is no law that compels a man to get boiling mad because a newspaperman writes a sordid and morbid article.

The Bible says, *No man takes it from me . . .* (John 10:18). The meaning is quite obvious that no man, news article or circumstance or condition can take away our peace or faith in God. We can give our peace away by giving up our control over our thoughts and emotions.

This man saw the point and decided then and there to let no article, news report or happening rob him of his inner peace, poise or serenity. When thoughts of fear, anger or hate came to his mind, he immediately supplanted them by affirming, "God's peace fills my soul." He made a habit of that (and prayer is a good habit), and he eventually had the joy of hearing his doctor tell him to discontinue the medicine as his blood pressure was normal. In two weeks he had accomplished a state of inner peace and perfect composure.

There is Always an Answer

A few nights ago I gave a lecture at Dr. Bitzer's Church of Religious Science in Hollywood. The subject, "The Wisdom of I Ching." After the lecture an old friend who was present told me that her husband had been promised by his brother a sum of money and that he would send it immediately. This would have solved his acute financial problem. The letter was to be sent air mail, and he expected it in a few days. When he failed to receive the letter, though, he became terribly depressed and allowed despair to overwhelm him, which brought on an acute heart attack. The next day the letter arrived Special Delivery Air Mail.

He had permitted anxiety to control him. Had he remained quiet, still and relaxed, trusting in the Divine Presence, he would have realized that the letter was on the way. When his wife showed him the letter and the contents, he had a marvelous and rapid recovery. His physician said that his brother's letter was the best medicine. Remain faithful to the end, every step of the way. There is always an answer.

Wealth is in you

I had a most interesting conversation with an oil man on the plane returning from a series of lectures at Unity Church in Phoenix, Arizona. He was what he termed an old-timer. His father had prospected for oil in Texas many years ago and had given up in disgust, saying there was no oil anywhere. He asked his son, "Why don't you try?" This oil man said that he went to the fields explored by his father and found oil, which netted him a small fortune over the years. His father had given up too soon.

The son's attitude was that God would guide him to the right place, and he discovered a profitable well in the same area where his father had explored. Wealth was in the mind of the son. It was also in the ground, but it took some intelligence and mental acumen to find it. He said to me that his Dad had a blind spot, since he was very jealous of his neighbors who had found oil and who had become rich. Looking through the eyes of jealousy and envy had blurred his father's vision, and he couldn't see the oil underneath his feet.

The Kingdom Is Within You

The Kingdom of intelligence, wisdom and power is within you. In other words, God indwells you, and all the wisdom, guidance, power and strength you need is instantly available to you. Your kingdom is an attitude of mind; a way of thinking, and an emotional accent whereby you know you can achieve and overcome any challenge through the power of the Almighty within you. Make it a habit during every day to affirm frequently, "Divine peace fills my soul. Divine love governs all my activities. Divine right action is mine. Divine guidance is mine."

Make it a habit to pray as above and you will find peace and rest generated from the depths of yourself. Conditions, circumstances, people, the mountains, the lakes or the sea will not by themselves give you peace of mind. The world is in constant turmoil, and this is why you go within and find and claim the peace that passeth understanding. Tune in with the Infinite, which lies stretched in smiling repose. Wonders will happen as you pray.

Overcoming the World

The Bible says: . . . In the world ye shall have tribulation: but be of good cheer; I have overcome the world (John 16:33). The world does not refer to material objects such as sticks and stones, trees and lakes. The world is the mass mind with its confusion, hate, jealousies, conflicts, dreams and aspirations, the good and the bad, and wars and strife. In other words, it is the thinking, acting and reacting of four billion people.

All of us are immersed in the mass mind, or law of averages. There is no use in getting excited, agitated and perturbed about the conflicts in the world. Furthermore, you cannot run away from the world. You can rise above it by thinking spiritually, constructively and harmoniously. Adopt an attitude of victory and triumph, and claim boldly: "God in the midst of me is guiding me, prospering me and giving me strength and power to overcome." Radiate love and goodwill to all. Claim poise, balance and equilibrium. As you claim these truths regularly, you will move through the maelstrom of this world's thinking into the experiences of satisfaction, contentment and accomplishment.

She Said, "I Can't Stand It"

A young nurse said to me after the service at the Saddleback Theatre in Laguna Hills that she had received her first appointment in a medical clinic but that there were constant complaints, interruptions, strife and contention. She was vexed and said to me, "The situation seems impossible. I can't stand it."

I suggested to her that it would do her no good to run away; that she was there to meet the challenges and difficulties and overcome them. Complaints, interruptions, contention and upset people are a part of the job. She listened and decided to remain calm and affirm frequently, "None of these things move me . . . (Acts 20:24). I am here to conquer, to serve, to radiate love and understanding and to gain experience."

She discovered that her changed attitude changed everything. She moves in the clinic now with a quiet mind . . . . (Isaiah 30:15). She discovered that the power of transcendence over turmoil and vexation was within her. She found there was a power within her greater than any situation. *Greater is he that is in you, than he that is in the world* (I John 4:4).

Everybody meets with difficulties, challenges, problems, strife and contention as an inevitable part of experience here on earth; but the man or woman who realizes that every problem is divinely outmatched wins victories and knows that joining up with the Infinite presence and Power brings about the joy of the answered prayer. Your knowledge of the Divine Presence within you forms the basis of faith and peace of mind.

Be a Good Gardener

Your mind is the garden where you sow seeds, or thoughts, impressions and beliefs. Your mind is called a vineyard in the Bible. The Bible deals with mental and spiritual laws under the guise and symbolism of physical and earthly things. Whatever we impress on our subconscious mind, good or bad, comes forth into our experience.

Man is forever blaming conditions, events and circumstances rather than looking within himself and realizing that he becomes what he things all day long. Your health, happiness and prosperity are not predicated upon events and actions of others but upon the way you think and feel. Your thought and feeling control your destiny. Remember, you are dealing with your own thoughts and your concept of yourself, which determine your future.

What Are You Projecting?

Recently I talked with a man who was projecting anger, resentment and hostility to his associates, and they were responding with similar attitudes toward him. He did not know that he was at fault himself and was blaming them.

I explained to him that his mind was like a motion picture machine, which projects images on the screen. Accordingly, he reversed his attitude and began to silently exude goodwill, love, harmony and peace toward all his associates and co-workers, and he discovered a different response. He perceived the cause within himself.

The Bible gives the answer in a beautiful way: *Judge not, that ye be not judged. For with what judgment ye judge, ye shall be judged* . . . (Matthew 7:1-2) . . . . *With the same measure that ye mete withal it shall be measured to you again* (Luke 6:38). It is said, and rightly so, "Beauty is in the eye of the beholder." If your eyes are identified with the lovely, you will see only the lovely. *Unto the pure all things are pure* . . . (Titus 1:15).

Remember, you have the authority, the dominion and the ruler ship over the government of your mind. You are the husbandman and the vineyard is your mind. Learn to possess your own mind and recall frequently that the treasure house of Infinity is within you. Learn to lay hold of the vast potentialities of the Infinite within you and move forward into a greater measure of health, happiness and peace of mind.

He Found the Treasure House

A young man of ninety years, chronologically speaking, told me after the service on Sunday at the Saddleback Valley Plaza Theatre that he had discovered hidden talents he never knew he had. He began praying that Infinite Intelligence would reveal to him new creative ideas, which would bless and inspire people. He showed me some beautiful poetry which came forth freely from his pen. He is submitting these poems to various spiritual publications. They are, indeed, spiritual gems of wisdom.

As a young man he wandered all over the country doubting, questioning, fearing, grieving, hating and fighting with others until, as he said, at the age of thirty, he discovered that life's greatest gifts were within himself and not in the fifty states of the Union. He is now living in Laguna Hills and contributing to the beauty and harmony of the area by giving of his wisdom and largess to all those around him.

Look Within Always

Contemplate the Living Presence of God within you. Realize you live, move and have your being in this Infinite Presence and Power. As you do this frequently, you will find yourself sustained, strengthened and protected in all your ways. Spend some time every day contemplating things Divine. Remember, it is not running to and fro but accomplishment and achievement that counts.

Every morning when you arise, give thanks for your many blessings and live in the joyous expectancy of the best, claiming it is the greatest day of your life because your Higher Self is revealing to you better ways to serve and grow spiritually. At night prior to sleep wrap yourself in the mantle of God's love, forgiving yourself for any errors of the day, and go off to sleep with the praise of God forever on your lips.

Mental Readiness

In a recent lecture I used the statement, "All things be ready if our mind be so." Shakespeare here points out a great truth dealing with mental and spiritual laws. A young lady present wrote me and said that she had never heard it explained before and that it applied to her. She had been constantly postponing marriage, since she felt she was not ready because she had been looking after her parents. Suddenly, she came to the conclusion, "I am ready now." She phoned the young man who wanted to marry her, and the author had the privilege of performing the ceremony.

You can be and you can do what you want to be and do if you are mentally ready. Your great opportunity in life is really your mental acceptance and readiness. This young woman's parents were not a stumbling block to her fulfillment in life. This was a blind spot in her own mind. Her parents were delighted, and they hired a nurse and a maid to help them in their home, which actually proved to be a far better arrangement for all concerned. When love comes into your life, it contributes to the peace and happiness of all those around you and all people everywhere.

Remember a simple truth: Whenever you are mentally ready, you will find that everything else is also ready. In the early days of America, the Pilgrims could have used the telephone, radio, automobile, cinemas, airplanes, etc., but they were not mentally ready. They believed that the horse and buggy was the only means of transportation. Moses, Elijah, Buddha and all the ancient teachers could have used radio and television to dramatize and portray the great truths of life had they been mentally receptive and ready.

The laws of nature never vary, however, and were the same then as now, but the minds of the ancient seers and prophets were not ready for these inventions. Supply and demand are one, but you must supply mental readiness and the answer will then come to you in Divine order.

She Was Using the Ouija Board

I receive many letters from men and women who live in different states, claiming that they hear voices at night shouting obscenities and vulgarities in their ears, as well as all kinds of profane language. One woman wrote saying that an entity had been telling her to commit suicide and join him in the next dimension.

She had been using the Ouija Board and lived in constant fear that some evil entity would take over. What she continually feared finally came upon her. She did not know that her subconscious mind accepts all kinds of suggestions, good or bad, and that her fear of an evil entity was a constant command to her subconscious mind, which responded and played the role of an evil spirit. Actually, it was her own subconscious mind talking back to her.

I gave her the following, which is very effective, telling her to repeat this prayer aloud many times, day or night, as often as needed, and she would feel the Presence of God. This awareness will dethrone from one's mind all negative influences that are bothersome. Make it real, affirm these truths and boldly assert:

"I mean this and I decree it. God lives in me. God talks and walks in me. My life is God's life, and God's peace fills my mind and heart. God's love saturates my soul. I am growing in wisdom, truth and beauty. I am whole, I am strong, and I am happy, joyous and free. I can do all things through the God-Power, which strengthened me. I know that whatever I attach to 'I AM,' I become. God careth for me. I am surrounded by the sacred circle of God's eternal love. The whole armor of God surrounds me. God is guiding me. His light shines in me."

Following this spiritual meditation, she was to issue this command to her subconscious mind boldly, incisively and decisively: "I decree you to get out now.

I mean this. I am sincere. Get thee hence. God is here now. Wherever God is, there is no evil. Are thou gone. I am free."

Following this technique, she became completely free in two weeks' time, and she no longer dabbles with the Ouija Board.

The First and the Last

In a recent Bible class on the inner meaning of the Book of Revelation, a man asked the meaning of . . . *I am Alpha and Omega, the first and the last* . . . (Revelation 1:11).

He was a businessman, and I explained it along these lines: I AM is the Presence of God in all of us. It is the unconditioned consciousness or awareness. It is the only Presence and Power and is the Cause of all manifestation. It is Omnipresent and the very Life of all of us. The individual I AM is the universal I AM conditioned by man's thinking and beliefs. It is our personal consciousness, which means the way we think, feel, and believe as well as to whatever we give our mental consent.

He began to see what the Bible meant by the statement *I AM the first and the last*, the beginning and the end, for our own consciousness is the beginning of every enterprise or undertaking. Our actions, experiences and results are secondary.

We may begin writing a book, which takes some time; then it comes to an end when finished. The same would apply to any invention, discovery or business. The beginning was in the mind of the person. If he began or started his new business with faith and confidence, the end, or result, would end up as a successful enterprise. The end would agree with the beginning.

This man said that he began making picture postal cards of a religious nature with great love in his heart, and he received loving letters from nearly everyone to whom he sent them. His present wife received one of the cards, and that his how his loved one came into his life.

Your Mood is Contagious

Everyone knows the workman or salesgirl who is sour, cynical and full of criticism of others and about everything else in general. This negative attitude is picked up subconsciously by others, and they find themselves in a daily rut, never moving up in the ladder of life. Many are bitter and jealous of those who have gone up the ladder of life. This mood of jealousy and envy robs them of life's energy, and they are always tired, exhausted and lethargic.

Warm, kind, understanding and outgoing people release the healing power of life, and they pour out the sunshine of Divine love into their works.

Know Who You Are

The Bible says: *A bastard shall not enter into the congregation of the Lord; even to his tenth generation shall he not enter the congregation of the Lord* (Deuteronomy 23:2). "Our Father" mentioned in the Bible means the Life Principle, which is the Progenitor or Father of us all. We are all brothers and sisters and are intimately related to one another.

Every man should know the Source from which he springs. The Bible deals with psychology and metaphysics and speaks in metaphors, similes and parables. We must see the hidden meaning. When a man does not know that God, or Infinite Intelligence indwells him, he is unable to meet life's challenges in the right way. He fails to see that there is a wisdom and power within him, enabling him to solve all problems and to rise triumphantly and express him at the highest level.

If a man looks at his human ancestors as the source of his being, he is indeed limiting himself and will feel restricted and circumscribed by his environment, upbringing and limited beliefs of his forebears. Knowing that God is his real Father and that he has inherited all the powers, qualities and attributes of the Infinite gives him the feeling and the awareness that he can do great things, and he will go forth conquering and to conquer.

To take the passage from Deuteronomy literally would be absurd, but when a man knows his true Source and tunes in with the Infinite, he rejects completely the illusions, false beliefs and superstitions of the masses and becomes master of his environment and conditions. Man comes of royal lineage, for his Father is God, and God is Spirit; and, as Emerson says, "Every spirit builds itself a house." Then he is in complete charge and molds and fashions his own destiny.

. . . And as thou hast believed, so be it done unto thee . . . (Matthew 8:13).

Chapter 6

THE WONDERFUL WILL OF GOD

Longfellow said, "To will what God wills is the only science that gives us rest." It is the will of God that we should all be healthy, happy and joyous, and that we led lives full of marvelous experiences; that we should express more and more wisdom, truth, and beauty, day by day and week by week, until we become the man that God intended us to be—the happy man, the joyous man, the free man who is illumined and inspired and walks the earth with the praise of God forever on his lips.

A tragic mistake, that is often made by many people, is to assume that the will of God for them is bound to be something evil and uninviting, if not downright unpleasant. One reason for this strange and weird concept is that these people look upon God as a hard taskmaster of some sort of a capricious tyrant living up in the skies, meting out punishment to disobedient children.

The marvelous and priceless truth is that the will of God for us means greater peace, greater self-expression, more wisdom, greater and brighter experiences, radiant health, prosperity along all lines, and the capacity to give wider and greater service to others. In short, the will of God for you is the life more abundant! If the will of God for you were sickness, then all the doctors, psychologists, nurses, ministers, priests, and rabbis would be working against the will of God—this, of course, is the quintessence of absurdity.

If a man is ill, frustrated, lonesome, bored, impoverished, or is a square peg in a round hole, he may be certain that he is not expressing the will of God. As long as man is not expressing His will, he will experience discord and confusion in his life. But when man unites with God and expresses His will, harmony, peace, vitality, and prosperity will come into his experience.

A man said to me one time that he would be happy, joyous, and successful if God would let him alone. This man really believed that God caused him to suffer. Somehow he believed that he could run the universe better than God. He said to me, "I hate God for all the failures, troubles and tragedies He has brought upon me."

I explained to this man that God had nothing to do with the misery, suffering, and tragedies of life. Man experiences sickness, pain, suffering, and failure because of his own negative, destructive thinking. Man punishes himself by the natural laws of cause and effect. Punishment ceases when man ceases wrongdoing. I also pointed out to him that it was blasphemy to say that God sent sickness, disease, and suffering on man. On the contrary, man brings these things on himself by his own wrong thinking and ignorance of the laws of his mind.

Man must not blame God because through ignorance and inexperience be made mistakes. The powers and forces of nature are not evil; they are neutral. Good and evil are in the movement of our own minds, in the way we think and act, and in the attitude we take towards things, not in the things themselves. The wind that blows a ship on the rocks will also bring it to a port of safety. Electricity is not evil, but man must use it the right way; otherwise, he may electrocute himself and others.

Man's subconscious mind is not evil, but if he thinks evil, evil will follow; if he thinks good, good will follow. Man must decide what kind of seeds (thoughts) he plants in the garden of his mind, because seeds (thoughts) grow after their kind. The ideas contained in this chapter will prove to be of priceless benefit to man as he reads and applies them.

Nothing Good or Bad

Shakespeare said, "There's nothing good or bad but thinking makes it so." The problem you have at this moment is a wonderful opportunity for you to overcome it. You can meet the challenge. There is a wisdom and power within you which will enable you to overcome the problem. If you had no problems, difficulties, and challenges in life, you would never grow. The problem is not bad; it depends how you think about it. Realize your difficulty or problem is a marvelous opportunity for you to transcend it and prove your capacity to overcome.

He Was Bitter and Resentful

Mr. Jones, almost deaf and nearly blind, for years felt bitter and resentful, saying, "Why did God do this to me?" He felt insecure and inferior. He had great difficulty in seeing, and his hearing aid was not satisfactory and caused him great annoyance. He did not want his friends to know he was gradually going blind and deaf and felt embarrassed when they said to him, "I met you yesterday at the club, but you never spoke to me." He made excuses, and his resentment and anger against his condition were intensified.

Mr. Jones made a list of all his blessings. He gave thanks for his lovely and faithful wife, for his three brilliant daughters, for a lovely home, for his marvelous friends and all his kind neighbors. He ceased blaming God, and admitted to himself that there were certain people he did not want to see and voices of certain relatives he did not want to hear. He overcame this by blessing and releasing them mentally, and his constant prayer was as follows:

"My vision is spiritual, eternal, and a quality of my mind. My eyes are divine ideas and they are always functioning perfectly. My perception of spiritual truth is clear and powerful. The light of understanding dawns in me; I see more and more of God's truth every day. I see spiritually; I see mentally; I see physically. I see images of truth and beauty everywhere. The Infinite Healing Presence is now, this moment, rebuilding my eyes. They are perfect, divine instruments enabling me to receive messages from the world within and the world without. The light of God is revealed in my eyes and ears.

"I hear the Truth; I love the Truth; I know the Truth. My ears are God's perfect ideas functioning perfectly at all times. My ears are the perfect instruments which reveal God's harmony to me. The love, beauty, and harmony of God flow through my eyes and ears; I am in tune with the Infinite. I hear the Still, Small Voice of God within me. The Healing Presence quickens my hearing, and my ears are open and free."

At the end of a month he experienced a great personality change, and his eyesight and hearing improved remarkably. In fact, he came to see and hear almost normally. He transcended his problem. He transmuted that which he had heretofore called evil to a great good, and now he is happy, joyous and free.

The Will or Tendency of God

The will of God, as Judge Thomas Troward, author of Edinburgh Lectures and other works on Mental Science, so eloquently puts it, is the tendency of God, and God being Life, cannot wish anything detrimental to itself. Life feels Itself to be Love, Joy, Peace, and Beauty, and Its tendency is to express Its own nature which is the same yesterday, today, and forever.

The will of God is the nature of God, and God is love; therefore, God cannot wish for you anything unloving. God is Absolute Peace, and God cannot wish for you discord, chaos, and confusion. God is Life, and Life cannot wish death; that would be a contradiction of its own nature. God is Absolute Joy and cannot wish grief or sorrow. God is Absolute and unalloyed Harmony and cannot wish sickness or disease. God is Infinite Riches of all kinds and cannot wish poverty; to think so would be a denial of His abundance. God's will for you is something transcending your fondest dreams. It is wrong, therefore, to say, "I am poor; I am weak; I am tired; I am broke," because you bring that condition on yourself by your negative, destructive statements which are lodged in your subconscious mind and which come forth as experiences and events in your life.

Your Power to Choose

You are here to grow, expand, and unfold, and if all your faculties were fully developed when you were born, you would never discover yourself. If, for example, you were compelled to love your husband or wife, you would have no free will. This is why you say, "I choose _____ from all the women in the world to be my lawful wedded wife." You are not an automaton; you have freedom to give love or retain it. You have the capacity to choose, select, and arrive at a decision through your capacity to reason.

In the beginning, man looks out at the three-dimensional world and is governed by appearances and conditions until he awakens to the fact that, through the medium of his own thought and feeling, he can control and direct his life. Gradually, man awakens to the truth that circumstances and conditions are effects and not causes. All outer conditions are subject to change. As man changes his mind he changes his body, environment, and conditions.

The Meaning of Will

The dictionary defines will as choice, intention, inclination, determination, and tendency, and in order to make it the will of Omnipotence you must animate it, make it alive within you by enthusiasm, feeling, and animation until it becomes embodied in the subconscious mind. When man learns to choose wisely, he will choose happiness, peace, security, joy, health, abundance, and all the blessings of life. He will enthrone the spiritual values and truths of God in his mind and will busy his mind with these eternal verities until they become part of his consciousness in the same manner that an apple becomes a part of his bloodstream. Choose Divine guidance, right action, Divine order, and Divine success in your life. What is true of God is true of you, for God dwells in you. God is always successful, whether making a star, planet, tree, or the cosmos. Therefore, you were born to succeed, because the Infinite cannot fail.

The worldly minded man who is a victim of the race mind unconsciously chooses sickness, misfortune, lack, and limitation of all kinds. He fails to realize that thoughts are things, that what he imagines, he becomes, and that what he feels he attracts. If man does not do his own thinking, the newspapers, the neighbors, and the race mind will do his thinking for him, and his life will be a mess. *"Choose you this day whom ye will serve."* (Joshua 24:15)

Let God's Will be done

Realize that God's will is being expressed through you at all times. Make a habit of affirming that God's will is being expressed in all departments of your life, making certain, of course, that you know what you mean when you say, "God's will be done."

God is Boundless Love, Absolute Bliss, Indescribable Beauty, Infinite Intelligence, Absolute Harmony, Omnipotent, Supreme, and Absolute Peace. There are no divisions or quarrels in the Absolute. God is Infinitely Good, Perfect, and the Author only of Perfect Good. Pray aright in this way: "God's will is being made manifest in my life as harmony, perfect health, happiness, peace, joy, abundance, love, and perfect Divine expression. It is wonderful."

If you meditate on this prayer regularly, your present environment and circumstances will magically change and be transformed into the likeness of what you are contemplating. Now, when you say, "God's will is operating in my life," it has a magnificent and beautiful significance full of spiritual precious stones. When you say, "God's plan is made manifest in my life," that, too, has a new and wonderful meaning. God's plan is God's will, and His plan can only be beauty, order, symmetry, love, health, and all the good things of life. God's plan for you could only be to express more of Himself through you, moving ever onward, upward, and God-ward.

If God Wants Me to Have It

I have heard this expression frequently: "I want it if God wants me to have it." If you really believe that God is the Divine Presence or Life within you and is Infinite Intelligence and All-Powerful and Boundless Love, why should you think that God does not want you to have it, whether it is health, peace, joy, true place, abundance, a new home, marriage, or what not?

Many people utter another superstitious phrase: "Maybe it isn't good for me." When people use such an expression, they are living in a world of duality, of two powers. They have God and a devil; they are double-minded. Isn't happiness good for you? Surely, you must agree that God wants you to be happy. If you pray for right action, why would you begin to think of wrong action? There is only a Principle of Right Action in the world; there is no principle of wrong action. There is a Principle of Joy, none of sadness. There is a Principle of Love, none of hatred. There is a Principle of Truth, and none of error. There is a Principle of Harmony, and none of discord.

What kind of a God would you have that did not want you to be joyous, free, radiant, and illumined? You are here to reproduce all the qualities, attributes, potencies, and aspects of God and to move from glory to glory.

God's Infinite Riches are yours

If you have a desire for healing, for true expression, for greater wisdom and spiritual understanding, or for greater wealth and expression to do the things you want to do, surely there is not a doubt in your mind but that God wants you to have all these things. If you think that God wants you to be sick or is testing you in some strange way, or if you think that God could create sickness, such a God is not worthy of your consideration and attention, and the belief is only a false, superstitious concept in your mind.

God wants you to be prosperous as well as healthy. Many people, because of false theological beliefs implanted in their subconscious minds when they were young and impressionable, believe that there is some virtue in lack and limitation. You must eradicate that false belief from your subconscious mind and realize that the infinite riches of God are all around you. You cannot count the sands on the seashore or the stars in the heavens above. Did you ever try to count the flowers by the wayside as you drive along the road? Everywhere you look you see a profusion of God's wealth.

God's ideas are infinite, and you can have an idea now that could put a million men to work. Ideas are wealth. An invention is an idea in the mind; so is a book, a new business venture, and a new real estate and make it rejoice and blossom as the rose. Nature is lavish, extravagant, and bountiful. Man in his greed and lust creates an artificial shortage, but there is no shortage of God's wisdom or creative ideas in the mind of man, if he will become open and receptive to the Divine Influx, which is always ready and available.

Your Will Becomes God's Will

You are not glorifying God when you are sick, frustrated, neurotic, unhappy, and poverty stricken. You are here to dramatize, portray, and express in your life that which is true of God. To believe in a God of Love is to express love, and to believe in a God of Abundance is to express the abundant life.

If you have a desire to write a play, write a novel, or build a new house, would it not be extremely foolish for you to think that God did not will these things? God is within you, and your desire to express is from God. God gave you your brain, your mind, the hands to write and build, and the urge to achieve and express, plus the intelligence and capacity to do all these things.

His Conscious and Subconscious Will

A man came to see me some time ago. He was an alcoholic and said that if he took one drink he would be compelled to keep on drinking until he fell unconscious on the floor. In other words, he had lost control and was compelled by the law of his subconscious mind to drink. His story was a familiar one. His wife divorced him because of his infidelity. He resented her action and hated her because she refused to take him back. Then he turned to drink to relieve the psychic pain in the same way you might take aspirin for a headache. He repeated this act over and over again, and each time he took a drink to bolster his spirits, he was rejecting the power of God within him and was suggesting weakness and inferiority to his subconscious mind.

Habits are formed by repeating certain thought patterns or actions over and over again until they establish patterns in the subconscious mind, where they grow until they reach the point of saturation. He now had a mental bartender established in his subconscious mind that reminded him repeatedly, "You need a drink." When he took one, he lost control. His wish or conscious will was not to drink, but the will of the subconscious took over and said, "You must drink." His choice to drink, which he had repeated over and over again until it became an established habit pattern, was now in control.

He Reversed the Pattern

This man reversed the pattern and freed himself by the use of the same law which made him a compulsive drinker. Regularly and systematically he contemplated freedom and peace of mind, claiming that his food and drink were God's ideas which constantly unfolded within him, bringing him harmony, health, and peace. He ran a movie in his mind several times daily by imagining himself free, happy, and joyous. He pictured himself doing what he longed to do and heard a friend congratulate him on his freedom and sobriety. Whenever he was tempted, he flashed the movie in his mind, knowing that the power of the Almighty was flowing through his mental movie and that by a process of mental and spiritual osmosis the mental image was sinking down into his subconscious where it was being developed in the darkroom of his mind.

Impressions are made in the subconscious by repetition, faith, and expectancy, and as he continued faithfully imagining his freedom and peace of mind, the dawn came and all the shadows flew away. His conscious will (desire for complete freedom from the destructive habit) became a subconscious will (his deep abiding conviction was lodged in his subconscious mind), and he was compelled to express freedom, for the law of the subconscious is compulsion. The law which held him in bondage is the same law which freed him, enabling him to enter into the glorious liberty of the sons of God.

The Meaning of Heaven

Thy will be done on earth as it is in Heaven is a wonderful prayer, as you now realize. Heaven means your own mind or mental and spiritual awareness. What you feel as true in the heavens of your own mind, you shall experience on earth or the objective plane (your body, world, environment, circumstances). Your will is your capacity to define your objectives, to choose your goal, ideal, or plan. Live with it mentally by loving it, nursing it, giving it your attention and whole-souled devotion. Finally, it becomes jelled within you, and your desert has become paradise, and *your will has become God's will* or the joy of the answered prayer. It is wonderful!

Highlights and Suggestions

1. God does not send sickness, disease, or suffering; we bring these on ourselves by our own wrong thinking.
2. The powers and forces of nature are not evil; it depends how man uses these powers or forces.
3. "There is nothing good or bad but thinking makes it so." Your problem is not bad—it is your opportunity to overcome.
4. Count your many blessings, bless the diseased organ, and you will be amazed at the wonders happening in your life.
5. To will what God wills is the only science that gives us rest.
6. It is the will of God that you lead a full, happy, and joyous life and that you experience the abundant life spoken of by Jesus.
7. A tragic error is to suppose that the will of God for you is something unpleasant or uninviting.
8. If you are ill or depressed, you are going contrary to the will of God.
9. The will of God is the tendency of God. God, being life, cannot wish anything detrimental to itself.
10. The will of God is the nature of God, and God is Love. Love cannot wish for you anything unloving.
11. You are here to reproduce the qualities, potencies, and aspects of God.
12. Your thoughts, imagery, and mental patterns mold, fashion, and shape your life.

13. You have the power to choose. Choose health, happiness, peace, guidance, and right action.
14. It is superb spiritual strategy to affirm "God's will be done," particularly when you understand the spiritual significance of these words.
15. To say, "If God wants me to have it," is rank superstition. God wants you to be happy. He gave you Himself and the whole world.
16. God wants you to be prosperous and successful. Nature is lavish, extravagant, and bountiful. Everywhere, you see a profusion of God's wealth.
17. The channels through which you receive your wealth are not the source, and you should not confuse the channel with the Eternal Source.
18. Your desire for growth, expansion, and unfoldment is from God. Accept your desire now, and Infinite Intelligence will bring it to pass.
19. Your will (desire, choice, plan, purpose) becomes God's will (conviction in your subconscious mind) when you feel the reality of your fulfilled desire. Your conscious wish or desire has now passed from wishing to a subconscious conviction.
20. The law which holds you in bondage or in any limitation is the same law which will free you as you entertain the concepts of freedom, peace, joy, and happiness. What you feel as true in your mind (heaven), you shall experience on earth (the objective world).
21. Let your will (your conscious choice or decision) become God's will (a subconscious conviction) by living with It mentally, by nursing it and giving it your attention, and you will experience the joy of the answered prayer.

Chapter 7

LIFE PLAYS NO FAVORITES

God is Life, and this Life-Principle is flowing through you this moment. God loves to express Himself as harmony, peace, beauty, joy, and abundance through you. This is called the will of God or the tendency of Life.

If you set up resistance in your mind to the flow of Life through you, this emotional congestion will get snarled up in your subconscious mind and cause all kinds of negative conditions. God has nothing to do with unhappy or chaotic conditions in the world. All these conditions are brought about by man's negative and destructive thinking. Therefore, it is silly to blame God for your trouble or sickness.

Many persons habitually set up mental resistance to the flow of Life by accusing and reproaching God for the sin, sickness, and suffering of mankind. Others cast the blame on God for their pains, aches, loss of loved ones, personal tragedies, and accidents. They are angry at God, and they believe He is responsible for their misery.

As long as people entertain such negative concepts about God, they will experience the automatic negative reactions from their subconscious minds. Actually, such people do not know that they are punishing themselves. They must see the truth, find release, and give up all condemnation, resentment, and anger against anyone or any power outside themselves. Otherwise, they cannot go forward into a healthy, happy, or creative activity. The minute these people entertain a God of love in their minds and hearts, and when they believe that God is their Loving Father who watches over them, cares for them, guides them, sustains and strengthens them, this concept and belief about God or the Life-Principle will be accepted by their subconscious mind, and they will find themselves blessed in countless ways.

Life Always Forgives You

Life forgives you when you cut your finger. The subconscious intelligence within you sets about immediately to repair it. New cells build bridges over the cut. Should you take some tainted food by error, Life forgives you and causes you to regurgitate it in order to preserve you. If you burn your hand, the Life-Principle reduces the edema and congestion, and gives you new skin, tissue, and cells. Life holds no grudges against you, and it is always forgiving you. Life brings you back to health, vitality, harmony, and peace, if you co-operate by thinking in harmony with nature. Negative, hurtful memories, bitterness, and ill will clutter up and impede the free flow of the Life-Principle in you.

How He Banished that Feeling of Guilt

I knew a man who worked every night until about one o'clock in the morning. He paid no attention to his two boys or his wife. He was always too busy working hard. He thought people should pat him on the back because he was working so arduously and persistently past midnight every night. He had a blood pressure of over two hundred and was full of guilt. Unconsciously, he proceeded to punish himself by hard work and he completely ignored his children. A normal man does not do that. He is interested in his boys and in their development. He does not shut his wife out of his world.

I explained to him why he was working so arduously, "There is something eating you inside, otherwise, you would not act this way. You are punishing yourself, and you have to learn to forgive yourself." He did have a deep sense of guilt. It was toward a brother.

I explained to him that God was not punishing him, but that he was punishing himself. For example, if you misuse the laws of life, you will suffer accordingly. If you put your hand on a naked charged wire, you will get burned. The forces of nature are not evil; it is your use of them that determines whether they have a good or evil effect. Electricity is not evil; it depends on how you use it, whether to burn down a structure or light up a home. The only sin is ignorance of the law, and the only punishment is the automatic reaction of man's misuse of the law.

If you misuse the principle of chemistry, you may blow up the office or the factory. If you strike your hand on a board, you may cause your hand to bleed. The board is not for that purpose. Its purpose may be to lean upon or to support your feet.

This man realized that God does not condemn or punish anyone, and that all his suffering was due to the reaction of his subconscious mind to his own negative and destructive thinking. He had cheated his brother at one time, and the brother had now passed on. Still, he was full of remorse and guilt.

I asked him, "Would you cheat your brother now?"

He said, "No."

"Did you feel you were justified at the time?"

His reply was, "Yes."

"But, you would not do it now?"

He added, "No, I am helping others to know how to live."

I added the following comment, "You have a greater reason and understanding now. Forgiveness is to forgive you. Forgiveness is getting your thoughts in line with the divine law of harmony. Self-condemnation is called hell (bondage and restriction); forgiveness is called heaven (harmony and peace)."

The burden of guilt and self-condemnation was lifted from his mind, and he had a complete healing. The doctor tested his blood pressure, and it had become normal. The explanation was the cure.

He was a Transformed Man

A man who murdered his brother in Europe visited me many years ago. He was suffering from great mental anguish and torture believing that God must punish him. He explained that his brother had been having an affair with his wife, and that he had shot him on the spur of the moment. This had happened about fifteen years previous to his interview with me. In the meantime, this man had married an American girl and had been blessed with three lovely children. He was a transformed man.

My explanation to him was that physically and psychologically he was not the same man who shot his brother, since scientists inform us that every cell of your bodies changes every eleven months. Moreover, mentally and spiritually he was a new man. He was now full of love and good will for humanity. "The "old" man who committed the crime fifteen years before was mentally and spiritually dead. Actually, he was condemning an innocent man!

This suggestion had a profound effect upon him, and he said it was as if a great weight had been lifted from his mind. He realized the significance of the following truth in the Bible: *Come now, let us reason together, saith the Lord: though your sins be as scarlet, they shall be as white as snow; though they be red like crimson, they shall be as wool.* Isaiah 1:18.

Criticism cannot hurt you without your Consent

A schoolteacher told me that one of her associates criticized a speech she had given, saying to her that she spoke too fast, she swallowed some of her words, she couldn't be heard, her diction was poor, and her speech ineffective. This teacher was furious and full of resentment toward her critic.

She admitted to me that the criticisms were just. Her first reaction was really childish, and she agreed that the letter was really a blessing and a marvelous corrective. She proceeded immediately to supplement her deficiencies in her speech by enrolling in a course in public speaking at City College. She wrote and thanked the writer of the note for her interest, expressing appreciation for her conclusions and findings which enabled the teacher to correct the matter at once.

How to be Compassionate

Suppose none of the things mentioned in the letter had been true of the teacher. The latter would have realized that her class material had upset the prejudices, superstitions, or narrow sectarian beliefs of the writer or the note, and that a psychologically ill person was simply pouring forth her resentment because a psychological boil had been hurt.

To understand this fact is to be compassionate. The next logical step would be to pray for the other person's peace, harmony, and understanding. You cannot be hurt when you know that you are master of your thoughts, reactions, and emotions. Emotions follow thoughts, and you have the power to reject all thoughts which may disturb or upset you.

Forgiveness is Necessary for Healing

And when ye stand praying, forgive, if ye have ought against any . . . Mark 11:25.

Forgiveness of others is essential to mental peace and radiant health. You must forgive everyone who has ever hurt you if you want perfect health and happiness. Forgive yourself by letting your thoughts in harmony with divine law and order. You cannot really forgive yourself completely until you have forgiven others first. To refuse to forgive you is nothing more or less than spiritual pride or ignorance.

In the psychosomatic field of medicine today, it is being constantly stressed that resentment, condemnation of others, remorse, and hostility are behind a host of maladies ranging from arthritis to cardiac disease. They point out that these sick people, who were hurt, mistreated, deceived, or injured, were full of resentment and hatred for those who hurt them. This caused inflamed and festering wounds in their subconscious minds. There is only one remedy. They have to cut out and discard their hurts, and the one and only sure way is by forgiveness.

Forgiveness is Love in Action

The essential ingredient in the art of forgiveness is the willingness to forgive. If you sincerely desire to forgive the other, you are fifty-one percent over the hurdle. I feel sure you know that to forgive the other does not necessarily mean that you like him or want to associate with him. You cannot be compelled to like someone, neither can a government legislate good will, love, peace, or tolerance. It is quite impossible to like people because someone in Washington issues an edict to that effect. We can, however, love people without liking them.

The Bible says, *Love ye one another.* This, anyone can do who really wants to do it. Love means that you wish for the other health, happiness, peace, joy, and all the blessings of life. There is only one prerequisite, and that is sincerity. You are not being magnanimous when you forgive, you are really being selfish, because what you wish for the other, you are actually wishing for yourself. The reason is that you are thinking it and you are feeling it. As you think and feel, so are you. Could anything be simpler than that?

The Secret of True Forgiveness

The following is a simple method which works wonders in your life as you practice it: quiet your mind, and let go. Think of God and His love for you, and then affirm, "I fully and freely forgive (mention the name of the offender); I release him mentally and spiritually. I completely forgive everything connected with the matter in question. I am free, and he/she is free. It is a marvelous feeling. It is my day of general amnesty. I release anybody and everybody who has ever hurt me, and I wish for each and everyone health, happiness, peace, and all the blessings of life. I do this freely, joyously, and lovingly, and whenever I think of the person or persons who hurt me, I say, 'I have released you, and all the blessings of life are yours." I am free and you are free. It is wonderful!"

The great secret of true forgiveness is that once you have forgiven the person, it is unnecessary to repeat the prayer. Whenever the person comes to your mind, wish the delinquent well, and say, "Peace is to you." Do this as often as the thought enters your mind. You will find that after a few days the thought of the experience will return less and less often, until it fades into nothingness.

The Acid Test for Forgiveness

There is an acid test for gold. There is also an acid test for forgiveness. If I should tell you something wonderful about someone who has wronged, cheated you, or defrauded you, and you sizzled at hearing the good news about this person, the roots of hatred would still be in your subconscious mind, playing havoc with you.

Let us suppose you had a painful abscess on your jaw a year ago, and you told me about it. I would casually ask you if you had any pain now. You would automatically say, "Of course not, I have a memory of it but no pain." That is the whole story. You may have a memory of the incident but no sting or hurt any more. This is the acid test, and you must meet it psychologically and spiritually, otherwise, you are simply deceiving yourself and not practicing the true art of forgiveness.

To Understand All is to Forgive All

When man understands the creative law of his own mind, he ceases to blame other people and conditions for making or marring his life. He knows that his own thoughts and feelings create his destiny. Furthermore, he is aware that externals are not the causes and conditioners of his life and his experiences. To think that others can mar your happiness, that you are the football of a cruel fate, that you must oppose and fight others for a living—all these and others like them are untenable when you understand that thoughts are things. The Bible says the same thing. *For as a man thinketh in his heart, so is he.* Proverbs 23:7.

Chapter 8

YOU HAVE THE POWER TO CONTROL SUGGESTIONS

If someone calls you a skunk, well, you know you are not a skunk, and the statement has no power. You are in charge of your mind, and you have the wonderful opportunity to affirm that God's peace and love fill the soul of the person in question. The power is always in you, and not in the other. You can curse or bless. Cease giving power and prerogatives to other people, conditions, and events which have no power and prerogatives to people, conditions, and events which have no power. Cease looking upon matter as evil or the world as evil. Spirit and matter are one. Matter is the lowest degree of Spirit, and Spirit is the highest degree of matter. Matter and Invisible Energy are one, and scientists inform us that energy and matter are interchangeable, that energy and matter are one—this is why thoughts are things. Thought is cause, and the manifestation is the effect.

Some years ago, I visited an old friend in Hawaii. He was, as he said, the victim of a curse by a Kahuna and was slowly dying. The doctors tried their best to alleviate the creeping paralysis to no avail.

I knew he was a victim of an ideological suggestion of a so-called death prayer. He had never reasoned out in his mind that there is only One Power, and that there are no divisions or quarrels in this Power. One part of God cannot be antagonistic to another part. Its fundamental nature is unity and love.

I explained to him that there was no evil power, no devil, save his own fear and ignorance. Gradually, he began to understand that he was the victim of autohypnosis that he had accepted the suggestion of death, made it his own, and his subconscious mind proceeded to bring about death of his body. This man was involved emotionally with a native Hawaiian woman on the Island who sought revenge when he married someone else of his own race and religion.

I visited him for several days and told him that I had seen his former girl friend and that everything was all right. The curse was lifted, and he would be perfect in a few days.

All of this was pure invention on my part. I had not seen his former girl friend or the Kahuna, or anybody connected with him. It was an old ruse which I employed. I gave him a counter-suggestion which neutralized the former one with which he had impregnated himself.

The suggestion of health and perfect recovery was now dominant in his mind. The subconscious mind accepts the dominant of two ideas at all times.

He made a full recovery, and is now home in Ireland with an Irish instead of a Hawaiian wife. According to his belief was it done unto him? He believed the so-called curse was lifted, he accepted my suggestion, and his subconscious mind responded accordingly.

All your fears, anxieties, and forebodings are caused by your belief in external powers and malevolent agencies. All this is based on ignorance. The only immaterial creative power you are aware of is your thought, and once, as Troward says, you are aware of the creative power of your thought, and that thoughts are things, you are at once delivered from all sense of bondage and the thralldom of the world.

The scientific thinker does not give power to things, conditions, people, or circumstances. He is full of poise, balance, and equanimity, because he knows that his thoughts and feelings mold, fashion, and shape his destiny. He is not afraid of anything or any person, for the only enemy he can ever have is his own negative or fearful thought. Think well, and good follows; think evil, and evil follows. Write the truths of this paragraph indelibly on your heart. Cease transferring the power, which is within you to sticks, stones, and the foolish opinions of others.

The Bible says, "Wilt thou be made whole?" Do you really believe the God-Presence can heal you now? Do you believe implicitly in the Infinite Healing Presence within you, or do you think disease is independent of your mind? Do you think you are incurable? Do you think the will of God for you is sickness, pain, and trouble? If so, these thoughts of impotence, sickness, and suffering are robbing you of health, vitality, and peace of mind. False ideas have no power other than the power you give them.

"Thy faith hath made thee whole."

Open your mind and heart to the Healing Power of God, and the Healing Power will flow into you as surely as the light and heat of the sun will come into your habitation when thrown open to receive the light and heat, in the same way as the surrounding air will rush in to fill a vacuum when the connecting hose is opened.

Have you taken inventory of the stock you are carrying in your mind? Is your mind cluttered up with a lot of false beliefs, concepts, and images of no value? Why not liquidate all your false traditional concepts of God and Life and buy the belief in the One Creative Power within you, that God's will for you is the life more abundant and good transcending your fondest dreams.

I chatted with a man last night at dinner here in Jasper Park Lodge. He told me that he had arthritis for twenty years and was told by a specialist in Germany that nothing could be done for him. He accepted the suggestion at that time, as it seemed to be one of authority, and he became wholly unresponsive to his wife and others who persistently kept prodding him, saying to him that God could heal him.

He visited the late Dr. Emmet Fox in New York at the insistence of his wife, and Dr. Fox told him that God's will for him was perfect health. Dr. Fox had him forgive many people whom he said he had hated for twenty years. Actually, he said he began to realize for the first time that hatred and hostility were reflected in his body as arthritis.

His simple prayer was, "God's Love fills my soul and automatically flows in my body."

"Look at me now," he said, "I swim,

He changed his mental image of himself and his thought patterns. He rejected the suggestion of incurability, dropped his hostility, and went from weakness to strength, from morbidity to the sunshine of God's Love.

"I am the Lord and there is none else." God will flow through your thoughts and images of wholeness, beauty, and perfection. Open your heart to the influx of the Holy Spirit now and become whole, vital, and strong.

Give your attention, love, reverence, and devotion to the All-Originating Intelligence as the source of your health, happiness, security, and peace of mind, and wonders will happen in your life.

Cease being hypnotized, brainwashed, and mesmerized by the fear, ignorance, and superstitions of the world. No one can hypnotize you without your mental participation. If you refuse to concentrate on what is said and feast on God and His illimitable power, you are free and cannot be brainwashed.

That disease you speak of has no power. There is no principle of sickness. It is a false pattern of thought lodged in your subconscious and it must pass away as you dwell on the wholeness, beauty, and perfection of god. A new cause is set in motion by your harmonious thinking which will produce a new effect, namely health.

Keep calm and balanced. A nervous neurotic person or a religious fanatic is highly suggestible. Truth is a paradox. Every truth is a half-truth because every truth has two sides.

You might insist that sitting by a fan caused you to have a stiff neck. This is a relative truth for you, because you believe it, but the fan is harmless and has no power. The power is in your mind and spirit, and in your thought-life and belief. If it were a truth that a fan gave one a stiff neck, all people would suffer accordingly. It is the subjective belief on the part of the individual that is the cause.

Your religion or knowledge of metaphysics counts for little unless you apply the truths in your daily life. The word (ideas, truths) must become flesh or embodied on the screen of space.

We know what your concept of God is by what you say, do, and express in your life. You are here to dramatize and portray God in your work, your relationship with others, and in all your functions and acts.

You become what you condemn. When you vilify, criticize, and find fault with others, you begin to exemplify what you criticize. When you are angry, hostile, and bitter, your mind is much more receptive to the negative, fearful, and hateful suggestions of the world.

The reason is obvious. You are operating at a very a very low vibration and you are opening your mind to all sorts of angry, hateful vibrations from the race mind. You are operating at a very low wave length and tuning in on all the negative currents of humanity at that level of vibration, because like attracts like.

Give all power to God and to God alone and begin now to turn your eyes to the hills from whence cometh your help. *"With my eyes stayed on Thee, there is no evil on my pathway."*

Chapter 9

MAN'S GREATEST ENEMY AND THE POWER OF SUGGESTION

It is said that fear is man's greatest enemy. Fear is behind failure, sickness, and poor human relations. Millions of people are afraid of the past, the future, old age, insanity, and death. Fear is a thought in your mind, and you are afraid of your own thoughts.

A little boy can be paralyzed with fear when he is told there is a boogie man under his bed who is going to take him away. When his father turns on the light and shows him there is no boogie man, he is freed from fear. The fear in the mind of the boy was as real as if there really was a boogie man there. He was healed of a false thought in his mind. The thing he feared did not exist. Likewise, most of your fears have no reality. They are merely a conglomeration of sinister shadows, and shadows have no reality.

Prayer, which is faith in God and all things good, casts out fear. Fear is the cloud that hides the sunshine of God's Love. Men have made personal devils of fear of the past, the present, and the future. Fear causes man to fail. It is fear that makes man angry and jittery, causes him to rub others the wrong way, and creates bad human relations. Men fear criticism so much that many of their most beautiful thoughts never see the light of day.

Fear is the cause of great misery, and untold suffering and fear come to all of us. Many are afraid of the future, old age, insecurity, some illness or incurable condition, or the verdict of the doctors. Many are full of fear regarding their families, newspaper reports and the media in general, all of which project fear propaganda of all kinds. Fear of nuclear warfare, inflation and crime disturbs the masses.

Great numbers of individuals are afraid of death and loneliness in their old age. There are countless thousands who face death with equanimity and serenity, because they know that there is no death, only life, and that they will live forever in the many mansions (dimensions) of our Father's house.

There is a limitless catalogue of fears that afflict the human mind. The answer to all fear is to turn to the God-Presence within. Faith in God casts out fear... *Fear hath torment. He that heareth is not made perfect in love* (I John 4:18).

You begin to think and speak in a new tongue when you turn to God within and mentally dwell on the promises of the Bible. As you continue to dwell on these great Truths, you will experience a sense of peace and security. Examine some of your fears and you will discover that many of them are groundless.

Master Your Fears

While speaking in a club here in Leisure World, a man had been a chronic worrier. His greatest worries were those that never came to pass, but these worries depleted his vitality and brought on ulcers and high blood pressure. On the advice of a spiritual practitioner, he began to study and apply the teachings of the 23rd and 27th Psalms, which brought about a remarkable healing. He began to control and discipline his thinking. When worry thoughts came to his mind he would recite a verse or two of one of the Psalms, and in time he overcame his worries. He had discovered that all of his worries were unfounded and groundless.

One of our students told me that he was invited to speak at a banquet. He said he was panic-stricken at the thought of speaking before a thousand people. He overcame his fear this way: For several nights he sat down in an armchair for about five minutes and said to himself slowly, quietly, and positively, "I am going to master this fear. I am overcoming it now. I speak with poise and confidence. I am relaxed and at east." He operated a definite law of mind and overcame his fear.

The subconscious mind is amenable to suggestion and is controlled by suggestion. When you still your mind and relax, the thoughts of your conscious mind sink down into the subconscious through a process similar to osmosis, whereby fluids separated by a porous membrane intermingle. As these positive seeds, or thoughts, sink into the subconscious area, they grow after their kind, and you become poised, serene, and calm.

Do The Thing You Fear

Ralph Waldo Emerson, philosopher and poet, said, "Do the thing you are afraid to do, and the death of fear is certain."

There was a time when the writer of this chapter was filled with unutterable fear when standing before an audience. The way I overcame it was to stand before the audience, do the thing I was afraid to do, and the death of fear was certain.

When you affirm positively that you are going to master your fears, and you come to a definite decision in your conscious mind, you release the power of the subconscious, which flows in response to the nature of your thought.

There is no occasion to feel ashamed of the fact that you experience fear or that you get frightened one in a while. The thing to do is to supplant the fear thoughts with God-like thoughts. Do not fight the fear in your mind; proceed at once to overcome it. You can do it, and it does not call for superhuman effort, only a redirection of your thought-life.

A Bible Prayer

One of the most beautiful and practical prayers in the Bible for the overcoming of fear is this:

The Lord is my light and my salvation; whom shall I fear? The Lord is the strength of my life; of whom shall I be afraid? Psalm 27:1. This verse might well be indelibly printed in the mind of every man and woman who walks the earth. Contemplate for a moment what it says. It postulates clearly that the Living Presence of God is within you. *Know ye that the Lord he is God.* Psalm 100:3. Another meaning for the word Lord in the Bible is Law, meaning your subconscious mind.

Learn the powers of your subconscious mind, and you will have light, salvation, and strength, which means understanding, power, and solutions to all your problems. Master the prayer processes elaborated in this chapter. Your subconscious mind will respond, and you will be free of all fears.

Become a habitual peruse of the 91st, 46th and 23rd Psalms, and you will gradually saturate your subconscious with the eternal verities and be free. The following verse will work wonders in your life: *There is no fear in love: but perfect love castes out fear; because fear hath torment. He that heareth is not made perfect in love* (I John 4:18).

Love is an emotional attachment. It is an outpouring of goodwill. Spiritually, it means that you recognize the Presence of God in all His creatures. A woman who was terrified of dogs (probably dating back to her childhood when she was bitten by a dog, since she had a faint memory of the incident) began to affirm: "I radiate love to all dogs. They love their masters and they save lives. The Presence of God is in all of his creatures. I love dogs. They are loving, kind and cooperative."

She kept affirming these truths and after a period of time she was at peace with dogs. She no longer feared them. You will lose fear as you grow in understanding that there is only One Power.

Dwell also on these wonderful words: The Lord is my light and my salvation; whom shall I fear? *The Lord is the strength of my life; of whom shall I be afraid?* (Psalm 27:1).

When fearful, reiterate these truths over and over again, and you will sense an inner peace and security. In the Bible it also says: *Fear not, for I am with thee* ... (Isaiah 43.5). *He shall not be afraid of evil tidings: his heart is fixed, trusting in the Lord* (Psalm 112:7). *Fear thou not; for I am with thee: be not dismayed; for I am thy God: I will strengthen thee; yea, I will help thee; yea, I will uphold thee with the right hand of my righteousness. For I the Lord thy God will hold thy right hand, saying unto thee, Fear not; I will help thee* (Isaiah 41:10,13).

Select some of these verses or all of them and recite them slowly, quietly and reverently, knowing that as you repeat these truths, they will sink down into your subconscious mind, eradicating and neutralizing all of the fear patterns. You will feel strengthened and enlightened.

A Bible Verse Saved Her Estate

A woman who was being sued falsely by some of her relatives over an estate adhered to this Truth: ... *In God I have put my trust; I will not fear what flesh can do unto me* (Psalm 56.4). She did not waver in her faith, and the case was dismissed.

Take refuge in the great Psalms. As you enthrone these Truths in your mind, you will discover that you refers will subside and give way to a sense of peace and security.

Eternal Source of Supply

If you devote some time and attention every day to scientific prayer and meditation, you will experience a changed mental attitude, and you cannot and will not suffer from the many hazards and unforeseen catastrophes.

Walk in the consciousness of God's eternal supply. Know in your heart that the Overshadowing Presence is watching over you in all your ways. Remember that as long as you maintain a prosperity consciousness you cannot suffer losses. For example, if your oil well suddenly dried up and this happened to be the channel through which your money comes to you, as much money as you need automatically would come to you from some other source. The amount you would receive definitely would be equal to the income you had previously derived from the oil well.

When you build into your mentality the awareness of the Eternal Source of supply, you cannot become impoverished, and no matter what form wealth takes you always will be amply supplied.

Prayer Controlled His Ups and Downs

I talked with a man a few weeks ago who complained bitterly about his ups and downs. He said, "Sometimes I make a small fortune in the stock market, and shortly afterward I experience a great loss. At times, I enjoy robust health, but periodically I find myself in the hospital for various ailments. Fortune and misfortune are my lot. Can't something be done to stop these great swings of fate?"

I explained to this man that it is possible to maintain a constant upbeat and to lead a balanced life in which serenity and tranquility reign supreme. It is true that most people swing form exhilaration one day to a mood of depression the next day when something goes wrong. Many people constantly are going from "black Monday" to "bright Tuesday."

This man realized that life would be very insipid, dull, and monotonous without any variations, challenges, or problems. Tragedies, emergencies, and exigencies come into the lives of nearly all people. It is possible to regulate our emotional reactions so that neither the upbeat nor the downbeat is overly accentuated.

The first step this man had to take was purposefully acquiring mental and emotional control. He soon realized that while he could preserve his equanimity regardless of circumstances. While speaking about man's vicissitudes and misfortunes, Marcus Aurelius said, "Nothing happens to any man which he is not formed by nature to bear." In Hawaii a guide will show you a hut where the great writer, Robert Louis Stevenson, wrote a masterpiece, Treasure Island, despite the fact that he was suffering from an acute case of tuberculosis!

I gave my friend a spiritual prescription to follow, whereby he would find strength and assurance from the kingdom of God within him. He prayed frequently during each day, dwelling on these eternal verities:

> "Thou wilt keep him in perfect peace, whose mind is stayed on thee: because he trusted in thee." (Isaiah 26:3) I know that the inner desires of my heart come from God within me. God wants me to be happy. God's will for me is life, love, truth, and beauty. I mentally accept my good now, and I become a perfect channel for the Divine. I am an expression of God. I am Divinely directed in all my ways, and I am always in my true place, doing the thing I love to do. I refuse to accept as truth the opinions of man, for my mind is a part of God's mind, and I am always reflecting Divine wisdom and Divine

intelligence. God's ideas unfold within my mind in perfect sequence. I am always poised, balanced, serene, and calm, for I know that God always will reveal to me the perfect solution to all my needs. The Lord is my shepherd; I shall not want for any good thing. I am Divinely active and Divinely creative. I sense and feel the rhythm of God. I hear the melody of God whispering its message of love to me.

A completely balanced life followed after he had made himself a part of God's fulfillment by thinking in the above manner.

Who is Your Lord?

For in the time of trouble he shall hide me in his pavilion: in the secret of his tabernacle shall he hide me: he shall set me up upon a rock (Psalm 27:5).

Who are your Lord and master this very moment? Your Lord is your predominant mental attitude; it is your conviction or belief about yourself, people and things. This Lord can be a tyrant. For example, if you mood is now one of resentment, that is your Lord or tyrant that governs all of your actions and all phases of your life. If you want to invest some money, buy a new home or buy some property while in this attitude, you will do and say the wrong thing because your predominant mood is negative. The law is: "As within, so without." You fear your good, and you would react negatively. Fear is a lack of faith or trust in God, which is a denial of His Omnipotence.

The Lord is my light and my salvation . . . (Psalm 27:1). The *Lord* referred to is the Lord God, or the law of God or good. To put the law of good into operation—thereby banishing fear once and for all—enthrone in you mind the thoughts of power, courage and confidence. These thoughts will generate a corresponding mood or feeling, which will banish the arch enemy of your success and health.

Fear, this self-made enemy of yours, must be completely destroyed before the Lord God can shine through you. Your fear is the cloud that hides the sunshine of God. Men have made personal devils out of fear of the past, the present and the future.

It is our attitude toward life that determines the experience we are to meet. If we expect misfortune, we shall have it. Knowing the law of God or good, the truth student expects only good fortune. The world is not harsh; it may seem to be, because we fail to affirm or claim the Presence of God. Men fear criticism so much that many of their most beautiful thoughts never see the light of day. To the man who believes that God is the only Presence and the only Power, there is no past; he knows that if he believes in the power of the past, he is disbelieving in God. God is the Eternal Now; there is no future and no past in God.

This is the Gospel—the good tidings. There is no such thing as past karma; there is only man's foolish, false belief in it . . . *Now is the day of salvation* (II Corinthians 6:2). The Kingdom of Heaven is at hand. Your good, your health and your success are here now; feel the reality of them; thrill to them. Enter into the conviction that you are now the being you long to be.

Guilt and What It Means

The only guilt there is, is the consciousness of guilt. . . . *Thou your sins be as scarlet, they shall be as white as snow; though they be red like crimson, they shall be as wool* (Isaiah 1:18). This is the good news. The only moment that matters is the present. You can live only in the now, experience in the now, plan in the now and think in the now. Whatever you are planning or dreading, you are planning it now. When you realize that every form of lack and limitation is the result of your wrong thinking and feeling, you shall know the Truth that sets you free. The mountains will be removed.

Aboriginal tribes and primitive man feared nature. Modern man fears his fellow man. To a great extent we have dispelled the ghosts of ancient days. We have combated the plagues, and we will soon control the elements. Man is doped by modern propaganda. Some men are afraid to live and afraid to speak. Mothers fear for their children. All this is due to superstitious belief that there is another power to challenge God.

The only evil there is, is due to a lack of knowledge of the laws of life. If we put our hand on an open wire we get a shock, but if it is insulated properly we do not. The evil or shock was due to our ignorance; yet any man will admit that electricity is not evil. It blesses man in countless ways. Electricity is used to play music, drive trains, fry eggs, vacuum the floors and light the world. Evil or fear is our misapplication and incomplete comprehension of the Omnipresence of God, or good. Where fear is, love cannot be; for error cannot dwell with understanding.

The wealthy fear they are going to lose; the poor fear they will not gain. The only wealth and the only security are found in the consciousness in which we abide. If we are conscious of being wealthy, nothing in the entire world can stop us from being prosperous in our bodies and affairs. The things men fear are unreal. Only the One alone is real; only the One alone is Law; only the One alone is Truth.

The jungle doctor of old has passed on many of his superstitions; consequently, countless cults today instill fear into the minds of many individuals. Let us face the facts. The cause of most fear is man's fear of his fellow man. Many men pray together on Sunday and prey on each other on Monday.

The answer to the fear problem understands. All fear is due to ignorance. In order to express harmony, we must think and feel harmonious thoughts.

When we enter into the mood of success, confidence and happiness, we will express similar results in all phases of our life. When man knows that every form of discord, sickness and lack is due to wrong thinking, he will know the Truth which sets him free.

You can learn to live so that fear will no longer dominate you, although your fear may reach back into the past, maybe even into the inheritance of the race mind. While there are many primitive fears in the subconscious of all of us, you can eradiate all those fears by joining mentally and emotionally with the God-Presence within you. As you learn to love God and all things good and as you trust Him implicitly, you will overcome your fears and become a free and fearless person.

How Prayer Freed Her from Panic

A few years ago, a girl named Anne, whom I did not know, phoned me at the Algonquin Hotel in New York City, saying, my father died. I know he has hidden a large sum of money in the house. I am panic-stricken, desperate, and full of fear; I need the money and I can't find it."

She did not know how to communicate with her subconscious mind, and I told her that I would pray about it. I asked her to visit me the next day.

That same night following her phone call I had a dream in which a man said, "Get up and write this down; you are seeing my daughter, Anne, tomorrow." I awoke and went to the desk and rustled through the drawer for a sheet of hotel stationery. He dictated to me as I wrote. I am sure that these instructions were not written by Joseph Murphy, even half asleep, even by my subconscious in a half-dream-world in which I was. I believe the author was the father of the girl whom I was to see the following day.

I definitely feel that it was the personality of her father, surviving so-called death, who gave me the instructions which explained in detail where a large sum of money was hidden in her home and of holdings in the Bahamas with explicit instructions to his daughter whom to contact, etc. All of this was subsequently verified.

The following day Anne visited me at the Church of Religious Science headquarters in New York City. I recognized her immediately, because I had seen her in my dream the night previously. There is a shining facet of our subconscious mind which reflects what is subjectively perceived and known, but which is not consciously known.

This girl was suffering from acute anxiety needlessly, because all the time her subconscious knew where the money was, and she could have communicated with it and received her answer. Knowledge of the laws of her mind has completely transformed the life of this girl, so that she is a vital and alive and presently accomplishing great thing.

Persistence Pays

A young lady in New York City opened a music studio. She advertised extensively; weeks passed and not one student appeared on the scene. The reason for this was because the music teacher had the attitude of mind that she would fail and that students would not come to her because she was unknown. Her basic trouble was fear. She reversed her mental attitude and came to a decision that a great number of students could be benefited by what she had to offer. The following technique worked wonders in her professional career:

Twice daily she imagined herself teaching students and saw them happy and pleased. She was the actress in the drama, "Act as though I am, and I will be." She felt herself to be the successful teacher, acting the role in her imagination, and focusing her attention on her ideal. Through her persistence she became one with the idea in her mind until she succeeded in objectively expressing what she subjectively imagined and felt. She attracted more students than she could handle and eventually had to have an assistant.

What she imagined her life to be, she felt it to be, and according to her new feeling or mental attitude was it done unto her.

Fear Causes Pain

Following a recent series of lectures at the Science of Mind headquarters in San Francisco, a man visited me at my hotel. The first thing he said was, "I am haunted by unknown fears. I wake up at night perspiring copiously and shaking all over." He suffered frequently from acute paroxysmal attacks of asthma.

I found in talking to him that he had hated his father for many years because his father had bequeathed all his estate to his sister. This hatred developed a deep sense of guilt in his subconscious mind, and because of this guilt he had a deep, hidden fear of being punished; this complex expressed itself in his body as high blood pressure and asthmatic attacks.

Fear causes pain. The fear and guilt which this man had were expressed as disease, or lack of ease and peace.

This young man realized that his whole trouble was caused by his own sense of guilt, self-condemnation, and hatred. His father long since had passed to a higher dimension of life. Actually, the man was poisoning himself through hatred.

He began to forgive himself. To forgive is to give something for. He affirmed as follows, "I completely forgive my father. He did what he believed right according to his light. I release him. I wish him peace, harmony, and joy. I am sincere, and I mean it."

The young man lanced his psychic wound, and all the psychic pus came forth. His asthma disappeared, and his blood pressure dropped to normal. The fear of punishment which was lurking in his subconscious mind has now disappeared.

As he saturated his mind regularly and systematically with these thoughts, he succeeded in bringing about a new mental attitude of a constructive nature which changed everything for the better in his life.

How to Realize Your Desire

No man can serve two masters. A man cannot expect to realize the desire of his heart if he believes there is a power which thwarts that desire. This creates a conflict, and his mind is divided. He stands still and he gets nowhere. His mind must move as a unity. Infinity cannot be divided or multiplied. The Infinite must be one—a unity. There cannot be two Infinities, as one would quarrel with the other; they would neutralize or cancel out each other. We would have a chaos instead of a cosmos. Unity of the spirit is a mathematical necessity, for there is no opposition to the one Power. If there were some power to challenge God, or the Infinite One, God would cease to be omnipotent or supreme.

You can see what confusion and chaos reign in the minds of people who believe in two opposing powers. Their minds are divided because they have two masters, and this belief creates a conflict, causing their power and strength to be divided. Learn to go in one direction only by believing that God who gave you the desire will also show you how to fulfill it.

Make a Habit of Prayer

Once an executive came to me and told me that he was terribly worried that he would not get the presidency at his company's next scheduled board meeting. He added that he was next in line and this constant fear and anxiety were about to give him a nervous breakdown.

In talking to him I discovered that he had been worrying most of his life, and I remarked that he just thought his fear was due to the possibility that he would not be promoted. He did not agree with this. I told him to picture himself as president and to imagine that his associates were congratulating him on his promotion. He faithfully followed these instructions, and he was duly installed as president at the next board meeting.

About a month later, however, he again came to see me. He was still worrying, and his doctor had said that his blood pressure was dangerously high. I reminded him that he had previously attributed his fear to the fact that he might not be made president of his organization, but now that he was president he had not stopped worrying. He was worrying about the fact that he might not live up to the expectations of the executive board, that his decisions might cause the company to go in the red, and that he might be asked to resign.

He began to look inside himself, and suddenly he realized that his whole trouble was due to the fact that he did not make a habit of prayer and had no real contact with Infinite Power from which he could draw strength and security. He had thought that he was cursed with these fears; but now he awakened to the naked truth that he alone was their creator, and that by deciding to establish a prayer pattern he could overcome his obsession.

I gave him this suggestion: "When you waken in the morning use the following prayer:"

> I know that the answer to my problem lies in the God-Self within me. I now get quiet, still, and relaxed. I am at peace. I know God speaks in peace and not in confusion. I am now in tune with the Infinite; I know and believe implicitly that Infinite Intelligence is revealing to me the perfect answer. I think about the solution to my problems. I now live in the mood I would have were my problem solved. I truly live in this abiding faith and trust which is the mood of the solution; this is the spirit of God moving within me. This Spirit is Omnipotent; it is manifesting itself; my whole being rejoices in the solution; I am glad. I live in this feeling and I give thanks.
>
> I know that God has the answer, for with God all things are possible. God is the Living Spirit Almighty within me; He is the Source of all wisdom and illumination.
>
> The indicator of the presence of God within me is a sense of peace and poise. I now cease all sense of strain and struggle; I trust the God-Power implicitly. I know that all the wisdom and power I need to live a glorious and successful life are within me. I relax my entire body; my faith is in the wisdom; I go free. I claim and feel the peace of God flooding my mind, my heart, and my whole being. I know that the quiet mind gets its problems solved. I now turn my request over to the God Presence, knowing it has an answer. I am at peace.

He repeated the above prayer three times each morning, knowing that through repetition these truths would sink into his subconscious and establish a healing, wholesome habit of constructive thinking. He also realized that he now was anchored to the God-Power within him in which he lived, moved, and had his being. His sense of union with God gave him confidence to overcome anything about which he had mistakenly worried. Through this shift in his mental attitude, he became a balanced man.

Overcome Problem

Do not spend time looking at your troubles or problems; cease all negative thinking. Your mind cannot function harmoniously when it is tense. It relieves the strain to do something soothing and pleasant when you are presented with a problem. You do not fight a problem—you can overcome it.

To release pressure, take a drive; go for a walk; play solitaire; or read a favorite chapter of the Bible, such as the Eleventh Chapter of Hebrews or Chapter Thirteen of I Corinthians. Or, read the Forty-Sixth Psalm; read it over carefully and quietly several times. An inner calm will steal over you, and you will become poised and peaceful.

Suggested Ways to Freedom from Fear

1. Do the thing you are afraid to do, and the death of fear is certain. Say to yourself and mean it, "I am going to master this fear," and you will.
2. Fear is a negative thought in your mind. Supplant it with a constructive thought. Fear has killed millions. Confidence is greater than fear. Nothing is more powerful than faith in God and the good.
3. Fear is man's greatest enemy. It is behind failure, sickness, and bad human relations. Love casts out fear. Love is an emotional attachment to the good things of life. Fall in love with honesty, integrity, justice, good will, and success. Live in the joyous expectancy of the best, and invariably the best will come to you.
4. Counteract the fear suggestions with the opposite, such as "I sing beautifully; I am poised, serene, and calm." It will pay fabulous dividends.
5. You were born with only two fears, the fear of falling and the fear of noise. All your other fears were acquired. Get rid of them.
6. Normal fear is good. Abnormal fear is very bad and destructive. To constantly indulge in fear thoughts results in abnormal fear, obsessions, and complexes. To fear something persistently causes a sense of panic and terror.
7. You can overcome abnormal fear when you know the power of your subconscious mind can change conditions and bring to pass the cherished desires of your heart. Give your immediate attention and devotion to your desire which is the opposite of your fear. This is the love that casts out fear.
8. If you are afraid of failure, give attention to success. If you are afraid of sickness, dwell on your perfect health. If you are afraid of an accident,

dwell on the guidance and protection of God. If you are afraid of death, dwell on the Eternal Life. God is Life, and that is your life now.

9. The things you fear do not really exist except as thoughts in your mind. Thoughts are creative. This is why Job said; *the thing I feared has come upon me.* Think good and good follows.

10. Look at your fears; hold them up to the light of reason. Learn to laugh at your fears. That is the best medicine.

11. Nothing can disturb you but your own thought. The suggestions, statements, or threats of other persons have no power. The power is within you, and when your thoughts are focused on that which is good, then God's power is with your thoughts of good. There is only one Creative Power, and it moves as harmony. There are no divisions of quarrels in it. Its source is Love. This is why God's power is with your thoughts of good.

CHAPTER 10

SUGGESTED WAYS TO GET RESULTS

Learn to Imagine

Learn to imagine the thing desired, and then feel the reality of the state sought. This is the easiest and quickest way to get results. Some get results by convincing themselves of the Truth that God is the only Presence and the only Power. This is one of the most wonderful things in the entire world to know.

Whatever you imagine a thing to be, there is a corresponding emotional reaction. A prominent eastern teacher of oriental philosophy while walking the streets of London in the twilight of the evening looked at a coiled rope on the street and imagined it to be a snake; he became paralyzed with fear. When he discovered his mistake, his true picture of the rope induced a new mental attitude and emotional response. What do you imagine yourself to be? What do you imagine Life to be? According to your imagination will it respond to you?

The power of your subconscious is enormous. It inspires you, it guides you, and it reveals to you names, facts, and scenes from the storehouse of memory. Your subconscious started your heartbeat, controls the circulation of your blood, and regulates your digestion, assimilation, and elimination. When you eat a piece of bread, your subconscious mind transmutes it into tissue, muscle, bone, and blood. This process is beyond the ken of the wisest man who walks the earth. Your subconscious mind controls all the vital processes and functions of your body and knows the answer to all problems.

Your subconscious mind is the source of your ideals, aspirations and altruistic urges. It was through the subconscious mind that Shakespeare perceived great truths hidden from the average man of his day. Undoubtedly, it was the response of his subconscious mind that caused the Greek sculptor, Phidias, to portray beauty, order, symmetry, and proportion in marble and bronze. It enabled the Italian artist, Raphael, to paint Madonna's, and Ludwig van Beethoven to compose symphonies.

Imagination, the Workshop of God

"Where there is no vision, the people perish..." (Proverbs 29:18) my vision is that I desire to know more of God and the way He works. My vision is for perfect health, harmony, and peace. My vision is the inner faith that Infinite Spirit heals and guides me now in all my ways. I know and believe that the God-Power within me answers my prayer; this is a deep conviction within me. I know that imagination is the result of what I image in my mind. Faith is, as Paul says, the substance out of which the image is formed. (Hebrews 11:1)

I make it my daily practice to imagine only for myself and for others also that which is noble, wonderful, and God-like. I now imagine that I am doing the thing I long to do; I imagine that I now possess the things I long to possess; I imagine that I am what I long to be. To make it real, I feel the reality of it, and I know that it is so. Thank you, Father.

You possess nothing but by right of consciousness. I explained the meaning of this to a young lady who wants to become a doctor. She was rejected by five different medical institutions so far, each claiming that it was full. She began to see that she must mentally act as thought it were already accomplished and pictured herself studying in medical school. I suggested that she look at a diploma on the wall, stating that she is a physician and surgeon in the State of California and hear the writer congratulate her on her graduation as a physician.

In prayer you always go to the end and, having seen and felt the end, you have willed the means to the realization of the end. She thus played the role in her mind and acted as though it were an accomplished fact. Our interview was about five months ago, and the way suddenly opened up for her to attend in Montreal, Canada.

In 1955 I lectured at the Yoga Forest University, Rishikesh, India, and there I chatted with a visiting surgeon from Bombay. He told me about Dr. James Escamilla, a Scotch surgeon, who worked in Bengal before ether or other modern methods of anesthesia were discovered. Between 1843 and 1846, Dr. Escamilla performed about four hundred major operations of all kinds, such as amputations, removal of tumors and cancerous growths, as well as operations on the eye, ear, and throat. All operations were conducted under mental anesthesia only. This Indian doctor at Rishikesh informed me that the postoperative mortality rate of patients operated on by Dr. Escamilla was extremely low, probably two or three percent. Patients felt no pain, and there were no deaths during the operations.

Dr. Escamilla suggested to the subconscious minds of all his patients, who were in a hypnotic state, that no infection or septic condition would develop. You must remember that this was before Louis Pasteur, Joseph Lister, and others who pointed out the bacterial origin of disease and causes of infection due to unspecialized instruments and virulent organisms.

This Indian surgeon said that the reason for the low mortality rate and the general absence of infection, which was reduced to a minimum, was undoubtedly due to the suggestions of Dr. Escamilla to the subconscious minds of his patients. They responded according to the nature of his suggestion.

It is simply wonderful, when you conceive how a surgeon, over one hundred twenty years ago, discovered the miraculous wonder-working powers of the subconscious mind. Doesn't it cause you to be seized with a sort of mystic awe when you stop and think of the transcendental powers of your subconscious mind? Consider its extrasensory perceptions, such as its capacity for clairvoyance and clairaudience, its independence of time and space, its capacity to render you free from all pain and suffering, and its capacity to get the answer to all problems, be they what they may. All these and many more reveal to you that there is a power and an intelligence within you that far transcends your intellect, causing you to marvel at the wonders of it all. All these experiences cause you to rejoice and believe in the miracle-working powers of your own subconscious mind.

Hypnotic Suggestion

The hypnotic operator takes "the cover" (conscious mind) off of the subconscious mind. He gives a suggestion directly to the subconscious, which acts immediately upon the suggestion. It has been demonstrated and proven that even a post hypnotic suggestion will be carried out to the consternation of even a recalcitrant hypnotized subject. Time is actually collapsed in experiments of this kind.

What does all this show? Simply that there is a creative medium in your subconscious that responds to the nature of your thought. When you find creativity, you have found God, or the One Power, in essence. God created the universe and all things therein contained. God created you, and the Creative Power is within you. You have freedom to use any power two ways. You have freedom to create sickness or health, failure or success, poverty or wealth by the nature of your habitual thinking and imagery. This is the ancient mystery of good and evil—never quite understood through the ages. The Bible points out that Moses drew forth his hand white with leprosy or glowing with health according to the way he used his mind. This applies to all of us.

Stop Negative Suggestion

The Truth is that there is no hell, devil, purgatory, limbo or damnation of any kind; moreover, there is no past karma for which we must expiate here and there is any future evil. God is the Eternal Now! This is one of the most dramatic and significant statements in the whole Bible: . . . *Now is the day of salvation* (II Corinthians 6:2). This very moment all that you need to do is to turn to God and claim for yourself that which you long to be. Accept it; believe it, and go thy way rejoicing . . . *Thou your sins be as scarlet, they shall be white as snow; though they be red like crimson, they shall be as wool* (Isaiah 1:18) . . . (Forgive) *Until seventy times seven* (Matthew 18:22) . . . *To day shalt thou be with me in paradise* (Luke 23:43).

Let us stop suggesting fear into the minds of the youth; let us teach them the real facts. We must not preach religious tolerance unless we live it. We must teach the Truth. We must not distort the Truth so that we may hold a position or because we are afraid that the people will not come back. This type of fear results in spiritual stagnation and frustration. We must keep our eye on the Kingdom of Heaven, not upon the kingdom of earth. We must teach man to know the Truth, and the Truth shall make him free. The Truth is: Man is belief expressed!

There is no fear where faith in God rules. There is no fear of man where integrity rules in one's consciousness. There is no fear of criticism where the consciousness of kindliness enters into the mind of man. Religion is goodwill in action or the application of the golden rule. We have seen, therefore, that fear is man's basic weakness, and it is based solely on ignorance.

. . . *In the time of trouble he shall hide me in his pavilion: in the secret tabernacle shall he hide me; he shall set me up upon a rock* (Psalm 27:5). The pavilion is a canopy or covering; this means the covering shall be the garment of God (mood of good). Think about God. Begin to ask yourself, "What does God mean to me?" Realize that God, or I AM, is the life in you, your own consciousness, and It is Omnipotent.

Kingdom is at Hand

God and good are synonymous. For example, if a man is in prison, he automatically desires freedom. He begins to think of this Infinite Power and Wisdom within him. He knows that it has ways of freeing him of which he has no knowledge. He imagines, therefore, the opposite, which is freedom. Though he is behind bars, in meditation he imagines that he is at home talking to his loved ones. He hears familiar voices and feels the welcoming kisses of his children on his cheek. This is hiding in the *pavilion*. The prisoner actualizes this state by feeling the joy of being home. It is possible to rise high enough in consciousness in five or ten minutes to bring about a subjective conviction. This is the meaning of. *In the secret of his tabernacle shall he hide me?* (Psalm 27:5). The law is: Whatever is impressed is expressed; consequently, the prison doors are open for him in ways of which he has no knowledge . . . *His ways are past finding out (Romans* 11:33).

We read in the Scriptures: *Fear not, little flock; for it is your Father's good pleasure to give you the kingdom* (Luke 12:32). Jesus tells us this Kingdom is within us—this Kingdom of Heaven or harmony is within every one of us. Infinite Wisdom, Divine Intelligence and Infinite Power are available to all men, because God is within them and He is the very life of them. Anyone can prove to himself that the kingdom of Heaven is at hand. It is right here now. Jesus saw it and lived in it. We are color blind; that is why we do not see it. The blindness is due to ignorance and fear. We are blinded by centuries of false beliefs, superstitions, creeds and dogmas. The Truth is so shrouded by false dogmas that we have created God and a heaven of our making. God is to us what we believe Him to be. Man has created a horrendous creature in the skies. He visualizes a God of caprice and vengeance, or an inscrutable being who sends wars, plagues, etc. We create our own hell and our own heaven, based upon our concept of God. Anyone can prove that the Kingdom of Heaven is at hand.

She Proved It

Let me tell you the story of a young girl who proved it. She was living with a father who came home drunk every night and who sometimes treated her brutally. She lived in constant fear of her father. She kept house for him. Due to frustration, her face was covered with acne.

We are not living with people; we are living with our concept of them. Realizing this truth, the girl closed her eyes in meditation and dwelt on the God Power within her. She no longer clothed her father in the garment or mood of a drunkard. Instead, she saw a loving, kind father, who had a perfect balance, poise and equilibrium. She clothed him in righteousness, and her . . . *judgment was a robe and a diadem* (Job 29:14), which means that she saw her father as he ought to be. The fact that her father was drinking heavily meant that he was seeking to escape to conceal an inferiority complex or a subjective sense of loss. In other words, he was trying to run away from himself.

This girl spoke the word which healed him. She relaxed her whole body, closed her eyes and began to say to her, "How would I feel if my father were loving, kind and peaceful?" She dwelt on the solution, which generated a mood of peace, confidence and joy within her. This was clothing him in righteousness. Her judgment was a robe and diadem.

When you pass judgment, you come to a decision. It is the final verdict, and you are the judge passing judgment . . . . *As I hear, I judge* . . . (John 5:30). Her verdict was an inner hearing or feeling, wherein she saw her father smiling, happy and joyous. She imagined he was telling her how wonderful he felt and that he had found peace, balance and poise. She also heard him telling her how wonderful she was. She thrilled to the fact that her father was healed and made whole. *He wore a seamless robe*—no holes, no patches and no seams. This means that she meditated on the mood of love, peace and oneness with her ideal. All doubts and fears were absent, which *means judgment as the robe. Judgment as the diadem* means that she gave beauty for ashes, which signifies that she saw beauty in her father and felt it.

After one week's treatment, her father was completely healed; moreover, he was a changed man. His attitude was completely transformed, and he and his daughter are now devoted to each other. She proved the Kingdom of Heaven (harmony and peace) is at hand NOW. What are we afraid of? If God be for us, who can be against us? (Romans 8:31). The thing you fear does not exist.

For example, a man might live in fear that his business will fail. His business is not failing; neither is he in bankruptcy. Business is as usual, and it may be booming. The failure does not exist except in his imagination. Job said, . . . *the thing, which I greatly feared, is come upon me* . . . . (Job 3:25). Job is every man who walks the earth. Therefore, as the successful businessman continues to sustain the mood of failure, sooner or later his mood crystallizes into a subjective conviction or impression.

Any feeling impressed on the subconscious mind is made manifest by an immutable law of life. The subconscious, being impersonal and no respecter of persons, says, "John wants to fail in business," so it proceeds in ways that he (John) knows not of to bring this failure to pass. Everyone realizes that he brought this failure on himself through imagination and feeling.

What Am I Aware Of?

I knew a lady who read of an airplane wreck. She was contemplating a trip by air to Los Angeles, but she lived in fear of an accident. A negative thought cannot do you any harm unless it is energized by a charge of fear. It must be emotionalized before it becomes subjective. This lady did not know what she was doing; she was ignorant of the laws of life. This ignorance is the cause of our accidents and misfortunes. Having imagined her in an airplane accident and having emotionalized this negative thought with fear, it became a subjective state. When she took the trip two months later, she had the accident that she "knew" she would have.

If a woman fears that her husband is going to leave her, this is how she conquers her moods. The fear is a negative feeling which is communicated to him. If he does not know the laws of life, her conviction of him will be made manifest. In other words, he will do the thing she feared he would do, because this was her conviction of him. Instead of this fear, she supplants it by seeing her husband radiating peace, health and happiness. In meditation morning and night, she radiates the mood of love and peace and feels that her husband is the most wonderful man in the entire world. She feels that he is loving, kind and devoted. She imagines he is telling her how wonderful she is and how happy, free and balanced he is. Her mood of fear is now changed to a mood of love and peace. This is the Spirit of God moving in her behalf. As she continues to do this, this mood gels within her. She now knows, *He never falleth* (Zephaniah 3:5), and that . . . *perfect love castes out fear* . . . (I John 4:18).

Our daily prayer or daily mood must be one of joyous expectancy or a confident expectancy of all good things. This is our greatest prayer. If we expect the best, the best will come to us. It is our mood that is vital.

The modern metaphysician teaches that God is the life principle within man. If you feel full of confidence and trust, this is the movement of the Spirit of God within You, and it is all-powerful . . . None can stay his hand, or say unto him, "*What doest thou?*" (Daniel 4:35). Man's own consciousness is God; there is no other God. By consciousness is meant existence, life and awareness.

You, the reader, know that you exist. This knowing that you exist is God. Each man must ask himself, "What am I aware of?" The answer to this question is his belief about God. It is what he knows about God. When he says, "I am aware of want, I am fearful, I am sick," these are lies and have no truth in them. When man says, "I am fearful," he is saying that God is full of fear, which is nonsensical. When he says, "I am in want," he is relating a lie and a denial of God's abundance and infinite supply. His faith is in failure, and he succeeds in being a failure. He believes in a lie, but he cannot prove the lie. The false conditions seem real as long as he dwells upon it. When he ceases to believe it, he is free and healed.

Within the Secret Place

He that dwelleth in the secret place of the most High shall abide under the shadow of the Almighty (Psalm 91:1). The secret place is your own mind. Turn within and realize that the Presence of God indwells you. You can communicate with this Divine Presence through your thought, and a definite response will come.

The word shadow means protection, somewhat similar to a woman's use of an umbrella to protect her from the penetrating rays of the sun. When fear thoughts come to you, repeat a few verses of the 91st Psalm many, many times. Do this quietly, feelingly and knowingly, and you will discover that a sense of peace and security will come quietly and gently into your mind and heart. When your mind is at peace, you are in the secret place, for God is absolute peace and harmony.

Regardless of the cause of the fear, you have no one to treat or heal but yourself. You have to convince yourself that you are now expressing life, love and truth. Let us not fear anything or anybody; let us be radiating courage, confidence and power. In this way we will crush all obstacles in our path, and the mountains will be cast into the sea.

We are one with Infinite Power. If we say we are weak or infirm, we are telling a falsehood about God. Fear turns the love of God or good away from us in the same way that a poverty consciousness attracts poverty in health, money, business and love relationships. Man must stop preaching fear to his fellow man and unite in teaching all of the Truth.

Fear may come to your mind again and again because of habit; but persist in supplanting the fear thoughts with a few verses of the 91st Psalm, such as the first and second verses, and you will find that you will gradually become the master of your fears. Every time you enthrone constructive thoughts, such as "God's love fills my mind and heart" or "God's peace fills my soul," you are wiping out your fear and strengthening your faith and confidence in God and His love. Your abnormal fear will then gradually diminish and vanish

Suggestion Controls

Fear and worry cause confusion in the conscious mind. This creates confusion in the subconscious mind, and nothing happens but confusion in man's affairs. Continue to trust in the Divine Power, and that which you desire will come to you in some manner. Have faith in God, in the Divine Power, in His Divine Love, and His Overshadowing Presence always watching over you, and you will become invincible. *"Trust in the Lord, and do good; so shalt thou dwell in the land, and verily thou shalt be fed."*

One of our students told me that he was invited to speak at a banquet. He said he was panic stricken at the thought of speaking before a thousand people. He overcame the fear this way: For several nights he sat down in an armchair for about five minutes and said to himself slowly, quietly, and positively, "I am going to master this fear. I am overcoming it now. I speak with poise and confidence. I am relaxed and at ease." He operated a definite law of mind and overcame his fear.

The subconscious mind is amenable to suggestion and controlled by suggestion. When you still your mind and relax, the thoughts of your conscious mind sink down into the subconscious through a process similar to osmosis, whereby fluids separated by a porous membrane intermingle. As these positive seeds or thoughts sink into the subconscious area, they grow after their kind, and you become poised, serene, and calm.

She Counteracted the Fear Suggestion

A young lady was invited to do an audition. She had been looking forward to the interview. However, on three previous occasions she failed miserably due to stage fright.

Here is the very simple technique which I gave her. Remember this young lady had a very good voice, but she was certain when the time came for her to sing that she would be seized with stage-fright. The subconscious mind takes your fears as a request, proceeds to manifest them, and bring them into your experience. On three previous auditions she sang wrong notes and finally broke down. The cause, as previously outlined, was an involuntary auto-suggestion; i.e., a silent fear thought emotionalized and subjectified.

She overcame it by the following technique. Three times a day she isolated herself in a room. She sat down comfortably in an armchair, relaxed her body, and closed her eyes. She stilled the mind and body as best she could. Physical inertia favors mental passivity, and renders the mind more receptive to suggestion. She counteracted the fear suggestion by its converse, saying to her, "I sing beautifully, I am poised, serene, confident, and calm." She repeated this statement slowly, quietly, and with feeling from five to ten times at each sitting. She had three such "sittings" every day and one immediately prior to sleep. At the end of a week she was completely poised and confident, and gave a remarkable, wonderful audition. Carry out the above procedure with assurance and conviction, and the death of fear is certain.

Suggestive Amnesia

Occasionally young men from the local university come to see me, and also school teachers, who seem to suffer from suggestive amnesia at examinations. The complaint is always the same—"I know the answers after the examination is over, but I can't remember the answers during the examination"

The idea which realizes itself is the one to which we invariably give concentrated attention. I find that each one is obsessed with the idea of failure. Fear is behind the temporary amnesia and is the cause of the whole experience.

One young medical student was the most brilliant in his class; yet he found himself failing to answer simple questions at the time of written or oral examinations. I explained to him that the reason was he had been worrying and fearful for several days previous to the examination; these constant negative thoughts became charged with fear. Thoughts enveloped in the powerful emotions of fear are realized in the subconscious mind. In other words, this young man was requesting his subconscious mind to see to it that he failed, and that is exactly what it did. On the day of the examination he found himself stricken with what is called in psychological circles "suggestive amnesia."

A French psychologist named Baudoin said, "What we have to work for in overcoming fear is education of the imagination."

Here is how the young man overcame his fear. He learned that his subconscious mind was the storehouse of memory, and had a perfect record of all that he had heard and read during his medical training. Moreover, he learned that the subconscious mind was responsive and reciprocal; the way to be in rapport with it was to be relaxed, peaceful, and confident.

Every night and morning he began to imagine his mother congratulating him on his wonderful record. He would hold an imaginary letter from her in his hand and read congratulatory words. He would also feel the letter in his hand. As he began to contemplate the happy result, he called forth a corresponding or reciprocal response or a reaction in himself. The all-wise and omnipotent power of the subconscious took over, dictated, and directed his conscious mind accordingly. He imagined the end. When he imagined and felt the end, he willed the means to the realization of the end. Following this procedure he had no trouble passing subsequent examinations. In other words, the subjective wisdom took over, compelling him to give an excellent account of himself. The law of the subconscious mind is compulsion.

New Attitude of Mind

There are many people who are afraid to go into an elevator, climb mountains, or even swim in the water. It may well be that the individual had unpleasant experiences in the water in his youth, such as having been thrown forcibly into the water without being able to swim.

I had an experience when I was about ten years of age. I fell accidentally into a pool and went down three times. I can still remember the dark water engulfing my head, and my gasping for air until another boy pulled me out at the last moment. This experience sank into my subconscious mind; for years I feared the water.

An elderly psychologist suggested to, "Go down to the swimming pool, look at the water, and say out loud in strong tones, 'I am going to master you, I can dominate you;' then go into the water, take lessons, and overcome it." This I did. I learned that when you do the thing you are afraid to do, fear disappears.

It was only a shadow in my mind. When I assumed a new attitude of mind, the omnipotent power of the subconscious responded, giving me strength, faith, and confidence, enabling me to overcome my fear. I used the subconscious mind to the point where it began to use me.

Following is a process and technique for overcoming fear which I teach from the platform—it works like a charm. Try it! Suppose you are afraid of the water, or a mountain, an interview, an audition, or you fear closed places. If afraid of swimming, begin now to sit still for five or ten minutes, for three or four times a day, and imagine you are swimming. Actually you are swimming in your mind; it is a subjective experience. Mentally you have projected yourself into the water. You feel the chill of the water and the movement of your arms and legs. It is all real, vivid, and a joyous activity the mind. It is not idle day dreaming, for you know that what you are subjectively experiencing in your imagination will be developed in your subconscious mind; then you will be compelled to express the image and likeness of the picture you impressed on your deeper mind; this is the law of the subconscious.

As you continue to discipline your mind this way, you are mentally immersed in the water and happy in it; consequently the fear passes, and you will enter the water physically. I might say you will be compelled to give a good performance. You have consciously called upon the wonderful power of your subconscious mind which is all wise and powerful; this power controls you and governs you according to the nature of your call or request.

Confidence is a Powerful Thought

The president of a large organization told me that when he was a salesman, he used to walk around the block five or six times before he called on a customer. The sales manager came along one day and said to him, "Don't be afraid of the boogie man behind the door, there is no boogie man; it's a false belief."

The manager told him that whenever he looked at his own fears he stared them in the face and stood up to them looking them straight in the eye; then they faded and shrank into insignificance.

Go out now and face that thing you are afraid of. If you are afraid to take a new position, take it. Say to yourself, "I can accomplish; I will succeed!" You will find a corresponding emotion or feeling generated by your subconscious.

You will induce the mood or feeling of confidence, faith in yourself, and the joy of accomplishment. Fear is a thought in your mind, but confidence is a far more powerful thought; it fills your mind with a positive, constructive feeling and drives out fear.

Auto-Suggestion Saved Him

A chaplain told me of one of his experiences in the Second World War He had to parachute from a damaged plane and land in a jungle. He said he was frightened, but he knew there were two kinds of fear, normal and abnormal. Normal fear is good; it is the law of self-preservation. It is the subconscious mind telling you something must be done. It is sort of an alarm system that tells you to get out of the way of an oncoming car.

The chaplain said, "I began to talk to myself, saying, 'John, you can't surrender to your fear; your fear is a desire for safety or security, for a way out.'"

He said that he knew there was a subjective intelligence which led the birds to their food and told them where to go in summer and winter. He began to claim, "Infinite Intelligence which guides the planets in their course is now leading and guiding me out of this jungle"

He kept saying this out loud to himself for ten minutes or more. "Then," he added, "something began to stir inside me, a mood of confidence began to seize me, and I began to walk. After a few days I came out miraculously, and was picked up by a rescue plane."

His changed mental attitude saved him. His confidence and trust in the subjective wisdom and power within him was the solution to his problem. He said, "Had I begun to bemoan my fate and indulge my fears, I would have succumbed to the monster *fear*, and probably have died of fear and starvation."

Whenever fear comes, go to the opposite immediately in your mind. To indulge in fear thoughts constantly and to engage your mind constantly with negative thoughts result in abnormal fear, obsessions, and complexes. To engage the mind with all the difficulties of your problem will only instill more fear until it assumes a size of catastrophic proportions. Finally there comes a sense of panic and terror, weakening and sickening you. You can overcome fear of this nature when you know that the power of your subconscious can always change the objective conditions. Go within, claim and feel your good—the solution. Know there is an Infinite Intelligence which responds and reacts to your thought and feeling.

Imagine the end; feel the thrill of victory. What you subjectively feel and imagine as true is the inner evidence of what will take place objectively. Your subconscious can free you. When fear thoughts come, contemplate the solution, the happy ending. Never fight negative or fearful thoughts. Always turn on the lamp of love, peace, and confidence within you. Most of our fears are imaginary.

Deep Sense of Guilt

I met a man who came to my hotel in New Delhi, India, for consultation. He was from the British Isles. He had acute sinusitis, a deep sense of grief, and was haunted by unknown fears. I found in talking to him that he had hated his father for many years, because the father bequeathed all his estate to his brother. This hatred developed a deep sense of guilt in his subconscious mind; because of this guilt he had a deep, hidden fear of being punished; this complex expressed itself as migraine and sinusitis in his body. Fear means pain. Love and good will mean peace and health. The fear and guilt which this man had were expressed as disease, or lack of ease and peace. The mucous membranes of his nose were always inflamed.

This young man realized that his whole trouble was caused by his own sense of guilt, self condemnation, and hatred. His father had long since passed on to a higher dimension of life. Actually he was poisoning himself through hatred. He began to forgive himself. *To forgive* is to give something for. He practiced saying "I completely forgive my father. He did what he believed right according to his light. I release him. I wish him peace, harmony, and joy. I am sincere, I mean it."

Then he cried for a long time. That was good. He lanced the psychic wound, and all the psychic pus came forth. His sinusitis disappeared. I have had a letter from him saying that the migraine attacks have ceased altogether. The fear of punishment, which was lurking in his subconscious mind, has now disappeared.

Use this perfect formula for casting out fear. "I sought the Lord, and He heard me, and delivered me from all my fears." The *Lord* is an ancient word meaning your subconscious mind.

Learn the powers of your subconscious, how it works and functions. Master the techniques given you in this chapter. Put them into practice now—today! Your subconscious will respond, and you will be free of all fears.

"I sought the Lord, and He heard me, and delivered me from all my fears."

The Lord is my light and my salvation; who shall I fears? The Lord is the strength of my life; of whom shall I be afraid? Psalm 27:1.

Negative Emotions are Harmful

Many medical doctors today are stressing the harmful effects of negative emotions. One of the foremost doctors on holistic medicine is Dr. Frank Varese,

24953 Paso De Valencia, and Laguna Hills, California. I had a very interesting conversation with him. He told me that he was at one time a pharmacist in New York, working for a chain organization for fifty dollars a week. His doctor told him he was a chronic worrier, which was the cause of his high blood pressure. He said that he worried about his two boys and that he would not be able to send them to college. He worried that he could not buy a fur coat for his wife. He worried about a holdup in the pharmacy and lived in constant fear that he might be fired from the job, as business was slow. He worried about long hours, his future, and the fact that he would never own his own pharmacy. He worried that he would never have the money to buy a car.

When World War II came, he joined the Navy and was promoted rapidly. He said that he enjoyed the Navy. "Towards the end of the war," he related, "our submarine was attacked from all sides and I submerged as we were hopelessly outmanned and outgunned. The enemy ships kept dropping depth charges and we remained submerged for 20 hours. There was nothing to do but wait and pray. At any moment I and the other men could have been annihilated. Some of the men said, 'This is the end.' I said, 'God help us. The Lord is our shepherd.'"

These were the only spiritual words he could think of, and in his extremity he kept repeating these words audibly. He began to think of all the other things in his life as a pharmacist that he had worried about. He saw that all of them were trivia and of no consequence compared to what he and his men were now experiencing. He silently said to him, "If I ever see the moon and the stars again, I'll never worry all the days of my life." And, as a matter of fact, he has not worried since and is full of faith in God and all things good.

His prayer was answered and they were not killed. All of his lesser fears had paled into insignificance compared to the terror and extreme danger of his submarine experience.

Remember this great truth: You do not have to go along with, believe in, nor consent to negative suggestions and reactions. Begin to positively refuse to react mechanically as you formerly did. React and think in a new way. You want to be peaceful, happy, radiant, healthy, prosperous, and inspired; therefore, from this moment forward you must refuse to identify with negative suggestions which tend to drag you down.

Being in Truth

Think about God's love. Analyze it, claim it, and begin to realize that all the love of men and women thought the world is but a faint reflection of the Infinite Ocean of love. God's love is written in our heart and inscribed in your inward parts.

The Unbelievable Power of Suggestion

A woman said to me that she had prayed for a healing for many months and there was not the slightest improvement. The world is governed by law, and there is no such thing as a broken law. When our prayers are not answered it must be because we have not fulfilled the conditions of the law. Ninety-nine times in a hundred it is because we lack a sense of love for all and the spirit of forgiveness. This woman had a deep-seated grudge against another woman who had deceived her and who had extracted a large sum of money from her under false pretenses.

Being in Truth, she realized she had attracted this experience to herself and admitted that she was so careless, negligent and gullible that she did not use common sense and investigate before she invested. The first step in healing is forgiveness. She knew how to forgive, and when she had really forgiven the woman by the simple procedure of knowing that when the thought of her came to her mind she no longer sizzled, then a healing followed.

You can never lose money unless you admit the loss in mind. Accordingly she affirmed knowingly and wisely as follows: "I am mentally and spiritually identified with the money I gave _____ and it comes back to me multiplied and magnified in Divine order." Your subconscious always magnifies what you dwell upon. She was not to think of how it would come, as that is the secret of the subconscious. It came back to her in a very unusual way. She won over $10,000 in Las Vegas, which more than compensated for her previous loss. Love heals; fear, hate and self-condemnation damage and destroy. Claim frequently: "Divine love fills my soul." Let your words be sweet to the soul and bring health to the bones. See the Presence of God where the problem is and claim that Divine love saturates your whole being.

Went To Pieces

A woman said to me that her husband was financially very successful, but he dominated those around him in his business by the force of his domineering attitude and willpower. She wondered why he suddenly cracked up and, in her words, "went to pieces."

In talking with him, I found that he was full of fear of the future and of failure, even though he was prospering. Actually, he was afraid of life and of death. His external attitude was all bluff and bluster. He was covering it up by riding roughshod over his employees and associates. He was outwardly compensating for his inner sense of insecurity and inadequacy.

At my suggestion he began to read frequently the 27th Psalm, the greatest antidote to fear in the world today. His inner fear was calling upon his Inner Power waiting to respond to his call. Every morning he sat down quietly and prayed for all his associates and employees, as follows: "All my associates and employees are known in Divine mind. God is guiding them in all ways. I radiate love, peace and goodwill to them, and I wish for them all the blessings of life. All those connected with me are spiritual links in the chain of growth, welfare and prosperity of our company. God thinks, speaks and acts through me."

This regular prayer every morning prior to work eventually changed his relationship with his associates and he became more amiable, affable and cordial. The mirror treatment every morning (an age-old truth) was practiced, which means he looked into the mirror every morning for about five minutes, affirming "I am a son of the Living God. I am peaceful, harmonious and successful. God loves me and cares for me." The practice of these simple prayers transformed and changed his whole life and relationships with others.

Practice Now

Use this perfect formula for casting out fear. *I sought the Lord, and He heard me, and delivered me from all my fears.* Psalm 34:4. The Lord is an ancient word meaning law—the power of your subconscious mind.

Learn the wonders of your subconscious, and how it works and functions. Master the techniques given to you in this chapter. Put them into practice now, today! Your subconscious will respond, and you will be free or full of fears. *I sought the Lord, and He heard me, and delivered me from all my fears.*

His Vivid Imagination

The general manager of an organization told me that for three years he feared he would lose his position. He was always imagining failure. The thing he feared did not exist, save as a morbid, anxious thought in his own mind. His vivid imagination dramatized the loss of his job until he became nervous and neurotic. Finally he lost his position; he was asked to resign.

Actually he dismissed himself. His constant, negative imagery and fear suggestions to his subconscious mind caused the latter to respond and react accordingly. It made him make mistakes and foolish decisions which resulted in his failure as a general manager. The thing this man feared did not exist. His dismissal would never have happened had he immediately moved to the opposite in his mind.

No thought or concept, constructive or negative, can ever manifest except we emotionalize such concepts. The thoughts, concepts, and ideas have to penetrate the subconscious before they can affect us for good or evil.

If you look back in your life, you will agree with the writer that most of your fears, worries, and anxieties never came to pass. The reason for this was that you did not retain them long enough; likewise, you did not charge them with a deep emotion. The general secret of banishing fear is to constantly fill your mind with constructive and positive thoughts. Fill the mind with thoughts of love, peace, and harmony. Give attention to your goal, ideal, the positive, the things you wish to experience in life. As you do this, an inner invisible movement of your subconscious mind will take place, changing your world into the likeness of your inner imagery and contemplation.

He Found the Still Water

During a recent round the world lecture tour, I had a two-hour conversation with a prominent government official. He had a deep sense of inner peace and serenity. He said that all the abuse he receives politically from newspapers and the opposition party never disturbs him. His practice is to sit still for fifteen minutes in the morning and realize that in the center of him is a deep, still ocean of peace. Meditating in this way, he generates tremendous power which overcomes all manner of difficulties and fear.

Some months ago, a colleague called him at midnight and told him that a group was plotting against him. This is what he said to his colleague, "I am going to sleep now in perfect peace. You can discuss it with me at ten A.M. tomorrow."

Notice how calm he was, how cool, how peaceful! He didn't start getting excited, tearing his hair, or wringing his hands. At his center he found the still water, an inner peace, and there was a great calm.

Your mind is composed of two areas, the conscious mind where we reason, and the great unconscious or subconscious depths which somewhat resemble the ocean into which many forgotten fears and false beliefs are lodged.

Fear is the cause of great misery, and untold suffering and fear come to all of us. Many are afraid of the future, old age, insecurity, some illness or incurable condition, or the verdict of doctors. Many are full of fear regarding their families, newspaper reports and the media in general, all of which project fear propaganda of all kinds. Fear of nuclear warfare, inflation and crime disturbs the masses.

Chapter 11

THE POWER IS IN YOU AND NOT IN OTHERS

No one can live successfully until he masters self-control. You can control your own thoughts and responses to life. You must remember that the suggestions of others have no power to create the things they suggest. The creative power is your thought and not in the thoughts or suggestions of others.

I am writing this at Jasper Park Lodge, Jasper National Park, Alberta, Canada. I checked in here on Sunday night. It was about twelve o'clock midnight and the lobby was packed, for there were a great number of tourists checking in. I joined the line, moving slowly toward the registration desk, and overheard the clerk trying to pacify a very angry irate woman. She called him stupid, a fool, and said that he was dumb and should be discharged.

It was interesting to see his reaction. He replied, "I am sorry, madam. There must be some mistake. Your name is not registered with us, and there is no reservation according to our records. I will do the best I can and certainly find something for you."

She went off into a strident-voiced tirade, punctuated at intervals by the clerk's, "Yes, madam," and "I'm very sorry about it all, and if I were on your side of the desk, I would feel just as you do."

I observed this young man. There was no angry retort. No color came to his cheeks; he revealed no annoyance or irritation. He looked calmly and dispassionately at the woman from New York, and was friendly, pleasant, courteous, and quite efficient.

When I reached the desk, I said to him, "I admire your composure. You are to be complimented."

The Unbelievable Power of Suggestion

Then he quoted a test, the 19th verse of the 21st, 6 chapter of Luke, "*In patience possess ye your soul.*"

This young university student did not allow the statement of the woman to ruffle him. He was master of his thoughts and responses. He told me that all the clerks in the hotel, the waitresses, bellhops, maids, chauffeurs, etc., were students form the various universities of Canada, working here for the summer months, trying to pay their way through their respective university. He had a patience which implies maturity, mental health, philosophical understanding, and will continue to climb upward.

Keep constantly in mind that the power is in you and not in others.

The writer was told one time by an instructor that he would never become a public speaker and to forget all about it. I was a young boy at that time and stuttered considerably. My reaction was one of anger, and I said to myself, "I will show him. I will speak in public and to thousands of people."

Instinctively I rejected his suggestion. If I had accepted his negative statement, I would be a victim of autohypnosis, and undoubtedly would never have become a public lecturer.

Madame Schumann-Heink was told by a professor in Vienna that she had no voice and to go back home and become a good hausfrau. She rejected his suggestion and refused to accept his verdict. She believed that God who gave her the voice to sing would show her the way and open up the door, which He did. All of us know the majestic cadences and songs of God which came through her.

I knew a young boy who was constantly told by his mother, "You are a liar like your father. You can't tell the truth. You are dumb and stupid."

This boy simply could not tell the truth and had great difficulty in learning. His nickname became "Dummy." Unwittingly and ignorantly, the mother placed her own son in mental shackles and bondage that prevented him from releasing his hidden talents.

The mind of the boy was highly impressionable, and he accepted the verdict of his mother as a fact, and his subconscious reacted according to the impression made upon it.

I said to a young girl in a store in the town of Jasper, "You are a very beautiful and charming young lady."

She replied, "Oh, don't say that. My mother says I'm the ugliest and most ungainly of all the members of the family."

This girl believed this, but changed her mind when she realized that she was the victim of negative suggestions on the part of her mother. She quickly grasped the working of her subconscious mind by my implanting in her mind the concept that she is a daughter of God and one with Infinite Power and Wisdom. She is now fashioning a true image of herself as a child of God and "a princess of Israel, and a daughter of Judah."

To affirm, "I am a child of God," and in the next breath say, "I am ugly and awkward," creates a conflict in the mind resulting in a deep inferiority and rejection complex.

"As a man thinketh in his heart, so is he." Thought is the only creative power you know. You should think from the standpoint of God and the eternal verities and not from the standpoint of human opinion, false beliefs, and world propaganda.

The truth about you is that God is seeking expression through you. You are an instrument of the Divine, and you should begin now to realize the power of your own thoughts, ideas, and mental pictures. Refuse to permit your mind to be cluttered up with false impressions and partial glimpses of the truths of God.

If you want to ascend spiritually, you must cease once and for all to give power to conditions, circumstances, people, or any external or created thing. The only power is God, and you are one with God when you think, "God is the only presence and the only power. My thoughts are God's thoughts, and God's power is with my thoughts of good."

God is the Living Spirit within you which created you and is seeking to express as harmony, joy, and peace through you. There is no power inherent in the suggestions of another person whether clergyman, doctor, newspaper reporter, or what not.

If you go up to a sailor on board a British ship and say to him, "You are going to be seasick; you don't look good," he would simply smile condescendingly at you. Your suggestion would have no power to upset him; actually you simply reinforced his conviction in his immunity to seasickness. The sailor has faith and confidence that he won't get sick and his response is one of confidence in his inner strength and power.

Suggestions of fear and impotence will have no effect upon a man full of faith in God and all things good.

The radio, television, and newspapers are constantly pouring forth suggestions of all kinds, both good and evil, but many people are not affected by them at all.

Supposing you were on a ship on the high seas and a fellow passenger said to you, "You look very pale; there is a yellow pigmentation in your eyes. You are getting sick." These suggestions could not affect you in the slightest, except they kindled a response from you based on fear and expectancy of seasickness. The suggestion of the other had to find some kindred thoughts or feeling within you before any results could follow.

Wise Thoughts

If your thought is wise, the reaction or response will be wise. Your action is only the outer expression of your thought. Your constructive action or decision is but the manifestation of a wise or true thought entertained in your mind.

After asking for guidance or an answer to a particular problem, do not neglect obvious or convenient stepping stones to your goal. You will avoid blocking your answer when you simply think about the solution, knowing that your thought activates your subconscious, which knows all, sees all, and has the "know-how" of accomplishment.

How He overcame the Feeling of Frustration

To be frustrated is to be confused, baffled, perplexed, or thwarted in reaching your goal. Fear really is behind all frustration, because man believes he is stymied, blocked, and inhibited by external forces, and therefore he can't realize his desire. In other words, he thinks his environment is grater than himself.

A young engineer said to me some months ago, "I have been working for a boss for over fifteen years; I have not been promoted. My talents are being wasted. I'm so frustrated! I hate my boss—he is an ignoramus—and I just walked out and got another job. But I went from the frying pan into the fire. This new job is worse."

This engineer feared that he would never be advanced in his work because of his age and racial background. He was brought up by a domineering, tyrannical, puritanical sort of father who was typical of his New England traditions. He had resented his father and had not written him for several years. Moreover, he had a guilt complex and feared punishment because of his hatred and resentment toward his father. He said to me, "I suppose God has it in for me."

Slowly but surely he began to see that he was rebelling against authority in the same way he had been rebelling inwardly against his father. It began to dawn on him that he was actually transferring the blame for his own shortcomings, mistakes, and misdeeds to his superiors in business. He was attributing to those in authority over him his unacceptable impulses and thoughts.

He overcame his sense of frustration by first perceiving that he was actually blocking his own promotion by his fear, resentment and hatred. He decided to pray morning and evening as follows: "I wish for everyone in the plant where I work health, happiness, peace, and promotion. My employer congratulates me on my work; I paint this picture in my mind regularly, and I know it will come to pass. I am loving, kind, and cooperative. I practice the golden rule, and I sincerely treat everyone in the same way that I would like to be treated. Divine Intelligence rules and guides me all day long, and I am prospered in all my ways."

Don't Compare Yourself with Others

God never repeats himself. You are unique, and there is no one in the entire world like you. Many men and women who were timid, shy and retiring have visited me for counseling, and I have always pointed out to them the vast potentials within them waiting only to be called upon, resurrected and utilized. I explained to them that when fear came to their mind, it meant that they were supposed to call on the Divine reserves within them, thereby enabling them to overcome fear.

As they practice calling on the God Presence for guidance, strength and wisdom, they rise from that sense of inadequacy and keep going when others give up. One man, who had been born into poverty, told me that the reason he had reached the presidency of his company was due to his tremendous drive to overcome poverty and achieve his true place in life. His lack urged him on and acted as a powerful incentive to his ascent up the ladder of life.

Many women with an inferiority complex have told me that it was this sense of insecurity, inadequacy and inferiority which acted as their main driving force to excel, advance and go up the ladder of life. A formula which I have suggested to many women is as follows: Stand before the mirror every morning for five or ten minutes and affirm our loud: "I AM a daughter of the Infinite. I AM a child of eternity. My father is God, and God loves me.

As they keep using this prayer regularly every morning, it gradually sinks down by a process of mental and spiritual osmosis into their subconscious mind. This new concept of themselves, being impregnated in their deeper mind, comes forth and their whole life is transformed.

Chapter 12

SUGGESTIONS FOR WEALTH AND PROSPERITY

You're Right To Be Rich

It is normal and natural for you to desire prosperity, success, achievement and recognition in your life. You should have all the money you need to do what you want to do, and when you want to do it. There is no virtue in poverty because poverty is a mental disease, and it should be abolished from the face of the earth. Wealth is a state of mind; likewise, poverty is a state of mine. We will never eradicate all the slums in the world until we first wipe out the slums and belief in poverty and lack in the mind of man.

During private counseling and when talking to people in foreign lands as well as during interviews with people following lectures, both here and abroad, I hear the constant old refrain: "There is nothing that $25,000 or $50,000 would not cure in my life." This refers, of course, to those who suffer from pecuniary embarrassment and who are financially handicapped. They fail to realize that wealth is really a thought-image in the mind, and that if they follow the suggested simple techniques in this book, in using their subconscious mind, wealth will flow to them in avalanches of abundance.

It is your right and that of your family to have excellent food, good clothes, an ideal home and all the money you need to buy the good things of life. You need a period every day for meditation, prayer, relaxation and recreation, and the time and facilities necessary should be available to you. To prosper means that you begin to advance mentally, spiritually, intellectually, socially, financially and along all lines.

If you are having financial difficulties, if you are trying to make ends meet, it means you have not convinced your subconscious mind that you will always have plenty and some to spare. You know men and women who work a few hours a week and make fabulous sums of money. They do not strive or slave hard. Do not believe the story that the only way you can become wealthy is by the sweat of your brow and hard labor. It is not so; the effortless way of life is the best. Do the thing you love to do, and do it for the joy and thrill of it.

I know an executive in Los Angeles who receives a salary of $75,000 yearly. Last year he went on a nine-month cruise seeing the world and its beauty spots. He said to me that he had succeeded in convincing his subconscious mind that he is worth that much money. He told me that many men in his organization getting about one hundred dollars a week knew more about the business than he did, and could manage it better, but they had no ambition, no creative ideas, and were not interested in the wonders of their subconscious mind.

Wealth Is of the Mind

Wealth is simply a subconscious conviction on the part of the individual. You will not become a millionaire by saying, "I am a millionaire, and I am a millionaire." You will grow into a wealth consciousness by building into you mentality the idea of wealth and abundance.

Your Invisible Means of Support

The trouble with most people is that they have no invisible means of support. When business falls away, the stock market drops, or they lose their investments, they seem helpless. The reason for such insecurity is that they do not know how to tap the subconscious mind. They are unacquainted with the inexhaustible storehouse within.

A man with a poverty type mind finds himself in poverty-stricken conditions. Another man with a mind filled with ideas of wealth is surrounded with everything he needs. It was never intended that man should lead a life of indigence. You can have wealth, everything you need, and plenty to spare. Your words have power to cleanse your mind of wrong ideas and to instill right ideas in their place.

She Had a Mental Picture of Failure

A real estate saleswoman said she had opened a different office three times and had failed miserably. She went to church, received the sacraments, and prayed regularly for prosperity and success. The explanation was the cure for this saleslady. She feared failure and expected to fail. She had a mental picture of failure. Her constant negativity undermined all her work. She attracted clients and opportunities came her way, but the pattern of failure persisted. Since she began with thoughts of failure, the result coincided with the beginning.

She learned to reverse her mental attitude and enthroned in her mind the pattern of success by affirming every morning and night: "Infinite Spirit attracts to me clients who have the money to buy and who want the homes I have for sale. They are blessed and prospered, and I am likewise blessed and prospered. I AM a tremendous success in all my undertakings. I AM born to win and succeed in life. I know that when I begin with the idea of success, the end will be successful."

When fear thoughts came to her, she supplanted them immediately by affirming, "Success is mine. It is wonderful." She made a habit of this, and since the subconscious is the seat of habit, she is now compelled to succeed and is moving onward and upward.

The Ideal Method for Building a Wealth Consciousness

Perhaps you are saying as you read this chapter, "I need wealth and success." This is what you do: Repeat for about five minutes to yourself three times a day, "Wealth-Success." These words have tremendous power. They represent the inner power of the subconscious mind. Anchor your mind on this substantial power within you; then conditions and circumstances corresponding to their nature and quality will be manifested in your life. You are not saying, "I am wealthy," you are dwelling on real powers within you. There is no conflict in the mind when you say, "Wealth." Furthermore, the feeling of wealth will well up within you as you dwell on the idea of wealth.

The feeling of wealth produces wealth; keep this in mind at all times. Your subconscious mind is like a bank, a sort of universal financial institution. It magnifies whatever you deposit or impress upon it whether it is the idea of wealth or of poverty. Choose wealth.

Why Your Affirmations for Wealth Fail

I have talked to many people during the past thirty-five years whose usual complaint is, "I have said for weeks and months, 'I am wealthy I am prosperous,' and nothing has happened." I discovered that when they said, "I am prosperous, I am wealthy," they felt within that they were lying to themselves.

One man told me "I have affirmed that I am prosperous until I am tired. Things are now worse. I knew when I made the statement that it was obviously not true." His statements were rejected by the conscious mind, and the very opposite of what he outwardly affirmed and claimed was made manifest.

Your affirmation succeeds between when it is specific and when it does not produced a mental conflict or argument; hence the statements made by this man made maters worse because they suggested his lack. Your subconscious accepts what you really feel to be true, not just idle words or statements. The dominant idea or belief is always accepted by the subconscious mind.

How to Avoid Mental Conflict

The following is the ideal way to overcome this conflict for those who have this difficulty. Make this practical statement frequently, particularly prior to sleep: "By day and by night I am being prospered in all of my interests." This affirmation will not arouse any argument because it does not contradict your subconscious mind's impression of financial lack.

I suggested to one businessman whose sales and finances were very low and who was greatly worried, that he sit down in his office, become quiet, and repeat this statement over and over again: "My sales are improving every day." This statement engaged the co-operation of the conscious and subconscious mind; results followed.

The Riches of the Listening Ear and Understanding Heart

Recently I had a wonderful letter from a widow who listens every morning to my radio program. The following is the essence of the letter. She pointed out that her husband had died a year previously and had left no insurance. She had three children to support, the house was mortgaged, and she had only $500 in the bank. Friends paid the funeral expenses for her deceased husband. She wrote: "I heard you quote from the Bible: But my God shall supply all your needs according to his riches in glory (Philippians 4:12), and you elaborated on this by telling us that if we tune in on the Infinite within us and believe in our hearts that no matter what it is we really need to bless us, comfort us, provide for us or inspire us, the Divine Presence would respond, as it is written: Before they call, I will answer; and while they are yet speaking, I will hear (Isaiah 65:24).

"I sat down and began to think of God supplying all my needs and hearing me as I was praying, and a great sense of peace and harmony came over me. About two hours later, in walked my brother-in-law, who said to me that he knew of my predicament and that he also was aware of the spending habits and profligacy of his brother."

He told her he wanted to take care of her and the three small children, assuring her that neither she nor they would ever want for the good things of life. He gave her a $10,000 cashier's check and set up an arrangement with his attorney and accountant to see to it that a weekly sum of money was sent to his sister-in-law for the rest of her life. This was in the form of a trust fund, legally instituted, which took care of the children also.

This widow, recognizing that God supplies all her needs, and that even before she asks, the answer is within her, proved to herself the existence of the inexhaustible reservoir within her.

She Decreed Prosperity

A woman wrote to me, saying, "I owe the bank a lot of money on my home, and bills are piling up." I replied to her, saying that she should decree with feeling several times a day, "My house is free from all debt, and wealth flows to me in avalanches of abundance." I pointed out that she was not to question the manner in which the answer to her prayer would come and that he subconscious intelligence would direct all her steps, for it knows everything necessary for the fulfillment of her desires.

A few weeks later, she was approached by a builder who wanted to put up an apartment house on her property, and he offered her far more than her property was worth. She accepted gratefully and was able to liquidate all of her debts. At the same time she secured a contract from the builder to act as a manager of the apartment for him at a good salary and with a fine apartment.

Your subconscious always magnifies. The Bible says, *"Thou shalt also decree a thing, and it shall be established unto thee . . ."* (Job 22:28)

An Effective Prosperity Prayer

"I know there is only one Source, the Life-Principle, from which all things flow. It created the universe and all things therein contained. I am a focal point of the Divine Presence. My mind is open and receptive. I am a free-flowing channel for harmony, beauty, guidance, wealth and the riches of the Infinite. I know that health, wealth and success are released from within and appear on the without. I am now in harmony with the Infinite riches within and without, and I know these thoughts are sinking into my subconscious mind and will be reflected on the screen of space. I wish for everyone all the blessings of life. I am open and receptive to God's riches—spiritual, mental and material—and they flow to me in avalanches of abundance."

CHAPTER 13

AFFIRMATION IS A FORM OF SUGGESTION

Have you ever said, "He bores me"? If so, it is an unconscious confession of guilt within yourself, indicating that you are all wrapped up in yourself and looking for someone to lift you out of your despondency or "self-centeredness." Every time you meet another person, stir up the gift of God within you and say to yourself, "I behold the Presence of God in the other, and I know that at this moment there is a rearrangement of the mental and emotional factors in both of us whereby we blend harmoniously, peacefully and lovingly." Thoughts are things, and whatever we think about another we are thinking about ourselves.

For as he thinketh in his heart, so is he ... (Proverbs 23:7). Many people cite this Biblical quotation from the Book of Proverbs of such a profound truth. The heart (in the Bible) means your subconscious mind. Whatever idea you have that is emotionalized or felt as true will be made manifest in your life. Whatever you give attention to and feel to be true will be impressed in your subconscious and brought to pass.

If, for example, you affirm with emphasis and feeling that you will always be poor, can't get ahead in life, that you will be discriminated against and can't do anything about it, you can rest assured that you will get the results suggested by yourself. Likewise, the inverse is true. Claim feelingly and knowingly that you are born to win and to triumph, and that it is your Divine right to be healthy, wealthy, and successful, and that God wants you to be happy, joyous and free. Claim boldly that Divine right action is mine, Divine law and order are mine, and Divine harmony is mine. Declare that God's riches are mine and I am expressing more and more of my Divinity everyday. Affirm these suggestions with feeling and understanding and your subconscious will compel you to express these in your life as experiences, conditions and events.

Your Focused Thought Takes Form

Some years ago Dr. Charles Littlefield, a scientist, discovered the truth of the Biblical quotation, *for as he thinketh in his heart, so is he.* While concentrating his thought on a saline solution by peering through a microscope, he discovered his focused thought took form. One day, he concentrated his attention on a frail, elderly lady. He stood gazing intently at her for some time. When he turned back to look at the saline solution, he was surprised to find there is a miniature form of this woman. Day after day he concentrated on certain mental pictures, and he was amazed to see his mental imagery take form in the shapes developed by the crystals in the saline solution under the microscope.

Man is what he thinks all day long. Our thoughts are the tools and instruments which fashion, mold and shape our destiny. Your thoughts can be photographed. They have form, shape and structure in your brain now, and are gradually being condensed into muscle, skin and cells, as well as into experiences, events and conditions.

For many years there has been a revolution going on in the field of chemistry and physics. For example, the postulate of immutable elements is gone; this dogma vanished with the discovery of radioactivity. Scientists today point out that we are living in a dynamic, evolving, changing universe. The late Robert Andrew Milliken, who was head of the California Institute of Technology at Pasadena for many years, said that the two fundamental principles, conversation of mass and conservation of energy, are now gone as distinct and separable verities.

Einstein and other scientists have also pointed out the inter-convertibility of energy into mass and mass into energy. Energy and mass are actually one and the same thing operating at different levels of vibration. Mater is energy reduced to the point of visibility. The conception of the conservation of energy and the conservation of mass is considered no longer sacrosanct.

Your body is plastic, porous and pliable. It consists of waves of light existing at different rates of vibration. Modern science teaches that the only difference between one substance and another is the number and rate of motion of the electrons revolving around a nucleus, proving the dictum of Pythagoras that the world is ruled by number and motion.

The Invisible Suggestion

You cannot measure love with a slide rule; neither can you measure peace, happiness, wisdom or understanding. We are dealing with the intangible, the invisible, the imponderable. You cannot see the power that moves your finger to write, nor do you see the power that lifts the chair or table. Your body moves as it is moved upon. Your body acts as it is acted upon. Your body is basically characterized by inertia and your thoughts, emotions, and imagery are played upon it for good or ill. You can play a melody of God on the tissues of your body or a song of hatred or ill will.

Six Days of Creation

Look at the six days of creation as six great stages in the evolution of the cosmos. The six days In Genesis have an inner meaning which portrays the six steps in prayer followed by the seventh day, or Sabbath, in which you reach the point of conviction or inner knowing that your prayer is answered. In psychological parlance, the six days represent the length of time it takes you to impress or convey your idea or concept in your subconscious mind. As soon as you succeed in impregnating the subconscious by imagining the reality of your desire and feeling the thrill of fulfillment, you have succeeded in impressing the subconscious. Impregnation has taken place. The work of the six days is finished, followed by a period of inner rest called the Sabbath, or seventh day, which is the interval between the impregnation and its manifestation.

Ideas Move Men and Nations

The most wonderful and valuable form of wealth is a good idea. The Magna Carta was an idea in the mind of man, as was the Declaration of Independence. Ideas move men and nations and inspire men and women to the heights of accomplishment and achievement. An idea is a thought, a mental conception, suggestion, an image in the mind, an intention.

When you stop to think, you begin to realize that all the great inventions in the world started as an idea in the mind of man. Look around you in Los Angeles, New York or any city, and you will perceive that all the major skyscrapers, major plants and industries, all the great institutions and organizations began as simple ideas and suggestions. In fact, everything you look at in this world came out of the mind of man, or the mind of God. The universe, the galaxies in space and the billions of stars and suns and worlds came out of the mind of God. The ancient Vedas said, "God thinks and worlds appear." Man thinks and his world appears. What the world needs are lofty, noble, Godlike ideas which heal, bless and inspire mankind.

One of the old writers on the laws of mind, Prentice Mulford, said, "Truth heals; lies breed disease." For example, a man is told that he can't walk again due to an accident. He believes this suggestion and remains incapacitated. Another man who is hurt even worse than the first is told by a spiritual counselor that through the power of the Infinite Spirit within him, he can walk again and be healed. His mind is stirred with faith and confidence, and he imagines himself doing all the things he would do were he whole and perfect. His mental image, being backed up by faith and expectancy in the God-Power within him, creates a wonderful demonstration and he is completely healed. This is the power of a transcendent idea lodged in the mind of man.

Phineas Parkhurst Quimby, who was America's greatest spiritual healer, began healing people of all manner of diseases in the year 1847. He possessed tremendous mental power and concentration and perceived intuitively the inner meaning of the bible. He used to explain the inner meaning to his very sick patients, because in many instances their maladies were due to false religious beliefs based on the literal interpretation of Scripture. When people had lost all hope and could not be healed by any orthodox procedure, they came to Quimby as a last resort, and he healed them all. He duplicated most of the so-called miracles of the Bible, and if he had lived long enough he would undoubtedly have duplicated all of them.

Supplant Negative Suggestions with Godlike Ideas

All of us tend to be influenced everyday by the propaganda of all sorts of news which tend to depress, excite and instill fear into the mind. You must learn to reject all these negative suggestions and supplant them with Godlike ideas which will raise your spirit. The false predictions of doom and gloom can influence you negatively and cause great trouble. Permit the truths of God to guide you to ways of pleasantness and paths of peace.

Fear and ignorance are rampant today, and if you permit these suggestions to enter your mind, you will develop what is called by psychologists an anxiety neurosis. Insist on governing your mind with true ideas, for then your talents and abilities are encouraged and you become imbued with the confidence and faith that lead you along the path of success and inner peace.

The Whole World Believes a Lie

Quimby said that "the whole world believes a lie, and when I tell it the truth, it thinks the truth is a lie." Millions are brought up in the belief that it is the will of God that they suffer, that externals are causative, that the night air will give them a cold, if they get wet they might catch pneumonia, or that when they grew old their vision, hearing and other faculties will weaken. Millions believe in evil entities, demons and voodooist, and black magic.

The scientific thinker does not give power to the phenomenalistic world. It is an effect, not a cause. The Supreme Power, I AM, is within you. There is nothing to oppose it, challenge it, thwart it or vitiate it. Otherwise, the word omnipotence would have no meaning. The propaganda of fear regarding cancer, the flu and other diseases has no power to disturb you. These are suggestions only and have no power unless they awaken a response within your own mind, which is the creative power of your own mind. Always remember that a suggestion has no power to create the thing it suggests. If someone suggests to you that you will get the flu, you can affirm boldly, "I am all health. God is my health." In that way you neutralize the suggestion and build up immunity to all disease.

Some say, "Roses give me hay fever." If that were really true, then all people throughout the world would get hay fever when in contact with roses. There are no exceptions to a law. It is obvious that the person who is allergic to roses has made a law for himself. Roses have no such power. The cause is in the subconscious of the person. He may be allergic to his wife or to the fellow next to him on the work bench. It is the things inside the mind that cause the things outside the mind. The inside is always the cause; the outside is the effect of the inner contents of the mind.

A man living in Leisure World, Laguna Hills, where I live, told me that for several years his right hand had been constantly shaking, actually trembling; it seemed to be full of tremors. He had been told it was due to a nerve in his hand that had been injured. He went to a woman who was noted for spiritual healing, and she gave him a prayer to use frequently. She told him point blank that if he continued using the prayer he would be healed. He had the prayer I suggested, in his billfold, which read as follows: "God has not given me the spirit of fear but the spirit of power, and of love, and of a sound mind. My faith is in the healing power of God, which created me. I am relaxed and at peace. All my nerves are God's ideas, and I am vitalized, energized, and healed through and through. I give thanks to God."

He saturated his mind with these simple truths and had a wonderful healing of the palsy. He turned to the Divine man (his Higher Self) within him, and as he called upon the presence, it responded to him. This is wisdom in action. Wisdom is an awareness of the Presence and Power of God within you, which responds when you call upon it.

Recently I talked with a woman over the phone, who said that she was ready to explode. She said that her husband was afflicted with a fatal illness, that he would take his medicine, and that he kept humming the same song all day long while sitting in a rocking chair and rocking continuously for hours on end. She said that she was turning to drink and that she had lost her buoyancy and resiliency altogether. She told me that she yells at him, saying, "For heaven's sake, stop it! You're driving me crazy!"

I suggested to her to sit down quietly and do what the Psalmist said. "*I will lift up mine eyes unto the hills, from whence cometh my help* (Psalm 121:1). *God gives me peace. God gives me joy, and God loves my husband and cares for him.*" She began to affirm these by actually singing the words. She climbed the mountain and rose above it. The hills mentioned by Psalmist represent the great truths of God, which heal, invigorate and bring peace to the troubled mind. She discovered then that the constant rocking had no further effect upon her. You can always climb the hills of God and find peace in this changing world.

The late Dr. Frederick Bailes told me that a number of helpless paralytics were confined to a hospital in South America and that somehow a boa constrictor had crawled into the ward through an open window. All the paralytics ran out of the ward into the yard outside, and all had become completely healed.

Amazing Stories

Many physicians in the United States and other countries have reported in medical journals extraordinary feats of strength, so called miraculous healings taking place in the presence of a great shock such as fire in the home, a sudden catastrophe or a great emergency. The following article appeared in the National Enquirer January 29, 1980:

Tiny Housewife Lifts 4,500-Pound Car to Free Child Pinned Under a Wheel

> In a rush of superhuman strength, a 118 pound woman lifted a 4,600 pound Cadillac with her bare hands to free an 8-year-old girl pinned under the front wheel.
>
> "All I can think is that God gave me the strength," says 44 year-old Martha Weiss, who stands 5 feet 3 inches.
>
> Now, children are calling her "Wonder Woman," and the police have given her a hero's citation.
>
> The gut-wrenching drama unfolded when Mrs. Weiss saw the car hit little Berta Amaral in front of Our Lady of Mount Carmel in San Diego, drag her 20 feet and stop on top of her.
>
> "Everyone seemed to freeze in horror, recalled Mrs. Weiss, who had just dropped of her own children at school.
>
> "The little girl's mother was crawling under the car trying to reach her.
>
> "All I could think of was that woman's desperation as she tried to pull her daughter out.

"I knew I had to do something. I ran over and grabbed the front side of the car.

"The girl was under the right front wheel. She couldn't breathe. I said a silent prayer and strained with all my might. I could feel the metal cutting into my fingers—but the car didn't move an inch.

"I looked down at the pitiful face lying under the car, and I knew I had to lift it off of her.

"I tried again and, at first, nothing happened. Then suddenly I felt a new strength rush into my body. It was as though an invisible hand was suddenly helping me—and the car started to lift. I couldn't believe that it was actually happening, but then I screamed at the girl's mother to pull her free.

"As her tiny body came free of the car, I suddenly felt its full weight cutting into my fingers again and I had to let it drop."

Young Berta was rushed to a nearby hospital following the December 6 accident and is now recovering.

San Diego Policeman Bill Robinson, who investigated the accident which earned Mrs. Weiss an official recommendation, told the Enquirer:

"The car weighed about 2 ½ tons—and she did lift the full weight of the front end off the child. I've heard of men managing to do something like this, with a rush of adrenaline, but never a woman. It's really amazing."

A Cadillac spokeswoman said the car, a 2968 Coupe De Ville weight 4,596 pounds. The driver was cited for reckless driving.

Reflecting on her accomplishment, Mrs. Weiss said: "I simply did it because it had to be done. My children are telling everyone that their mother is "Wonder Woman"—God must have worked through me that day."

—Malcolm Boyes

The late Henry Hamblin, Editor of the Science of Thought Review, Chichester, England, told me of a man who had lived a short distance from him. He was completely paralyzed due to polio and could move only rather slowly with two crutches. His two boys, ages six and seven, had been in the next room when the house caught on fire. He had rushed in and raised his two boys on his shoulders and run down the stairs. He had run into the street and asked a neighbor to call the fire brigade. He had walked for years after that incident, completely cured. The idea to save the lives of both of his little boys had sized his mind, and the power of the Almighty had moved on his behalf and he had responded accordingly.

Husband Has Morning Sickness

Recently I counseled with a man who had suffered with his wife the pangs of what he called "morning sickness" during her pregnancy. I sent him to a doctor friend of mine, who could fine nothing physically wrong with him. This is not a strange phenomenon; it was due to his subconscious rapport with his wife. The constant telepathic communication brought on the same symptoms. It could be psychological sympathy between husband and wife.

I suggested that he use the following prayer three or four times a day:

> Thou wilt keeps him in perfect peace, whose mind is stayed on thee: because he trusted in thee (Isaiah 26:3). I know that the inner desires of my heart come from God within me. God wants me to be happy. The will of God for me is life, love, truth, and beauty. I mentally accept my good now and I become a perfect channel for the Divine.
>
> I come into his Presence singing; I inter into His courts with praise; I am joyful and happy; I am still and poised.
>
> The Still Small Voice whispers in my ear revealing to me my perfect answer. I am an expression of God. I am always in my true place doing the thing I love to do. I refuse to accept the opinions of man as truth. I now turn within and I sense and feel the rhythm of the Divine. I hear the melody of God whispering its message of love to me.
>
> My mind is God's mind, and I am always reflecting Divine wisdom and Divine intelligence. My brain symbolizes my capacity to think wisely and spiritually. God's ideas unfold within my mind with perfect sequence. I am always poised, balanced, serene and calm, for I know that God will always reveal to me the perfect solution to all my needs.
>
> Whenever I think of my wife I will affirm immediately, "God's peace fills your soul. God loves you and cares for you."

Following this procedure, he became completely free from all symptoms.

Never Admit a Loss

In Zurich, the home of the late Carl Jung, there is a great spiritual awareness. Dr. Fruitage frequently speaks to audiences in Switzerland and has a large following in several of the major cities. I experienced overflow audiences in all the cities visited, including Zurich.

In consultation with a woman in the hotel in Zurich, she said that she had given 100,000 francs to a con man. Apparently, she had experienced difficulty gaining admission to the United States, and he had told her he could fix it up for that sum of money. This was negligence, careless and indifference on her part. She had not consulted an attorney nor asked representatives in the office of the American Consulate about this proposed bribe. In other words, she did not use common sense.

She admitted that she had been foolish and gullible and a victim of a negative suggestion. Con men succeed many times in defrauding their victims because the victims don't reason things out and are greedy and looking for something for nothing. There is no free lunch. The suggestion of the con man that he could bribe an official and get her the visa and necessary papers triggered her false belief and ulterior motivation. Had she been honest, upright and on the level, the suggestion of bribing would have been rejected. It is rare that a con man can cheat an honest person. Remember that the suggestions of another have no power to create what he suggests. You can reject it. If accepted by you, then it becomes a movement of your own thought. The local authorities in Zurich informed this young woman that the same man had swindled many widows and was now in East Germany.

I suggested that she could not lose the money unless she admitted the loss mentally. I further suggested that she apply the following formula or prayer: "I am mentally and spiritually united with the 100,000 francs I gave up_____. It comes back to me multiplied in Divine order." I explained to her that she was not to subsequently deny what she affirmed and that her subconscious always magnifies what she contemplates. The return of the money will come to her in ways she knows not of. The ways of the subconscious are past finding out.

This took place about a month ago, and as of this writing I have not heard from her, but I know that as she remains faithful to her prayer, she will receive the answer, magnified and multiplied. Never admit a loss. You can always go back to the Center and claim your good from the Infinite Storehouse within, and the Spirit within will honor and validate your claim.

Marvelous Power

Over 90 percent of your mental life is subconscious, so men and women who fail to make use of this marvelous power live within very narrow limits.

Your subconscious processes are always life ward and constructive. Your subconscious is the builder of your body and maintains all its vital functions. It is on the job 24 hours a day and never sleeps. It is always trying to help and preserve you from harm.

Your subconscious mind is in touch with infinite life and boundless wisdom, and its impulses and ideas are always life ward. The great aspirations, inspirations, and visions for a grander and nobler life spring from the subconscious. Your profoundest convictions are those you cannot argue about rationally because they do not come from your conscious mind; they come from your subconscious mind. Your subconscious speaks to you in intuitions, impulses, hunches, intimations, urges, and ideas, suggestions and it is always telling you to rise, transcend, grow, advance, adventure, and move forward to greater heights. The urge to love, to save the lives of others comes from the depths of your subconscious. For example, during the great San Francisco earthquake and fire of April 18, 1906, invalids and cripples who had been confined to bed for long periods of time, rose up and performed some of the most amazing feats of bravery and endurance. The intense desire welled up within them to save others at all costs, and their subconscious responded accordingly.

Great artists, musicians, poets, speakers, and writers tune in with their subconscious powers and become animated and inspired. For example, Robert Louis Stevenson, before he went to sleep, used to charge his subconscious with the task of evolving stories for him while he slept. He was accustomed to ask his subconscious to give him a good, marketable thriller when his bank account was low. Stevenson said the intelligence of his deeper mind gave him the story piece by piece, like a serial. This shows how your subconscious will speak lofty and wise sayings through you which your conscious mind knows nothing about.

Mark Twain confided to the world on many occasions that he never worked in his life. All his humor and all his great writings were due to the fact that he tapped the inexhaustible reservoir of his subconscious mind.

How the Body Portrays the Workings of the Mind

The interaction of your conscious and subconscious mind requires a similar interaction between the corresponding systems of nerves. The cerebrospinal system is the organ of the conscious mind, and the sympathetic system is the organ of the subconscious mind. The cerebrospinal system is the channel through which you receive conscious perception by means of your five physical senses and exercise control over the movement of your body. This system has its nerves in the brain, and it is the channel of your volitional and conscious mental action.

The sympathetic system, sometimes referred to as the involuntary nervous system, has its center in a ganglion mass at the back of the stomach known as the solar plexus, and is sometimes spoken of as the abdominal brain. It is the channel of that mental action which unconsciously supports the vital functions of the body.

The two systems may work separately or synchronously. Judge Thomas Troward* says, "The vague nerve passes out of the cerebral region as a portion of the voluntary system, and through it we control the vocal organs; then it passes onward to the thorax sending out branches to the heart and lungs; finally, passing through the diaphragm, it loses the outer coating which distinguishes the nerves of the voluntary system and becomes identified with those of the sympathetic system, so forming a connecting link between the two and making the man physically and single entity.

"Similarly different areas of the brain indicate their connection with the objective and subjective activities of the mind respectively, and Speaking in a general way we may assign the frontal portion of the brain to the former and the posterior portion of the latter, while the intermediate portion partakes of the character of both."

A rather simple way of looking at the mental and physical interaction is to realize that your conscious mind grasps an idea which induces a corresponding vibration in your voluntary system of nerves. This is in turn causes a similar current to be generated in your involuntary system of nerves, thus handling the idea over to your subconscious mind which is the creative medium. This is how your thoughts become things.

Every thought entertained by your conscious mind and accepted as true is sent by your brain to your solar plexus, the brain of your subconscious mind, to be made into your flesh, and to be brought forth into your world as a reality.

Suggestion of the Master Mind

When you study the cellular system and the structure of the organs, such as eyes, ears, heart, liver, bladder, etc., you learn they consist of groups of cells which form a group intelligence whereby they function together and are able to take orders and carry them out in deductive function at the suggestion of the master mind (conscious mind).

A careful study of the single-celled organism shows you what goes on in your complex body. Though the mono-cellular organism has no organs, it still gives evidence of mind action and reaction performing the basic functions of movement, alimentation, assimilation, and elimination.

Many say there is an intelligence which will take care of your body if you let it alone. That is true, but the difficulty is that the conscious mind always interferes with its five-sense evidence based on outer appearances, leading to the sway of false beliefs, fears, and mere opinion. When fear, false beliefs, and negative

---

* The Edinburgh Lectures on Mental Science (New York: Robert McBride & Co., 1909).

patterns are made to register in your subconscious mind through psychological, emotional conditioning, there is no other course open to the subconscious mind except to act on the blueprint specifications offered it.

Works Continually for the Common Good

The subjective self within you works continuously for the general good, reflecting an innate principle of harmony behind all things. Your subconscious mind has its own will, and it is a very real something in itself. It acts night and day whether you act upon it or not. It is the builder of your body, but you cannot see, hear, or feel it building, as all this is a silence process. Your subconscious has a life of its own which is always moving toward harmony, health, and peace. This is the divine norm within it seeking expression through you at all times.

Know the Truth

To think correctly, scientifically, we must know the "Truth." To know the truth is to be in harmony with the infinite intelligence and power of your subconscious mind, which is always moving life ward.

Every thought or action which is not harmonious, whether through ignorance or design, will result in discord or design, will result in discord and limitation of all kinds.

Scientists inform us that you build a new body every eleven months; so you are really only eleven months; so you are really only eleven months old from a physical standpoint. If you build defects back into your body by thoughts of fear, anger, jealousy, and ill will, you have no one to blame but yourself.

You are the sum total of your own thoughts. You can keep from entertaining negative thought and imagery. The way to get rid of darkness is with light; the way to overcome cold is with heat; the way to overcome the negative thought is to substitute the good thought. Affirm the good, and the bad will vanish.

The Innate Principle of Harmony

The average child born into the world is perfectly healthy with all its organs functioning perfectly. This is the normal state, and we should remain healthy, vital, and strong. The instinct of self preservation is the strongest instinct of your nature, and it constitutes a most potent, ever-present, and constantly operative truth, inherent in your nature. It is, therefore, obvious that all your thoughts, ideas, and beliefs must operate with greater potentiality when they are in harmony with the innate life-principle in you, which is forever seeking to preserve and protect you along all lines. It follows from this that normal conditions can be restored with greater ease and certainty than abnormal conditions can be induced.

It is abnormal to be sick; it simply means you are going against the stream of life and thinking negatively. The law of life is the law of growth; all nature testifies to the operation of this law by silently, constantly expressing itself in the law of growth. Where there is growth and expression, there must be life; where there is life there must be harmony, and where there is harmony, there is perfect health.

If your thought is in harmony with the creative principle of your subconscious mind, you are in tune with the innate principle of harmony. If you entertain thoughts which are not in accordance with the principle of harmony, these thoughts cling to you, harass you, worry you, and finally bring about disease, and if persisted in, possibly death.

In the healing of disease, you must increase the inflow and distribution of the vital forces of your subconscious mind throughout your system. This can be done by eliminating thoughts of fear, worry, anxiety, jealousy, hatred, and every other destructive thought which tends to tear down and destroy your nerves and glands—body tissue which controls the elimination of all waste material.

Faith and Perseverance

In the Nautilus magazine of March 1917, there appears an article about a boy suffering from Pot's disease, or tuberculosis of the spine, who had a remarkable healing. His name was Frederick Elias Andrews of Indianapolis, now minister of Unity School of Christianity, Kansas City, Missouri. His physician pronounced him incurable. He began to pray, and from a crooked, twisted cripple going on about on hands and knees, he became a strong, straight, well-formed man. He created his own affirmation, mentally absorbing the qualities he needed.

He affirmed over and over again many times a day, "I am whole, perfect, a strong, powerful, lowing, harmonious, and happy." He persevered and said that this prayer was the last utterance on his lips at night and the first in the morning. He prayed for others also by sending out thoughts of love and health. This attitude of mind and way of prayer returned to him multiplied many times. His faith and perseverance paid off with big dividends. When thoughts of fear, anger, jealousy, or envy drew his attention, he would immediately start his counteracting force of affirmation gong in his mind. His subconscious mind responded according to the nature of his habitual thinking. This is the meaning of the statement in the Bible, *Go thy way, thy faith hath made thee whole*. Mark 10:52.

What Happened?

A young man, who came to my lectures on the healing power of the subconscious mind, had severe eye trouble which his doctor said necessitated an operation. He said to himself, "My subconscious made my eyes, and it can heal me."

Each night, as he went to sleep, he entered into a drowsy, meditated state, the condition akin to sleep. His attention was immobilized and focused on the eye doctor. He imagined he heard the doctor saying to him, "A miracle has happened!" He heard this over and over again every night for perhaps five minutes or so before going to sleep. At the end of three weeks he again went to the ophthalmologist who had previously examined his eyes, and the physician said to this man, "This is a miracle!" What happened? This man impressed his subconscious mind using the doctor as an instrument or a means of convincing it or conveying the idea. Through repetition, faith, and expectancy he impregnated his subconscious mind. His subconscious mind made his eye; within it was the perfect patterns, and immediately it proceeded to heal the eye. This is another example of how faith in the healing power of your subconscious can make you whole.

Suggested Pointers

1. Your subconscious is the builder of your body and is on the job 24 hours a day. You interfere with its life-giving patterns by negative thinking.
2. Charge your subconscious with the task of evolving an answer to any problem, prior to sleep and it will answer you.
3. Watch your thoughts. Every thought accepted as true is sent by your brain to your solar plexus—your abdominal brain—and is brought into your world as a reality.
4. Know that you can remake yourself by giving a new blueprint to your subconscious mind.
5. The tendency of your subconscious is always life ward. Your job is with your conscious mind. Feed your subconscious mind with premises which are true. Your subconscious is always reproducing according to your habitual mental patterns.
6. You build a new body every eleven months. Change your body by changing your thoughts and keeping them changed.
7. It is normal to be healthy. It is abnormal to be ill. There is within the innate principle of harmony.

8. Thoughts of jealousy, fear, worry, and anxiety tear down and destroy your nerves and glands bringing about mental and physical diseases of all kinds.
9. What you affirm consciously and feel as true will be made manifest in your mind, body and affairs. Affirm the good and enter into the joy of living.

CHAPTER 14

SUGGESTED PRAYER TECHNIQUES TO ACHIEVE YOUR GOALS IN LIFE

An engineer has a technique and a process for building a bridge or an engine. Like the engineer, your mind also has a technique for governing, controlling, and directing your life. You must realize that methods and techniques are primary.

In building the Golden Gate Bridge, the chief engineer understood mathematical principles, stresses and strains. Secondly, he had a picture of the ideal bridge across the bay. The third step was his application of tried and proven methods by which the principles were implemented until the bridge took form and we drive on it. There are also techniques and methods by which your prayers are answered. If your prayer is answered, there is a way in which it is answered, and this is a scientific way. Nothing happens by chance. This is a world of law and order. In this chapter you will find practical techniques for the unfolding and nature of your spiritual life. Your prayers must not remain up in the air like a balloon. They must go somewhere and accomplish something in your life.

When we come to analyze prayer, we discover there are many different approaches or methods. We will not consider in this book the formal, ritual prayers used in religious services. These have an important place in group worship. We are immediately concerned with the methods of personal prayer for use in your daily life and in helping others.

Prayer is the formulation of an idea concerning something we wish to accomplish. Circumstances and individuals suggest different approaches, but all must establish a clear statement of the benefit, the healing, and the purpose for which the prayer is offered.

The Visualization Technique

The easiest and most obvious way to formulate an idea is to visualize it, to see it in your mind's eye as vividly as if it were alive. We can see with the naked eye only what already exists in the external world; in a similar way what we can visualize in the mind's eye already exists in the invisible realms of our mind. Any picture which we have in the mind is the substance of things hoped for and the evidence of things not seen. What we form in our imagination is as real as any part of our body. The idea and the thought are real and will one day appear in our objective world if we are faithful to our mental image.

This process of thinking forms impressions on the mind; these impressions in turn become manifested or expressed on the screen of space as forms, functions, facts, and experiences The builder visualizes the type of building he wants; he sees it as he desires it to be completed. His imagery and thought-processes become a plastic mold from which the building will emerge—a beautiful or an ugly one, a skyscraper or a very low one. His mental imagery is projected as it is drawn on paper; eventually the contractor and his workers gather the essential materials, and the building progresses until it stands finished, conforming perfectly to the mental patterns of the architect.

Each Sunday I use the visualization technique prior to speaking from the platform. I quiet the wheels of my mind in order that I may present to the subconscious mind my images of thought; then I picture the entire auditorium and the seats filled with men and women, and each one of them illumined and inspired by the Healing Presence. I see them as radiant, happy, and free.

Having first built up the idea in my imagination, I quietly sustain it there as a mental picture while I imagine I hear men and women exclaiming aloud, "I am healed," "I feel wonderful," "I've had an instantaneous healing," "I'm transformed," etc. I keep this up for about ten minutes or more, knowing and feeling that each person is a tabernacle of God's Presence, and that Divine Love saturates each mind and body making them whole, pure, relaxed, and perfect. I see to the point where I actually can hear the imaginary voices of the multitudes proclaiming the glory of God; then I release the whole picture and go onto the platform. Almost every Sunday some people stop and say that their prayers were answered.

Use of Mental Picture

The Chinese say, "A picture is worth a thousand words." William James, the father of American psychology, stressed the fact that the subconscious mind will bring to pass any picture held in the mind backed by faith. "Act as though I am, and I will be."

A number of years ago, I was in the Middle West lecturing in several states and I desired to have a permanent location. One evening in a hotel in Spokane, Washington, I relaxed completely on the couch, immobilized my attention, and in a quiet, passive manner imagined that I was talking to a large audience, saying in effect, "I am glad to be here. I have prayed for this ideal church and opportunity." I saw in my mind's eye the imaginary audience and I felt the reality of it all. I played the role of the actor, dramatized this mental movie, and felt satisfied that his picture was being conveyed to my subconscious mind which would bring it to pass in its own way. The next morning on awakening I felt a great sense of peace and satisfaction, and in a few days' time I received a telegram asking me to take over a church in the East which I did, and enjoyed immensely for several years.

The method outline here appeals to many who have described it as the "mental movie method." I have received numerous letters from people who listen to my radio lectures and Sunday morning talks, telling me of the wonderful results they get using this technique in the sale of their property for sale that they satisfy themselves in their own mind that their price is right; then claim that Infinite Intelligence is attracting to them the buyer who really wants to have the property, and who will love it and prosper in it. After having done this I suggest that they quiet their mind, relax, let go, and get into a drowsy, sleepy state which reduces all mental effort to a minimum; then they are to picture the check in their hands, rejoice in the check, give thanks for the check, and go off to sleep feeling the naturalness of the whole mental movie created in their own mind. They must act as though it were an objective reality, and the subconscious mind will take it as an impression, and through the deeper currents of the mind the buyer and the seller are brought together. A mental picture held in the mind backed by faith will come to pass.

Charles Boudoir's Formula

Charles Baudoin was a professor of Rousseau Institute in France. He was a brilliant psychotherapist, and a research director of the New Nancy School of Healing, who in 1910 taught that the best way to impress the subconscious mind was to enter into a drowsy, sleepy state, or a state akin to sleep, in which all effort was reduced to a minimum; then in a quiet, passive, receptive way, by reflection, convey the idea to the subconscious. The following is his formula: "A very simple way of securing this (impregnation of the subconscious mind) is to condense the idea which is to be the object of suggestion, to sum it up in a brief phrase which can be readily graven on the memory, and to repeat it over and over again as a lullaby."

Baudoin emphasized the fact that when we enter into "the state akin to sleep" (between the waking and sleeping state), effort is reduced to a minimum, and we can focus our attention on our good with ease and without strain. We induce this state by feeling sleepy.

Innumerable experiences on persons have shown that the subconscious mind will accept any idea, suggestion, or mental picture which is felt as true by the conscious mind, and works out every suggestion to the minutest detail in the results which flow from it. The subconscious mind is entirely under control of the conscious or objective mind. With the utmost fidelity it reproduces and manifests in the final consequences whatever conscious mind impresses upon it.

Application of Baudoin Technique

A lady in one of our classes was engaged in a prolonged, bitter family lawsuit over a will. Her husband had bequeathed his entire estate to her, and his sons and daughters were bitterly fighting to break the will. The Baudoin technique was outlined in detail to her, and this is what she did: She relaxed her body in an armchair, entered into the sleepy state, and as suggested, condensed the idea of her need into a phrase consisting of six words easily graven on the memory. "It is finished in Divine Order." The significance of these words to her meant that Infinite Intelligence operating through Law (the subconscious mind) would bring about a harmonious adjustment in Divine Order. She continued this procedure every night for about ten nights; after she got into a sleepy state she would affirm slowly, quietly, and feelingly the statement: "It is finished in Divine Order." Over and over again, feeling a sense of inner peace and a letting go; then she went off into her deep, normal sleep.

On the morning of the eleventh day following the use of the above technique, she awakened with a sense of well-being, a conviction that it was finished. Her attorney called her the same day, saying that the opposing attorney and his clients were willing to settle. A harmonious agreement was reached, and litigation was discontinued.

The Sleeping Technique

By entering into a sleepy, drowsy state, effort is reduced to a minimum. The conscious mind is submerged to a great extent when in a sleepy state. The reason for this is that the highest degree of outcropping of the subconscious occurs prior to sleep and just after we awaken. In this state the negative thoughts which tend to neutralize your desire and so prevent acceptance by the subconscious no longer present themselves.

Assume a comfortable posture, relax your body, and be still. Get into a sleepy state and in that sleepy state, say quietly, over and over again as a lullaby, "I am completely free from this habit, sobriety and peace of mind reign supreme." Repeat the above slowly, quietly, and lovingly for five or ten minute's night and morning. Each time you repeat the above statement its emotional value becomes greater. When the urge comes, repeat the above formula out loud to yourself. By this means you induce the subconscious to accept the idea and a healing follows.

The Bible Inspirations

What things sever ye desire, when ye pray, believe that ye receive them, and ye shall have them. Mark 11:24. Note the difference in the tenses. The inspired writer tells us to believe and accept as true the fact that our desire has already been accomplished and fulfilled, that it is already completed, and that its realization will follow as a thing in the future.

The success of this technique depends on the confident conviction that the thought, the idea, the picture is already a fact in the mind, and in order for anything to have substance in the realm of the mind, it must be thought of as actually existing there.

Here in a few cryptic words is a concise and specific direction for making use of the creative power of thought by impressing upon the subconscious the particular thing which we desire. Your thought, idea, plan, or purpose is as real on its own plane as your hand or your heart. In following the Bible technique you completely eliminate from your mind all consideration of conditions, circumstances, or anything which might imply adverse contingencies. You are planting a seed (concept) in the mind which if you leave undisturbed, will infallibly germinate into external fruition.

I am writing this chapter at the beautiful Wishing Well, Rancho Santa Fe, a few hundred miles from Los Angeles. One of the guests lost a very valuable diamond. She had gone horseback-riding and discovered the loss when she returned. At my suggestion she prayed as follows: "Infinite Intelligence knows where the ring is. There can be no loss except I admit the loss in my mind, as all experiences come through my mind. I know Infinite Intelligence will now reveal the whereabouts of the ring to me. I see it on my finger. I feel and I know it is mine. I believe I have it now. I accept it mentally, for my thought is as real as the ring."

She quietly affirmed the above for a few minutes, and immediately afterwards she had an inner feeling or urge to drive back along one of the paths she had taken. Her horse stopped at the very spot where her ring was. The subjective mind operates throughout all nature, and in the horse also. The ways of the subconscious mind are not always obvious. This incident illustrates the law of belief and the results which must inevitably follow.

Paul's Suggestion

Paul recommends that we make known our requests to God with praise and thanksgiving. Some extraordinary results follow this simple method of prayer. The thankful heart is always close to the creative forces of the Universe, causing countless blessings to flow toward us by the law of reciprocal relationship based on a cosmic law of action and reaction.

A father promises his son a car for graduation; the boy has not yet received the car, but is very thankful and happy and is as joyous as though he had actually received the car. He knows his father will fulfill his promise, and is full of gratitude and joy even though he has not yet received the car, objectively speaking. He has, however, received it with and thankfulness in his mind. Oftentimes you have gone to a store and ordered a fur coat or hat, although they did not have exactly what you wanted. But you specified where you wanted and paid for it, and the clerk said they would send it. You thanked the clerk or owner and walked away without the coat or hat. You were absolutely sure of receiving the merchandise ordered in the near future because you trusted and believed in the integrity and honesty of the man who operated the business. How much more should we trust the Infinite and the Creative Law which never changes and responds with absolute fidelity to our trust and belief in It!

It is amazing how the thankful attitude improves every department of your life, including your health and happiness as well as your prosperity.

A real broker proved this in a wonderful way. He had been having a great deal of difficulty in selling homes and properties which were listed with him, and he was frustrated and unhappy. Convinced of the prosperity-power of the grateful heart, however, he began to pray every night, affirming as follows: *"Father, I thank thee that thou hast heard me, and I know that thou hearest me always."* John 11:41-42. Then, just prior to sleep, he condensed the phrase to two words: "Thank you." He repeated them over and over again, as a lullaby; he continued to speak these two words silently until he fell asleep.

One night, in a dream, he saw a man who gave him a check for fourteen lots and a home which he particularly desired to sell. In a week's time, the man whom he had seen in his dream came into his real estate office and bought the property which he had previously foreseen in his dream.

This real estate broker has made a habit of feelingly repeating every night the words, "Thank you," until he falls off into the deep of sleep. His health has remarkably improved, his wealth is soaring, and, quite frequently in his dream life, he has a preview of the sale of certain properties which subsequently is verified objectively in all details.

As this man does, silently decree morning and night that God is prospering you in mind, body, and affairs; feel the reality of it, and you will never want for anything. Repeat over and over again as a lullaby, "Thank you, Father," as you prepare for sleep; this means that you are thanking your Higher Self for abundance, health, wealth, and harmony. It may also happen that the Lord (your subconscious mind) may answer you in a vision and speak to you in a dream.

"Thank You, Father"

I shall illustrate how Mr. Broke applied this technique with excellent results. He said, "Bills are piling up, I am out of work, I have three children and no money. What shall I do?" Regularly every night and morning for a period of about three weeks he repeated the words, "Thank you, Father, for the Law of Opulence," in a relaxed, peaceful manner until the feeling or mood of thankfulness dominated his mind. He imagined he was addressing the Infinite, knowing, of course, that he could not see God. He was seeing with the inner eye of spiritual perception, realizing that his thought-image of wealth was the first cause relative to the money, position, and food he needed. His thought-feeling was the substance of wealth untrammeled by antecedent conditions of any kind.

By repeating, "Thank you, Father," over and over again, his mind and heart were lifted up to the point of acceptance, and when fear, thoughts of lack, poverty, and distress came into his mind, he would say, "Thank you, Father," as often as necessary. He knew that as he kept up this thankful attitude he would recondition his mind to the idea of wealth, which is what happened. Mr. Broke met on the street a former employer of his whom he had not seen for twenty years; the man offered him a very lucrative position and advanced him $500.00 as a temporary loan. Today Mr. Broke is vice president of the corporation for which he works. His recent remark to me was, "I shall never forget the wonders of 'Thank you, Father.' It has worked wonders for me."

He Followed My Suggestion

I shall now proceed to show you how you may definitely and positively convey an idea or mental image to your subconscious mind.

Your conscious mind is personal and selective. It chooses, selects, weighs, analyzes, dissects, and investigates. It is capable of inductive and deductive reasoning. The subjective, or subconscious, mind is subject to the conscious mind. It might be called a servant of the conscious mind. The subconscious obeys the order of the conscious mind. Focused, directed thoughts reach the subjective level; they must be of a certain degree of intensity. Intensity is acquired by concentration.

A man who owned a hamburger stand in the Middle West wrote me and said that he had read The Power of Your Subconscious Mind when it first came on the market. He wrote that he had decided to concentrate on a million dollars, as he wished to expand his business and have several restaurants; he also wanted to establish a branch in his native country in Europe.

He followed the technique of impregnating his subconscious mind by concentrating on a million dollars. To concentrate is to come back to the center and to contemplate the infinite riches of the subconscious mind. Every night he stilled the activity of his mind and entered into a quiet, relaxed, mental state. He gathered all his thoughts together and focused all his attention on a million dollar deposit in his bankbook. He gave all his attention to this mental image. His steadied attention made a deep, lasting impression on the sensitive plate of his subconscious mind.

He repeated this drama every night, and at the end of one month things began to happen. He married a very wealthy woman who loved his ambition, zeal, enthusiasm, and dreams for accomplishment. She bought a restaurant for him which, within a few months' time, proved to be a tremendous success; he has opened two branches. He has made some investments in oil stock which is pyramiding fantastically. He sent me a gift of five hundred dollars for having written the book, which was one of the most delightful presents I have ever received.

This man has over a million dollars in the bank at the time of this writing, and, in addition, his subconscious has furnished him extra dividends, including a beautiful and fabulously wealthy wife, a newborn baby, and a life more abundant.

Why His Technique Worked

All material things must have their origin in the Invisible or Spirit; all of creation is evidence of thought-images and ideas in the Mind of God which became form according to the Creative law. There is only one Creative process, and man through his thoughts sets in motion the Creative Law. We may be using it consciously or unconsciously; nevertheless we are always using the Creative Law for the simple reason that we are always impressing some sort of ideas and mental pictures upon It, whether we are aware of it or not. All our existing limitations result from our having habitually impressed upon our subconscious mind ideas of limitation, restriction, and bondage of all kinds. When we realize that our conditions and circumstances are never real causes in themselves, but only the result of prior thinking, we reverse our method of thinking and regard our ideal as real, and as we mentally and emotionally unite with the ideal in our mind, we change the outer manifestations to agree with the inner thought-images and thus change our world.

Affirmative Method

The effectiveness of affirmation lies in its intelligent application of definite and specific positives. For example, a boy adds three and three and puts down seven on the blackboard. The teacher affirms with mathematical certainty that three and three are six; therefore, the boy changes his figures accordingly. Likewise when we affirm the Truth about a person, we must conform to the Principles of Truth regardless of appearances. The power of the affirmation process depends on the faith and understanding of the person affirming.

The Affirmative Method Heals Acute Gall Bladder Trouble

This method was chosen by the writer for use on his sister, who was to be operated on for the removal of gallstones, based on the diagnosis of hospital tests and the usual X-ray procedures. She asked me to pray for her. We are separated geographically about 6,500 miles, but there is no time or space in Mind. Spirit or Mind is present in its entirety at every point simultaneously. In prayer treatment for another, you withdraw all thought from the contemplation of symptoms and from the corporeal personality altogether, and think of the individual as pure spirit and expressing the vitality, wholeness, beauty and perfection of that Spirit. I affirmed as follows: this prayer treatment is for my sister Kate. She is relaxed and at peace, poised, balanced, serene, and calm. Her mind and spirit are the Mind and Spirit of God. The healing Intelligence which created her body is now transforming every cell, nerve, tissue, muscle, and bone of her being into God's Perfect Pattern. Silently, quietly, all distorted thought patterns are removed and dissolved, and the vitality, wholeness, and beauty of the Spirit are made manifest in every atom of her being. She is now open and receptive to this Healing Presence which flows through her like a river, restoring her to perfect health, harmony, and peace. All distortion and ugly thought images are now washed away by the Infinite Ocean of love and Peace flowing through her, and it is so."

I affirmed the above several times a day, and at the end of two weeks my sister had an examination which showed a remarkable healing, and the X-rays proved negative.

To affirm is to state that it is so, and as you maintain this attitude of mind as true, regardless of all evidence to the contrary, you will receive an answer to your prayer. Your thought can only affirm, for even if you deny something you are actually affirming the presence of what you deny. Repeating an affirmation, knowing what you are saying and why you are saying it, leads the mind to that state of consciousness where it accepts that which you state as true. Keep on affirming the Truth until you get the subconscious reaction which satisfies.

The Argumentative Technique

This method is just what the word implies. It stems from the procedure of Dr. Phineas Parkhurst Quimby of Maine. Dr. Quimby was a pioneer in mental and spiritual healing and lived and practiced in Belfast, Maine, about one hundred years ago. He studied mesmerism for about seven years in order to discover how the mind worked, and thereafter discarded it in favor of spiritual healing. He had most remarkable results in prayer therapy in all kinds of so-called incurable diseases. A book called Quimby's Manuscripts edited by Horatio Dresser is available in your library. This book gives newspaper accounts of the man's remarkable results in prayer-treatment of the sick. Quimby duplicated many of the miracles of healing recorded in the Bible. Quimby used to ask patients sick with tuberculosis and other malignant diseases to let him plead their case before the Great Tribunal, which is God, because if they had faith and confidence in him, he would prove that they were innocent of the charge.

In brief, the argumentative method consists of spiritual reasoning, where you convince yourself that the patient is a victim of false beliefs and groundless fears, and that the disease or ailment is due only to a distorted, twisted pattern of thought which has taken form in his body. The wrong belief in some external power and external causes has now externalized as sickness and can be changed through a knowledge of the Law, which shows there is only One Primary Cause—Living Spirit or God, and spirit can't be sick, frustrated, or unhappy. Spirit is unconditioned, not hampered by conditions of any sort, and is not subject to illness.

The basis of all healing is a change of belief. You reason out in your mind that the Infinite Intelligence created the body and all its organs; therefore it knows how to heal it, can heal it, and is doing so now as you speak. You argue in the courtroom of your mind that the disease is a shadow of the mind, based on disease-soaked, morbid thought-imagery. You continue to build up all the evidence you can muster on behalf of the power of the healing Presence which created all the organs in the first place and has a perfect pattern of every cell, nerve, and tissue within it; then you render a verdict in the courthouse of your mind in favor of your patient. You liberate the sick one by faith and spiritual understand. Your mental and spiritual evidence is overwhelming; there being but One Mind, what you feel as true will be resurrected in the experience of the other. There is but One Mind common to all individual men.

She Won the Argument

Recently, a listener of our radio programs in Los Angeles prayed for her mother in New York City who had a coronary thrombosis. She prayed as follows: "God is the only presence and the only Power, the only Living Reality, the Living Spirit Almighty. This Presence and power is right where my mother is. God is her Life, and that Life is her Life now. The bodily condition is but a reflection of her thought-life, like shadows case on the screen. I know that in order to change the images on the screen, I must change the projection reel. My mind is the projection reel, and I now project in my own mind the image of wholeness, harmony, and perfect health for my mother. The Infinite Healing Presence which created my mother's body and all her organs is now saturating every atom of her being, and His River of Peace flows through every cell of her being. The doctors are divinely guided and directed, and whoever touches my mother is governed over by the overshadowing presence. I know that disease has no ultimate reality; if it had, no one could be healed. I now align myself with the Infinite Principle of Love and Life, and I know and decree that harmony, health, and peace are now being expressed in my mother's body. There is no power to challenge Omnipotence. The healing Presence of God is now flowing through her. It is wonderful!"

Her mother had a most remarkable recovery after a few days, much to the amazement of the specialist who complimented her on her faith in God. The argumentative method of prayer on the part of her daughter produced certain conclusions in her mind and set the Creative law of Mind in motion on the subjective side of life, which manifested through her mother's body as perfect health and harmony. There is only One Mind, and what the daughter felt as true about her mother was simultaneously resurrected in the experience of the mother.

The Absolute Method

The person practicing this form of prayer treatment mentions the name of the patient, such as John Jones; then quietly and silently thinks of God and His qualities and attributes, such as God is All Bliss, Boundless Love, Infinite Intelligence, All peaceful, Boundless Wisdom, Absolute Harmony, and Indescribable Beauty and Perfection. As he quietly thinks along these lines, he is lifted up in consciousness into a new spiritual wave length, at which time he feels that the Infinite ocean of God's Love is now dissolving everything unlike Itself in the mind and body of John Jones for whom he is praying. He feels all the Power and Love of the Godhead is now focused on john Jones, and whatever is bothering or vexing him now is completely dissolved in the Presence of the Infinite Ocean of God's Love.

Modern Sound Wave Therapy

The absolute method of prayer might be likened to the sound wave or sonic therapy recently shown me by a distinguished physician in Los Angeles. He has an ultra sound wave machine which oscillates at a tremendous speed and sends sound waves to any area of the body to which it is directed. These sound waves can be controlled and he told me of remarkable results in dissolving arthritic calcareous deposits and the healing and removal of other disturbing conditions.

To the degree that we rise in consciousness by contemplating the qualities and attributes of God, do we generate spiritual electronic waves of harmony, health, and peace? Many instantaneous healings follow the absolute method of prayer.

A Cripple Walks

Dr. Phineas Parkhurst Quimby, of whom we spoke previously, used the absolute method almost exclusively in the latter years of his healing career. He was really the father of psychosomatic medicine and the first psychoanalyst. He had the capacity to diagnose clairvoyantly the cause of the patient's troubles, pains, and aches. Quimby would tell the patient where the pain was and the cause behind it. In order to cure him Quimby said, "I must go to Him who sent me, and there I will contemplate your Divine perfection; if I succeed, you will be healed." The phrase, "I must go to Him Who sent me," is taken from the Bible. Yet a little while I am with you, and then I go unto Him who sent me, *you shall seek me and shall not find me: and where I am, thither you cannot come.* John 7:33, 34. You will see the wonderful meaning of this as we proceed.

Quimby was called on to visit a woman who was lame, aged, and practically bedridden. He sates that her ailment was due to the fact that she was imprisoned by a creed so small and contracted that she could not stand upright or move about. She was living in the tomb of fear and ignorance; furthermore, she was taking the Bible literally and it frightened her. "In this tomb," Quimby said, "was the presence and Power of God trying to burst the bars, break through the bonds, and rise from the dead." When she would ask others for an explanation of some passage of the Bible, the answer would be a stone; then she would hunger for the bread of life. Dr. Quimby diagnosed her case as a mind cloudy and stagnated due to excitation and fear caused by the inability to see clearly the meaning of the Scriptural passages she had been reading. This showed itself in the body by her heavy and sluggish feeling which would terminate in paralysis.

At this point, Quimby asked her what was meant, A little while I am with you and then I go to Him that sent me. She replied that it meant Jesus went to heaven. Quimby explained what it really meant by telling her that being with her a little while meant his explanation of her symptoms, feelings, and their cause; i.e., he had compassion and sympathy for her momentarily, but he could not remain in that mental state. The next step was to go to Him that sent us, which is the Presence of God in all of us.

Quimby immediately traveled in his mind and contemplated the Divine Ideal; i.e., the Vitality, Intelligence, Harmony and Power of God functioning in the sick person. This is why he said to the woman, "Therefore where I go, you cannot come for you are in your narrow, restricted belief, and I am in health." This prayer and explanation produced an instantaneous sensation, and a change came over her mind. She walked without her crutches! She was as it was dead in error and to bring her to life or truth was to raise her from the dead. "Quoted the resurrection Christ and applied it to her own Christ or health; it produced a powerful effect on her." (Quimby's Manuscripts).

The Decree Method

Thou shalt also decree a thing, and it shall be established unto thee: and the light shall shine upon thy ways. Job 22:28.

Power goes into our word according to the feeling and faith behind it. When we realize the Power that moves the world is moving on our behalf and is backing up our word, our confidence and assurance grow. We do not try to ad power to Power; therefore, there must be no mental striving, coercion, force, or mental wrestling.

A young girl used the decree method on a young man who was constantly phoning her, pressing her for dates, and meeting her at her place of business; she found it very difficult to get rid of him. She decreed as follows: "I release—unto God. He is in his true place at all times. I am free, and he is free. I now release this word into the Ocean of Infinite Mind which is the Mind of the almighty. Infinite Mind is the Only Power operating and it brings this to pass. I have decreed this and it shall come to pass. It is so." She said he vanished and she has never seen him since, adding, "It was as though the ground swallowed him up."

How a Minister Got a Car

A young, struggling minister recently told me that he read the above-mentioned verse in the Bible, Thou shalt also decree a thing.... He decreed as follows: "I am one with all the automobiles in the world. They are all God's ideas made manifest. I decree that Infinite Mind through the Law of Right Action reveals to me the ideal car suitable for my work. I trust the Deeper Mind implicitly. It knows how to bring it to pass in its own way."

The sequel to this decree was most interesting. Secretly, members of his congregation collected a sum of money and presented him with a new Chevrolet car after his church service. They said, "We have a surprise for you!" He was not surprised, because he knew the Deeper Mind has ways we know not of. The Infinite Intelligence acted on their mind causing them to fulfill what the minister had accepted as true in his own mind.

You can never know how your prayer will be answered. Man must never say, "I don't have the money to buy a car; therefore I must do without it." He can decree what he wants, and Infinite Mind will bring it to pass.

Chapter 15

THE SUGGESTED WAY IS SPIRITUAL

If you think, pray, and act in a spiritual way while you are in a predicament, you will turn it to good account. A girl in our audience told me that she believes she will always be pleasantly and wondrously surprised wherever she goes. She has marvelous and unique experiences in all her travels. She has suggested this idea to her subconscious mind by repetition, and her subconscious mind responds accordingly. She has conditioned her subconscious to good fortune.

Be alert and alive, and feel quickened by the Holy Spirit within you. Realize that God will put the words into your mouth and that they will be right for the occasion.

"One with God is a majority." "If God be for you, who can be against you?" Believe this wholeheartedly, and all things will work together for your good, and all your experiences will be filled with joy and good fortune.

The Seeds of Opportunity

No matter how bad the situation, you can turn it to good account and profit by it. You can make an opportunity out of every problem to serve life and rise higher. "In every adversity there is the seed of opportunity." When you pray, accept as true what your reason and five senses deny and reject. Remain faithful to your idea for being full of faith every step of the way. When your consciousness is fully qualified with the acceptance of your desire, all the fear will go away. Trust in the reality of your ideal or desire until you are filled full of the feeling of being it; then the day will break and all shadows will flee away.

Yes, the answer to your prayer will come and light up the heavens of your mind bringing you peace.

No matter what the problem is, how acute, dark, or hopeless things seem to be, turn now to God, and say, "How is it in God and Heaven?" The answer will softly steal over your mind like the dew from heaven: "All is peace, joy, bliss, perfection, wholeness, harmony, and beauty"; then reject the evidence of your senses, and feed among the lilies of God and Heaven, such as peace, harmony, joy, and perfection. Realize what is true of God must be true of you and your surroundings.

Size is Not a Problem

The late Dr. Harry Gaze told about Dan Morgan, a splendid speaker, who went to a small town in New England one Sunday evening for the purpose of collecting funds in a church for a special project. A terrible storm came up, and the snow and sleet were so heavy that no one was out on the street. The speaker decided to brave the storm, although he doubted that anyone would come to church. At first, no one came but the janitor. Finally, two old ladies came in and sat down. Dan Morgan said, "I came here to speak, and I will speak." Dr. Gaze said that Mr. Morgan gave a splendid lecture, and one of the ladies donated $15,000! The other woman said, "Well, it's for a good cause, and if you can give $15,000, I can, too." Mr. Morgan said he received more money from that congregation than from any other meeting of any size at any time during his lecture tour.

Oneness With God

"Pitch a lucky man into the Nile," says the Arabian proverb, "and he will come up with a fish in his mouth." Through faith in God and all things good, you can reap a profit out of any situation and grow in wisdom and strength. You can receive your good by going within and claiming what you want in consciousness. Feel it and thrill to it, and the Spirit within you will bring your request to pass. Knowing that you can go to the Spirit within for what you want and knowing that you will receive it voids your mind of anger, hate, ill will, and resentment.

Emerson said, "The Over-Soul had need of an organ where I am, else I would not be here." You are an organ of God, and God needs you and wants to express His power and wisdom through you. Think of yourself now in terms of your oneness with God and how every problem is Divinely outmatched, and you will always be victorious and triumphant.

Trouble Was In His Own Mind

Mr. Block said that he had been making an annual income of $20,000, but for the past three months all doors seemed to jam tightly. He brought clients up to the point where they were about to sign on the dotted line, and at the eleventh hour the door closed. He added that perhaps a jinx was following him.

In discussing the matter with Mr. Block, I discovered that three months previously he had become very irritated, annoyed, and resentful toward a dentist who, after he had promised to sign a contract, had withdrawn at the last moment. He began to live in the unconscious fear that other clients would do the same, thereby setting up a history of frustration, hostility, and obstacles. He gradually built up in his mind a belief in obstructions and last minute cancellations until a vicious circle had been established. "What I fear most has come upon me." Mr. Block realized that the trouble was in his own mind, and that it was essential to change his mental attitude.

His run of so-called misfortune was broken in the following way: "I realize I am one with the Infinite which knows no obstacle, difficulty, or delay. I live in the joyous expectancy of the best. The deeper mind responds to my thoughts. I know that the work of the Infinite cannot be hindered. God always finishes successfully whatever He begins. God works through me bringing all my plans and purposes to completion. Whatever I start, I bring to a successful conclusion. My aim is to give wonderful service, and all those whom I contact are blessed by what I have to offer. All my work renders full fruition. I thank God for this."

He repeated his prayer every morning before going to call on his customers and he prayed also each night prior to sleep. In a short time he was back in his old, accustomed stride as a successful salesman.

Mr. Block removed the mental road blocks after he realized that whatever he experienced in his life was really the out picturing of his own thought and belief. When he changed his thought, the outer picture changed also. He found that the story of his life was really the story of the relations between himself and God.

The Alcoholic's Road Block

Mr. Barleycorn visited me one day when I was giving some lecture in Auckland, New Zealand. A chronic alcoholic, he had tried all the "cures" to no avail, asserting that an uncontrollable passion seized him periodically to drink. He was a victim of a habit, and because the acts leading to intoxication where repeated so often, he had established a subjective pattern in his subconscious mind.

Because the alcoholic has yielded so many times to his craving, he fears that he will yield once more; this contributes to his repeated falls due to the suggestions given to his subconscious mind. It is his imagination which causes the alcoholic to return to drinking intermittently. The images which have been impressed on his subconscious mind begin to bear fruit. He imagines a drinking bout in which glasses are filled and drained; then he imagines the following sense of ease and enjoyment, a feeling of relaxation. If he lets his imagination run wild, he will go to the bar or buy a bottle.

The drinker uses effort and will power to overcome the habit, or 'cause," as he is likely to call it. But the more effort or will power he uses, the more hopelessly does he become engulfed in the quicksand of good intentions.

The Real Cause

The real cause of alcoholism is negative and destructive thinking; for as a man thinketh so is he. The alcoholic has a deep sense of inferiority, inadequacy, defeat, and frustration, usually accompanied by a deep inner hostility. He has countless alibis as to his reasons for drinking, but the sole reason is in his thought life. If you are an alcoholic, admit it; do not dodge the issue. Many people remain alcoholics because they refuse to admit it.

Your disease is instability, an inner fear. You are refusing to face life and so you try to escape your responsibilities through the bottle. The interesting thing about an alcoholic is that he has no free will; he thinks he has; he boasts about his will power. The habitual drunkard says bravely, "I will not touch it any more," but he has no power to back up his statement.

There are many people who find themselves in the same condition as Mr. Barleycorn. As soon as they are made to realize that the problem of alcoholism is of their own making and that they are living in their own psychological prison of fear, false beliefs, resentment, hostility, they are ready to recondition themselves to react in a constructive way. The minute they express a keep desire to free themselves from previous habits, they are fifty-one percent healed. Now they can follow a program of prayer to remove the mental blocks.

Opposite of Desire

Effort is invariably self-defeated, eventuating always in the opposite of what is desired. The reason for this is obvious. The suggestions of powerlessness to overcome the habit dominate his mind; the subconscious mind will accept the stronger of two contradictory propositions. The effortless way is the best.

In 1910 the French School of Therapeutics explained what they termed the law of reversed effort. When your desire and your imagination are in conflict, the imagination invariably gains the day. For example, you will hear an alcoholic say, "I took a lot of pains, I tried so hard, I forced myself, and I used all the will power I had." He has to be made to realize that his error lies in the effort; then he begins to conquer the habit.

If, for example, you were asked to walk a plank on the floor, you would do without question. Now suppose the same plank were placed twenty feet up in the air between two walls, would you walk it? Your desire to walk it would be counteracted by your imagination—your mental road block would be your fear of falling. The dominant idea would be reversed, and the dominant idea of failure would be reinforced.

If a man says, "I want to give up alcohol, but I cannot," he may wish to give up, but the harder he tries the less he is able to do so. Never try to compel the subconscious mind to accept your idea by exercising will power. Such attempts are doomed to failure. The subconscious mind accepts the dominant of two contradictory statements. It is like the man who is poverty-stricken saying, "I am wealthy." In most instances his statement makes him poorer. The simple reason for this is that his belief in poverty is so much greater than his belief in abundance that he is suggesting more lack to himself each time he makes the statement. This illustrates the law of reversed effort. In other words his subconscious mind reacts with the opposite result from that which was intended.

Repeated Failures

I told Mr. Barleycorn about an alcoholic in Rochester, New York, whom I had treated some years earlier. That man said to me, "I would not drink a drop of liquor for six months and I would congratulate myself. All my friends would pat me on the back telling me what wonderful will power I had."

"Then," he added, "an uncontrollable urge would seize me, and I would be drunk for two weeks." This had happened time and again with this man. The efforts of his will power would suppress his desire temporarily, but his continued efforts to suppress the many urges made matters worse. His repeated failures convinced him that he was hopeless and powerless to control his urge or obsession. This idea of being powerless operated, of course, as a powerful suggestion to his subconscious mind, increased his impotence, and made his life a succession of failures.

I taught him to harmonize the functions of the conscious and subconscious mind. When these two cooperate, the idea or desire implanted in the subconscious mind is realized. His reasoning mind admitted that if he had been conditioned negatively, he could be conditioned positively. His mind entertained the idea that he could succeed. He ceased thinking of the fact that he was powerless to overcome the habit. Moreover, he understood clearly that there was no obstacle to his healing other than his own thought; therefore, there was no occasion for great mental effort or mental coercion. To se force is to pre-suppose that there is opposition. When the mind is concentrated on the means to overcome a problem, it is no longer concerned with the obstacle.

The Power of His Mental Picture

This man made a practice of relaxing his body, getting into a relaxed, drowsy, meditative state; then he filled his mind with the picture of the desired end, knowing that the subconscious mind would bring it about in the easiest way. He imagined his daughter congratulating him on his freedom, saying to him, "Daddy, it's wonderful to have you home!" He had lost his family through drink. He was not allowed to visit them; his wife would not speak to him.

Regularly, systematically, he used to sit down and meditate in the way outlined. When his attention wandered, he brought it back to the picture of his daughter with her smile, and the scene of his own home enlivened by her cheery tonal qualities. All this brought about a reconditioning of his mind. It was a gradual process. He kept it up; he persevered knowing that sooner or later he would succeed in impregnating his subconscious mind with the mental picture. I had told him that the conscious mind was the camera, and his subconscious mind was the sensitive plate on which he registered and impressed the picture. This had made a profound impression on him; his whole aim was to impress the picture and develop it in his mind. Films are developed in the dark; likewise, mental pictures are developed in the darkroom of the subconscious mind.

Focused Attention

Realizing that his conscious mind was simply a camera, he used no effort. There was no mental struggle. He quietly adjusted his thought and focused his attention on the scene before him until he gradually became identified with the picture. He became absorbed in the mental atmosphere, repeating the mental movie frequently. There was no room for doubt that a healing would follow. When there was any temptation to drink, he would switch his imagination from any reveries of drinking bouts to the feeling of being at home with the family. He was successful because he confidently expected to experience the picture he was developing in his mind. Today he is the president of a multimillion dollar concern and is radiantly happy.

Techniques of Healing Used

There is nothing new about the following technique which Mr. Barleycorn used. It is as old as a man. The most ancient wisdom available said, "As a man imagines and feels, so is he."

The Unbelievable Power of Suggestion

The first step: Get still; quiet the wheels of the mind. Enter into a sleepy, drowsy state. In this relaxed, peaceful, receptive state you are preparing for the second step.

The second step: Take a brief phrase which can readily be graven on the memory and repeat it over and over again as a lullaby. (Nancy School Technique). Use the phrase, "Sobriety and peace of mind are mine now, and I give thanks." To prevent the mind from wandering, repeat it aloud or sketch its pronunciation with the lips and tongue as you say it mentally. This helps its entry into the subconscious mind. Do this for five minutes or more. You will find a deep emotional response from the subconscious mind.

The third step: Just before going to sleep, practice what Goethe used to do: Imagine a friend, a loved one in front of you. Your eyes are closed; you are relaxed and at peace. The loved one is subjectively present and saying to you, "Congratulations!" You see the smile; you hear the voice. You touch the hand and the face; it is all so real and vivid. The word congratulations imply complete freedom. Hear it over and over again until you get the reaction which satisfies.

Use the above technique three or four times a day and at night prior to sleep. Imagine the end—victory. See fulfillment and accomplishment and maintain this faith every step of the way, knowing that having imagined and felt the end, you have willed the means to the realization of the end.

I am now thinking of a married man with four children, supporting and secretly living with another woman during his business trips. He was ill, nervous, irritable, cantankerous, and could not sleep without drugs. He had pains in numerous organs of his body which doctors could not diagnose. He was a confirmed alcoholic when I saw him. The reason for his periodic sprees was a deep, unconscious sense of guilt. He had violated the ancient code and this troubled him. The religious creed he was brought up on was deeply lodged in his subconscious mind; he drank excessively to heal the wound of guilt. Some invalids take morphine and codeine for severe pains; he was taking alcohol for the pain or wound in his mind. It was the old story of adding fuel to the fire.

He listened to the explanation of how his mind worked; he faced his problem, looked at it, and gave up his dual role. He knows that his drinking was an unconscious attempt to escape. The hidden cause lodged in the subconscious mind had to be eradicated; then the healing followed.

When he began to look at his problem in the light of reason, it was dissipated. He began to use this treatment three or four times a day. "My mind is full of peace, poise, balance, and equilibrium. The Infinite Power lies stretched in smiling repose within me. I am not afraid of anything in the past, the present, or the future. Infinite Intelligence leads, guides, and directs me in all ways. I now meet every situation with faith, poise, calmness, and confidence. I am now completely free from the habit; my mind is full of inner peace, freedom, and joy. I forgive myself; then I am forgiven. Peace, sobriety, and confidence reign supreme in my mind."

He repeated this frequently, knowing what he was doing and why he was doing it. Knowing what he was doing gave him the necessary faith and confidence. I explained to him that as he spoke these statements out loud, slowly, lovingly, and meaningfully, they would gradually sink down into his subconscious mind; like seeds, they would grow after their kind. I explained to him that his subconscious mind was like a garden; by planting lovely seeds he would reap a wonderful harvest. It is the nature of an apple seed to bring forth an apple tree. These truths on which he concentrated went in through his eyes, his ears heard the sound, the healing vibrations of these words reached his subconscious mind and obliterated all the negative mental patterns which caused all the trouble. Light dispels darkness; the positive thought destroys the negative. He became a transformed man within a month.

When fear knocks at your door or when worry, anxiety, and doubt cross your mind, behold your vision. Think of god, believe in Him, and an Almighty Power will be generated by your subconscious mind, giving you full confidence and strength. Keep on keeping on "Until the day breaks and the shadows flee away."

You Can Overcome Worry

Do not spend time looking at your troubles or problems; cease all negative thinking. Your mind cannot function harmoniously when it is tense. It relieves the strain to do something soothing and pleasant when you are presented with a problem. You do not fight a problem—you *can* overcome it.

To release pressure, take a drive; go for a walk; play solitaire; or read a favorite chapter of the Bible, such as the Eleventh Chapter of Hebrews or Chapter Thirteen of I Corinthians. Or, read the Forty-Sixth Psalm; read it over carefully and quietly several times. An inner calm will steal over you, and you will become poised and peaceful.

How Often Should I Pray About a Problem?

I am often asked that question. You can't make a universal rule for prayer-therapy or scientific prayer. The particular person has to be considered, together with the way he looks at the problem or difficulty. You can pray in different ways at different times. For example, you might use the 91st Psalm in the morning, the 23rd Psalm at noon and the 27th Psalm at night.

If you are praying for your mother for peace and harmony and healing, the best way would be to mention your mother's name and contemplate peace, harmony, wholeness, beauty and the vitality and life of the Infinite flowing through her making her whole and perfect. You should also claim that Infinite Intelligence is guiding the doctors and nurses and all who minister to her. Surround her and all who are helping her with light, love, truth and beauty. Continue praying along these lines until you feel relaxed and satisfied.

Decree that your prayer is working now. Don't say, "This prayer will do now. I will pray again in a couple of hours." This attitude neutralizes your prayer. Know that your prayer is effective now, and pray later on when you have gotten away from the previous prayer session. This means that in a normal day you are busy about other things—your business, home profession, etc. In other words, you will have forgotten about it for several hours. Then you can begin prayer-therapy for your mother once again, and continue in like manner until she is well and happy. Each time you pray you are reinforcing the idea of wholeness and perfect health in your subconscious, which will be resurrected in your mother's mind and body.

Be sure to avoid picking and nagging at the problem from time to time. Relax and believe, and wonders will happen as you pray. Realize it is the Infinite Presence thinking and healing through you.

Suggested Steps to Peace of Mind

The First Step: Every morning when you awaken, turn to God in prayer and know that God is your loving Father. Relax your body; then have a dialogue with God, which is your Higher Self. Become as a little child; this means that you trust the God-Presence completely and you know that God is healing you now.

The Second Step: Affirm lovingly: "Thank you, Father, for this wonderful day. It is God's day: it is filled with joy, peace, happiness, and success for me. I look forward with a happy expectancy to this day. The wisdom and inspiration of God will govern me during the entire day. God is my partner; everything I do will turn out in a wonderful way. I believe that God is guiding me, and His love fills my soul."

The Third Step: Claim boldly: "I am full of confidence in the goodness of God. I know that He watches over me at all times. I let go; I am poised, serene, and calm. I know that it is God in action in all phases of my life, and Divine law and order reign supreme."

Make a habit of dwelling on these three steps to prayer, and when worry thoughts come to your mind, substitute any of the spiritual thoughts from the above three steps; gradually, your mind will be conditioned to peace.

God's Business

"*... Thou shalt make thy way prosperous, and then thou shalt have good success.*" (Joshua 1:8) I now give a pattern of success and prosperity to the deeper mind within me. I now identify myself with the Infinite Source of supply. I listen to the still, small voice of God within me. This inner voice leads, guides, and governs all my activities. I am one with the abundance of God. I know and believe that there are new and better ways of conducting my business; Infinite Intelligence reveals the new ways to me.

I am growing in wisdom and understanding. My business is God's business. I am Divinely prospered in all ways. Divine Wisdom within me reveals the ways and means by which all my affairs are adjusted in the right way immediately.

The words of faith and conviction which I now speak open up all the necessary door or avenues for my success and prosperity. I know that "*the Lord (Law) will perfect that which concerned me . . .*" (Psalm 138:8) my feet are kept in the perfect path, because I am a son of the living God. In prayer or treatment, if you want to help another, turn your mind completely toward God; this is the first step in the treatment process. The second step is to contemplate the solution of the problem (the answer). Do these frequently until you arrive at a conviction. This is symbolized by Jesus in the Scriptures who is "the one who should come" or the manifestation of your ideal. Your desire objectified is your Jesus—your solution. Jesus and Joshua are identical in the Bible, both mean God is the savior or emancipator. In another sense Jesus represents the Truth which, when it ascends into working consciousness in a man, begins a series of acts which are the result of the descent of a Holy (whole) spirit.

In prayer we call forth our disciples, which is a disciplining of our faculties—in other words, sight (Andrew) and faith in God (Peter). At first we are perhaps afraid, but as we meditate upon God, we intone our consciousness to a sense of peace and understanding; then Peter's name is changed to Cephas (a rock). This is the rock of Truth, which is impregnable—meaning and unassailable faith in the God power, which comes when we realize that it is supreme and *that there is no other*.

We also call Philip who, our concordance informs us, is a lover of horses. A trainer of horses is kind but firm. He never beats the animal, but rather he leads him. The horse, sensing that there is a master on his back, obeys and takes the trainer whosoever he wishes to go. All of us certainly need this mental quality sadly lacking in most of us. We quit after a few days and say, "What's the use? It doesn't work for me." Instead, we should ride our mood or feeling of acceptance until it takes root within us, then we have disciplined our mind through Phillip's qualities of character and action.

Most of the disciples were fishermen—which means that we draw the fish (or ideas) out of the Infinite Deep within us. We are all fishermen and we are afloat in the great deep. "I am the fish that swimmiest in the great deep." (Tarot teaching).

Philip finds Nathanael, the latter meaning "the gift of God" (our desire). Jesus of Nazareth, the son of Joseph, means this very gift of God—the consciousness of Emmanuel (god within). Joseph is our faculty of disciplined imagination. "Jesus" is our solution to that which we want it comes from Nazareth (a stem or sprout). If we will take that sprout or idea, no matter how fantastic it is, and see it clearly as a fact now existing in consciousness, we have psychologically called Andrew.

If we will have faith in God to bring it to pass, we have called Peter (the faculty of hearing or feeling the good tidings within). We *sustain* or *ride that mood* until it becomes a subjective embodiment within us. We are now calling Philip.

Then appears Nathanael (the gift of God), our desire made manifest. We say "Yes, this is Jesus (my answered prayer, my salvation), and he is of Nazareth (that idea or desire that I nourished). Yes, verily, it is the son of Joseph, the manifestation of what I imagines subjectively in the Greater Now (where past, present and future co-exist)." When we completely accept our desire in consciousness without any reservations, we are, indeed, an Israelite without guile.

The Holy Spirit always manifests as wholeness, completeness and perfection—but we are all, at times, under the fig tree of limitation, sorrow or lack. Consciousness possesses the answer to our need, did we but know where and hoe to seek and find it.

The metaphysical key to demonstration is offered in the following statements: *Before we ever pray for a thing, "it is." Creation is finished.* We simply give expression to that which has already been formed, subjectively and spiritually. We can go to I AM NOW and claim what we want, and *it will answer us!* The Truth student sees what he wants in a meditative state and *becomes one with it*. Having seen and felt what he wants subjectively, when he opens his eyes again, he knows what he must experience it objectively—since the latter is but the inevitable result of the subjective state.

Hence, do not fail to dream lofty dreams and make them come true. In moments of high meditation—when we become lost in the boundless One—we may see the Angels of God (divine truth and holy ideas) ascending and descending. We then become illumines by the radiance of the Light Limitless—"the true Light which lightest every man that cometh into the world" of spiritual understanding and illumination.

(1)—And the third day there was a marriage in Cana of Galilee; and the mother of Jesus was there: (2)—And both Jesus was called, and his disciples, to the marriage. (3)—And when they wanted wine, the mother of Jesus saith unto him, they have no wine. (4)—Jesus saith unto her, Woman, what have I to do with thee? Mine hour is not yet come. (5)—His mother saith unto the servants, whatsoever he saith unto you, do it. (6)—And there were set there six water pots of stone, after the manner of the purifying of the Jews, containing two or three firkins apiece. (7)—Jesus saith unto them, fill the water pots with water. And they filled them up to the brim. (8)—And he saith unto them, Draw out now, and bear unto the governor of the feast. And they bare it. (9)—When the ruler of the feast had tasted the water that was made wine, and knew not whence it was: (but the servants which drew the water knew;) the governor of the feast called the bridegroom, (10)—And saith unto him, Every man at the beginning doth set forth good wine; and when men have well drunk, then that which is worse: but thou hast kept the good wine until now. (John 2)

We will now proceed to give you the inner meaning of the first miracle performed by Jesus. The first thing we must remember in the interpretation of the Bible, is that it is a psychological drama-taking place within the consciousness of man. You, the reader, have all these psychological states of "character" within you.

Prayer is a marriage feast. The feast, of course, is a psychological one as you meditate on your good or your ideal, until you become one with it.

"And the third day there was a marriage in Cana of Galilee; and the mother of Jesus was there." Galilee is consciousness, and Cana means rod, or stem—desire; So the marriage is the embodiment of our desire in consciousness. The mother means feeling, warmth and emotion—and Jesus is our own I AM-ness. In other words it is you, the reader, and your feeling out yourself which are symbolized in the dramatic scenes to follow.

"And both Jesus was called, and his disciples, to the marriage." The twelve disciples represent the twelve powers of mind. The twelve faculties are disciples resident in all beings. These faculties must always be disciplined in true prayer. That is, we must become still, relaxed and contemplate God; then we are imbued with the Power from on high, and the feeling of "I AM God" steals over us and we are at peace! Peace be still and know that I AM God.

"And when they wanted wine, the mother of Jesus saith unto him, they have no wine." "Wine" represents answered prayer or the objectification of our ideal. The mother in this instance represents the feeling of lack or limitation or bondage. Jesus is reminded of lack. The answer of the disciplined mind is, *"Woman, what have I to do with thee?"* It is a complete rejection of the suggestion of lack—the recognition of the Omnipresence of Good and the availability of Truth at all times, in all emergencies and in every crisis.

"Mine hour is not yet come." This means that he has not yet reached conviction in his own mind. "His mother saith unto the servants, whatsoever he saith unto you, do it." The spiritual man in prayer moves from the mood of lack to the mood of confidence, peace and trust in the only Power there is—his own I AM-ness. His trust being in God, his faith is well founded. His mother registers the feeling of triumph, and his inner tone says to the servants (ideas of peace, happiness, harmony, success etc.), *"Whatsoever he saith unto you, do it."* When man realizes his oneness with the Father, he is now on the mountain top. This mood of victory, which is the mother, will bring about the solution, or the answer to his prayer.

"And there were set their six water pots of stone, after the manner of the purifying of the Jews, containing two or three firkins apiece." This is the symbol of the Divine creative fiat taking place within the womblike consciousness of man. Six and sex are synonymous; the six water pots refer to the psychological cycle that man goes through to bring about the subjective realization of his desire. This may endure for a moment, an hour, days, weeks or months, Depending on the faith and state of consciousness of the student.

In spiritual creation, we must always cleanse our minds from false beliefs, fear, doubt and anxiety and become completely detached from our external world with all its noise and confusion. In the stillness and quietue of our own soul, we must meditate on the joy of the answered prayer until that inner certitude comes whereby we know that we know. After the creative act is finished, there is no desire to pray any more about it, consequently, we know that "it is finished." This is the meaning of, "They filled them up to the brim."

"And he saith unto them, draw out now, and bear unto the governor of the feast." Whatever is impregnated in our subconscious mind is always objectified on the screen of space. Therefore, when we enter a state of conviction and our prayer is answered, we have given the command: "Bear unto the governor of the feast." The governor of the feast is the conscious mind which controls the subconscious. Now we are consciously aware of that which we formerly only felt subjectively as true.

"When the ruler of the feast had tasted the water that was made wine, and knew not whence it was: (but the servants which drew the water knew;) the governor of the feast called the bridegroom." The "ruler" of the feast is the conscious mind and its five senses, through which we are impregnated by hundreds of thoughts, concepts and ideas. When the conscious mind becomes aware of water made wine, it becomes aware of the answered prayer. Water is unconditioned consciousness, and wine is conditioned consciousness. The "servants" which drew the water represent the mood of peace and confidence, and we know that our prayer is answered. The governor of the feast calling the bridegroom means the thrill

and joy of satisfaction (the new state of consciousness), *whereby man is married to his highest ideal.*

"And saith unto him, Every man at the beginning doth set forth good wine; and when men have well drunk, then that which is worse: but thou hast kept the good wine until now." This is true of every man when he first enters into Truth. He sets out with high spirits and ambitions. He is the new broom that sweeps clean, and he is full of good intentions. Oftentimes he forgets the source of his power. Overlooking the fact that there is no honor to be given by man—for all honors comes from and is due to God—he becomes drunk with power. In other words, he misuses the law and selfishly takes advantage of his fellow man.

We find that many times men in high places become conceited, opinionated and arrogant. This is all due to ignorance of the law. The law is that power, security and riches are not to be obtained externally. They must come from the treasure house of consciousness. So the wine they drink is not of the Holy Spirit.

The point to remember in prayer is this: "In the beginning God," and God is good and life is good. When we realize this basic oneness with all good, we are "in tune with the infinite," rejecting all superficial suggestions of fear, doubt and anxiety. Our desire or ideal will bless ourselves and others. *It is good and very good.* We should realize that the good wine is *always present now,* for God is the Eternal Now, and regardless of how drunk we become with fear, grief or other discordant states, we should understand that the only factor that matters is the Eternal Now.

To reach this realization, we have to detach ourselves from the old state of consciousness; enter on the High Watch, and know that we are God and "about the Father's business." *When we have no desire to repeat any of the former mistakes, we are dead completely to the old state.*

We now dwell on the new concept of ourselves and our true love—we become married to it; the past is forgotten and remembered no more. We are transfigured and transformed and come down from the mountain a changed man. Now we know that water truly becomes wine—the wine of joy, the spirit of God manifesting itself in man. "Now is the day of salvation!" "This day thou shalt be with me in Paradise!" The kingdom of heaven is at hand!" *"Thou hast kept the good wine until now!"*

All our good is in the "greater now!" We have to leave the present "now" (our limitation); enter into the beatific vision and in that ecstatic state become one with our ideal. Having seen and felt it in the moments of high exaltations, we are operating the very law of God. We know that in a little while we shall see our ideal objectively as we walk through time and space. "As within, so without. As above, so below. As in heaven so on earth!" In other words, we will see our beliefs expressed. Man is belief expressed.

(11)—This beginning of miracles did Jesus in Cana of Galilee, and manifested forth his glory; and his disciples believed on him. (12)—After this he went down to Capernaum, he, and his mother, and his brethren, and his disciples: and they continued there not many days. (13)—And the Jews' Passover was at hand, and Jesus went up to Jerusalem, (14)—And found in the temple those that sold oxen and sheep and doves, and the changers of money sitting: (15)—And when he had made a scourge of small cords, he drove them all out of the temple, and the sheep, and the oxen; and poured out the changers' money, and over-three the tables; (16)—And said unto them that sold doves, Take these things hence; make not my Father's house an house of merchandise. (17)—And his disciples remembered that it was written; the zeal of thine house hath eaten me up. (John 2)

The Passover represents a change of consciousness. Jesus going up to Jerusalem represents the spiritually minded man entering into a state of peace. Before we can arrive at that "peace that passeth understanding," we must cleanse our consciousness.

The money changers that we throw out are the false values we have placed on external conditions and circumstances. We have given power to things outside ourselves, but the only power—I AM—is within. Through fear we transfer the power that is within us to external things. Man's false opinion, for example, believes a fan will give him a cold. The fan never said to any man, "If you sit under me, I will give you a cold!" This is the merchandise as mentioned in verse 16, which we must get rid of.

The " . . . scourge of small cords . . ." signifies the definite, absolute pronouncements of the Truth in our minds, which cut into the negative states like whip cords, and sever our connection with them completely.

(18)—Then answered the Jews and said unto him, *what sign she west thou unto us, seeing that thou doest these things?* (John 2)

The only sign is your inner feeling or conviction. The evidence or sign is within, as indicated by the surge or wave of peace that follows true prayer. This is the sign and there is no other.

Chapter 16

AUTO SUGGESTION AND THE WONDERS OF SLEEP

"When thou goes, it shall lead thee, when thou sleepiest, it shall keep thee; and when thou awakes, it shall talk with thee." (PROVERBS 6:22)

You spend about eight out of every twenty-four hours, or one-third of your entire life, in sleep. This is an inexorable law of life. This also applies to the animal and vegetable kingdoms. Sleep is a divine law, and many answers to our problems come to us when we are sound asleep upon the bed.

Many people have advocated the theory that you get tired during the day, that you go to sleep to rest the body, and that a reparative process takes place while you sleep. Nothing rests in sleep. Your heart, lungs, and all your vital organs function while you are asleep. If you eat prior to sleep, the food is digested and assimilated; also, your skin secretes perspiration, and your nails and hair continue to grow.

Your subconscious mind never rests or sleeps. It is always active, controlling all your vital forces. The healing process takes place more rapidly while you are asleep as there is no interference from your conscious mind. Remarkable answers are given to you while you are asleep.

In sleep we are united with our Father every night; we become one with the Ancient of days. Prior to falling asleep, students of the mysteries must learn to behold the scintillating white light that shines forever on the great white throne, which is the Secret Place of the Most High, or the Holy of Holies within man. We can imagine that we see this white light and this will completely still the mind. Nothing can appear on this white screen without our permission.

Now we are first in the pool. No man can get into this pool of silence but our "I AM" which is first person and present tense. *"But while I am cometh another stepped down before me."* (John 5:7) That which steps down before you are the idle thoughts such as fear, doubt, despair, self-pity and similar moods. If you banish these evil spirits or moods, Jesus, your own I-AM-NESS will speak softly and say "Rise, take up thy bed and walk." Then the healing comes. Meditating on the eternal verities and the inner glory and beauties of the Deity, man feels a movement within him, this is the Divine Light and it is visible as a golden yellow light. Words cannot always define and formulate the things behind the veil; there are of course many mystical experiences which we cannot express with words, the ecstasy of heavenly bliss, of love and happiness. Meditation is that inner communion which works like a thief in the night, silently in man's own soul. This mood cannot be expressed in words or language as it is beyond all formulation into word symbolism. To enter into the Silence, is intercommunion with the Self or Christ within. This is the nearest approach to the invisible.

To receive inspiration in Bible passages, the following procedure will be found very helpful. Begin to imagine and dwell on the fact that in the deep of yourself sits the King of Kings, the Lord of Lords and the prince of Peace whose dress is white, so also is the appearance of the light of his face. Imagine this Being sitting upon a throne of scintillating light that He may give Light to you. Realize now that your intellect is being anointed by the Christ or Truth. You will find your spine tingles and your forehead becomes moist—this is the "dew from heaven." "My head is filled with dew," "Aloha shall give thee of the dew of heaven."

Solving Problems While You Sleep

During the course of an interview, a young man asked me how he could locate his father's will. His father had passed on and apparently had left no will. The young man's sister told him that their father had confided to her that a will had been executed which was fair to all. All attempts to locate the will had failed. I suggested he turn his request over to his subconscious mind at night before sleep. This is the method he followed: "I now turn this request over to the subconscious mind. It knows just where the will is. It reveals it to me." Then he condensed his request into one word, "Answer."

He repeated this prayer over and over again as a lullaby. He lulled himself to sleep for several nights with the word, "Answer." A few nights later he had a very vivid, realistic dream. He saw the name and address of a certain bank. He went there and found a safe deposit vault registered in the name of his father. This was the answer to his prayer.

How a Famous Naturalist Solved His Problem

Professor Agassiz, a distinguished American naturalist, discovered the indefatigable activities of his subconscious mind while he slept. The following has been reported by his widow in her biography of her famous husband.

"He had been for two weeks striving to decipher the somewhat obscure impression of a fossil fish on the stone slab in which it was preserved. Weary and perplexed, he put his work aside at last, and tried to dismiss it from his mind. Shortly after, he woke up one night persuaded that while asleep he had seen his fish with all the missing features perfectly restored. But when he tried to hold and make fast the image it escaped him. Nevertheless, he went early to the Jardin des Plantes, thinking that on looking anew at the impression he should see something which would put him on the track of his vision. In vain—the blurred record was as black as ever. The next night he saw the fish again, but with no more satisfactory result. When he awoke it disappeared from his memory as before. Hoping that the same experience might be repeated, on the third night he placed a pencil and paper beside his bed before going to sleep.

"Accordingly, toward morning the fish reappeared in his dream, confusedly at first, but at last with such distinctness that he had no longer any doubt as to its zoological characters. Still half dreaming, in perfect darkness, he traced these characters on the sheet of paper at the bedside. In the morning he was surprised to see in his nocturnal sketch features which he thought it impossible the fossil itself should reveal. He hastened to the Jardin des Plantes, and, with his drawing as a guide, succeeded in chiseling away the surface of the stone under which portions of the fish proved to be hidden. When wholly exposed it corresponded with his dream and his drawing, and he succeeded in classifying it with ease."

An Outstanding Physician Solved the Problem of Diabetes

Some years ago I received a clipping from a magazine describing the origin of the discovery of insulin. This is the essence of the article as I recall it.

About forty years ago or more, Dr. Frederick Banting, a brilliant Canadian physician and surgeon, was concentrating his attention on the ravages of diabetes. At that time medical science offered no effective method of arresting the disease. Dr. Banting spent considerable time experimenting and studying the international literature on the subject. One night he was exhausted and fell asleep. While asleep, his subconscious mind instructed him to extract the residue from the degenerated pancreatic duct of dogs. This was the origin of insulin which has helped millions of people.

The Unbelievable Power of Suggestion

You will note that Dr. Banting had been consciously dwelling on the problem for some time seeking a solution, a way out, and his subconscious responded accordingly.

It does not follow that you will always get an answer overnight. The answer may not come for some time. Do not be discouraged. Keep on turning the problem over every night to the subconscious mind prior to sleep, as if you had never done it before.

One of the reasons for the delay may be that you look upon it as a major problem. You may believe it will take a long time to solve it.

Your subconscious mind is timeless and space less. Go to sleep believing you have the answer now. Do not postulate the answer in the future. Have an abiding faith in the outcome. Become convinced now as you read this book that there is an answer and a perfect solution for you.

Your thought, as you go to sleep, arouses the powerful latency which is within you. For example, let us suppose you are wondering whether to sell your home, buy a certain stock, sever partnership, move t New York or stay in Los Angeles, dissolve the present contract or take a new one. Do this: Sit quietly in your armchair or at the desk in your office. Remember that there is a universal law of action and reaction. The action is your thought. The subconscious mind is reactive and reflexive; this is its nature. It rebounds, rewards, and repays. It is the law of correspondence. It responds by corresponding. As you contemplate right action, you will automatically experience a reaction or response in yourself which represents the guidance or answer of your subconscious mind.

The subconscious mind will always answer you if you trust it.

In seeking guidance, you simply think quietly about right action which means that you are using the infinite intelligence resident in the subconscious mind to the point where it begins to use you. From there on, your course of action is directed and controlled by the subjective wisdom within you which is all-wise and omnipotent. Your decision will be right. There will only be right action because you are under a subjective compulsion to do the right thing. I use the word compulsion because the law of the subconscious is compulsion.

Your Thought is Your Prayer

When your conscious mind deliberately accepts a creative idea or plan and turns it over to the subconscious with confidence, the intelligence of your subconscious brings it to pass in your experience. Your subconscious mind acts as a law and produces with mathematical exactitude the equivalent of your idea in your experience.

Do everything from the standpoint of the One God and His Love. For instance, when you shop, pray before purchasing. Say, "God guides me in all my purchases." Say quietly to the saleslady or salesman, "God is prospering him."

Whatever you do, do it with love and good will. Pour out love, peace, and good will to all. Claim frequently that God's Love and Transcendent Beauty flow through all my thoughts, words, and actions. Make a habit of this. Fill your mind with the eternal verities; then you will see that "the flowers appear on the earth; the time of the singing of *birds* is come!" You will begin to *flower*, yes, you will begin to blossom forth.

The earth means your body, environment, social life, and all things necessary on this objective plane.

The flowers you witness will be the birth of God in your mind. The *flowers* of God's guidance will watch over you, and lead you to green pastures and still waters. The flowers of God's Love will fill your heart. Now when you see discord anywhere, you will see the Love of God operating in all His Creation; as you realize It, you will see love come forth and flower in the other.

When you go into a home, and you see confusion, quarrelling, and strife, you will realize within yourself, that the peace of God reigns supreme in the minds and hearts of all those in this house; you will see the flower of peace made manifest and expressed.

Where you see financial lack and limitation, you will realize the infinite abundance and wealth of God forever flowing, filling up all the empty vessels, and leaving a Divine surplus. As you do this, you will live in the garden of God where only orchids and all beautiful flowers grow; for only God's ideas circulate in your mind.

As you go to sleep every night, you will clothe yourself with the garment of love, peace, and joy. *When thou go, it shall lead thee; and when thou awake, it shall talk with thee* (Proverbs 6:22).

Why We Sleep

Dr. John Bigelow, a famous research authority on sleep, demonstrated that at night while asleep you receive impressions showing that the nerves of the eyes, ears, nose, and taste buds are active during sleep, and also that the nerves of your brain are quite active. He says that the main reason we sleep is because "the nobler part of the soul is united by abstraction to our higher nature and becomes a participant in the wisdom and foreknowledge of the gods."

Dr. Bigelow states also, "The results of my studies have not only strengthened my convictions that the supposed exemption from customary toils and activities was not the final purpose of sleep, but have also made clearer to my mind the conviction that no part of a man's life deserves to be considered more indispensable to its symmetrical and perfect spiritual development than the while he is separated from the phenomenal world in sleep."

Prayer, a Form of Sleep

Your conscious mind gets involved with vexations, strife, and contentions of the day, and it is very necessary to withdraw periodically from sense evidence and the objective world, and communicate silently with the inner wisdom of your subconscious mind. By claiming guidance, strength, and greater intelligence in all phases of your life, you will be enabled to overcome all difficulties and solve your daily problems.

This regular withdrawal from sense evidence and the noise and confusion of everyday living is also a form of sleep, i.e., you become asleep to the world of the senses and alive to the wisdom and power of your subconscious mind.

Startling Effects of Sleep Deprivation

Lack of sleep can cause you to become irritable, moody, and depressed. Dr. George Stevenson of the National Association for Mental Health says, "I believe it can safely be said that all human beings need a minimum of six hours' sleep to be healthy. Most people need more. Those who think they can get along on less are fooling themselves."

Medical research scholars, investigating sleep processes and deprivation of sleep, point out that severe insomnia has preceded psychotic breakdown in some instances. Remember, you are spiritually recharged during sleep, and adequate sleep is essential to produce joy and vitality in life.

Listen to Your Subconscious Mind

I will illustrate how the wisdom of your subconscious mind can instruct you and protect you relative to your request for right action as you go to sleep.

Many years ago, before the Second World War, I was offered a very lucrative assignment in the Orient, and I prayed for guidance and the right decision as follows: "Infinite intelligence within me knows all things, and the right decision is revealed to me in divine order. I will recognize the answer when it comes."

I repeated this simple prayer over and over again as a lullaby prior to sleep, and in a dream came the vivid realization of things to come three years hence. An old friend appeared in the dream and said, "Read these headlines—do not go!" The headlines of the newspaper which appeared in the dream related to war and the attack on Pearl Harbor.

Occasionally, the writer dreams literally. The aforementioned dream was undoubtedly a dramatization of the subconscious mind which projected a person whom I trusted and respected. To some a warning may come in the form of a mother who appears in a dream. She tells the person not to go here or there, and the reason for the warning. Your subconscious mind is all-wise. It knows all things. Oftentimes it will speak to you only in a voice that your conscious mind will immediately accept as true. Sometimes your subconscious will warn you in a voice which sounds like that of your mother or some loved one which may cause you to stop on the street, and you find, if you had gone another foot, a falling object from a window might have struck you on the head.

My subconscious mind is one with the universal subconscious, and it knew the Japanese were planning a war, and it also knew when the war would start.

Dr. Rhine, director of the Department of Psychology at Duke University, has gathered together a vast amount of evidence showing that a great number of people all over the world see events before they happen, and in many instances are, therefore, able to avoid the tragic event which was foreseen vividly in a dream.

The dream which I had showed clearly the headlines in *The New York Times* about three years prior to the tragedy of Pearl Harbor. In consequence of this dream, I immediately cancelled the trip as I felt a subconscious compulsion to do so. Three years later the Second World War proved the truth of the inner voice of intuition.

A Cat Nap Nets Him $15,000

One of my students mailed me a newspaper clipping three or four years ago about a man called Ray Hammerstrom, a roller at the steel works in Pittsburgh operated by Jones and Laughlin Steel Corporation. He received $15,000 for his dream.

According to the article, the engineers could not fix a faulty switch in a newly installed bar mill which controlled the delivery of straight bars to the cooling beds. The engineers worked on the switch about eleven or twelve times to no avail.

Hammerstrom thought a lot about the problem and tried to figure out a new design which might work. Nothing worked. One afternoon he lay down for a nap, and prior to sleep he began to think about the answer to the switch problem. He had a dream in which a perfect design for the switch was portrayed. When he awoke, he sketched his new design according to the outline of his dream.

This visionary catnap won Hammerstrom a check for $15,000; the largest award the firm ever gave an employee for a new idea.

How a Famous Professor Solved His Problem in Sleep

Dr. H.V. Helprecht, Professor of Assyrian at the University of Pennsylvania, wrote as follows: "One Saturday evening . . . I had been wearying myself, in the vain attempt to decipher two small fragments of agate which were supposed to belong to the finger rings of some Babylonians.

"About midnight, weary and exhausted, I went to bed and dreamed the following remarkable dream: A tall, thin priest of Nippur, about forty years of age, led me to the treasure chamber of the temple . . . a small, low-ceilinged room without windows, while scraps of agate and lapis-lazuli lay scattered on the floor. Here he addressed me as follows: "The two fragments which you have published separately on pages 22 and 26 belong together, are not finger rings . . . The first two rings served as earrings for the statue of the god; the two fragments (you have) . . . are the portions of them. If you will put them together you will have confirmation of my words." . . . I awoke at once. I examined the fragments. And to my astonishment found the dream verified. The problem was then at last solved."

This demonstrates clearly the creative manifestation of his subconscious mind which knew the answer to all his problems.

How the Subconscious Worked for a Famous Writer While He Slept

Robert Louis Stevenson in one of his books, *Across the Plains*, devotes a whole chapter to dreams. He was a vivid dreamer and had the persistent habit of giving specific instructions to his subconscious every night prior to sleep. He would request his subconscious to evoke stories for him while he slept. For example, if Stevenson's funds were at low ebb, his command to his subconscious would be something like this: "Give me a good thrilling novel which will be marketable and profitable." His subconscious responded magnificently.

Stevenson says, "These little brownies [the intelligences and powers of his subconscious] can tell me a story piece by piece, like a serial, and keep me, its supposed creator, all the while in total ignorance of where they aim." And he added: "That part of my work which is done when I am up and about [while he is consciously aware and awake] is by no means necessarily mine, since all goes to show that the *brownies* have a hand in it even then."

Sleep in Peace and Wake in Joy

To those who suffer from insomnia, you will find the following prayer very effective. Repeat it slowly, quietly, and lovingly prior to sleep: "My toes are relaxed, my ankles are relaxed, my abdominal muscles are relaxed, my heart and lungs are relaxed, my hands and arms are relaxed, my neck is relaxed, my brain is relaxed, my face is relaxed, my eyes are relaxed, my whole mind and body are relaxed. I fully and freely forgive everyone, and I sincerely wish for them harmony, health, peace, and all the blessings of life. I am at peace; I am poised, serene, and calm. I rest in security and in peace. A great stillness steals over me, and a great calm quiets my whole being as I realize the Divine Presence within me. I know that the realization of life and love heals me. I wrap myself in the mantle of love and fall asleep filled with good will for all. Throughout the night peace remains with me, and in the morning I shall be filled with life and love. A circle of love is drawn around me. *I will fear no evil, for Thou art with me.* I sleep in peace, I wake in joy, and *in Him I live, move, and have my being.*"

In sleep your conscious mind is creatively joined to your subconscious mind. Many good people think that sleep is intended only for rest of the body, but nothing rests while you are asleep, as your subconscious and all the vital processes of your body, though slowed down considerably, continue to function. A restorative process sets in during sleep resulting in a feeling of well-being due to the fact that there is a restoration of physical energy. Another reason we go to sleep is to develop spiritually; therefore, it is of paramount importance that we avoid all discordant states prior to sleep. The Divinity that shapes our ends is all wise and has so arranged it that man is compelled to withdraw from the world of noise, which is not conducive to spiritual unfoldment.

From now on you always go to sleep feeling that you now are what you long to be. Your last concept as you fall asleep is etched on your deeper mind; you shall resurrect it. Always take into the *banquet house* of your Lover a noble, Christ like concept of yourself; your Lover will always give you what you conceive and believe as true. Anything you can conceive, your Lover can give conception. Love gives birth to all things. Your tomorrows are determined by your concept of yourself as you fall asleep in the arms of your Love (your ideal).

The Gift of Intuition

The time of the singing of birds is at hand for you when you cease singing that old song of lack. You have listened to people sing this kind of song: It is like an old gramophone record: "I'm so lonesome; things never went right for me. I never had a chance. I have been cruelly treated." "I have been operated on three times." "You should hear about all the money I lost." Yes, then they tell about the fear on the lonely road, plus their likes, dislikes, pet peeves, and hates. Imbued with God's love, you will no longer sing that song again. You will sing the new song; for God's ideas and truths (birds) will sing in you.

Then you will speak in a new tongue which means the mood of peace, joy, good will, and love. You will no longer react to people and conditions like you did. The Song of God is now heard. Now when someone says something mean or nasty to you, you will immediately transform it by realizing God's peace fills your soul. You will consume it with the fire of right thoughts; the birds will truly sing in your mind and heart as you do. You are happy; you are bubbling over with enthusiasm, and you are looking forward with a joyous expectancy to all good things. Wherever you go, you carry peace with you; all those who come within your orbit are blessed by your inner radiance. You begin to see sermons in stones, tongues in trees, songs in running brooks, and God in everything. The voice of the turtle dove is now heard in your land!

Tennyson said, "Speak to Him thou, for he hears, spirit with spirit shall meet, closer is He than breathing, and nearer than hands and feet."

The voice of the turtle dove is the voice of peace, the voice of intuition, and of God's inner guidance. You can hear it by slowly listening. You breathe air without effort; likewise, you should learn to let the intelligence within your subconscious mind flow through your intellect without tension. Your subjective mind perceives by intuition. It does not have to reason or inquire, as it is an all-wise and an infinite intelligence. If you say to your subconscious, sometimes referred to as the subjective mind (it is subject to the conscious mind), "Wake me up at 6:00 o'clock," you know that you will awaken exactly at the time specified. It never fails. We must realize that herein lays a source of power, which is omnipotent. Many good people have erroneous ideas about the gift of intuition. Many believe that it is an extraordinary event, to be experienced only by highly spiritual people. This is not true. Any businessman or housewife can receive an answer by turning to the infinite intelligence of the subconscious mind, and guidance may be received for any problem. For instance one time as a boy I was lost in the woods. I sat down under a tree, and remembered a prayer which starts with, "Our Father, He will show us the way; let us be quiet, and He will lead us." I quietly repeated, "Father, lead us."

A wave of peace came over me which I can still recall. The voice of the turtle dove became real. The turtle dove is intuition which means being taught from within. An overpowering feeling came over me to go in a certain direction as if I were being pushed ahead. Two of the boys came with me; the others did not. We were led out of that thick jungle, as if by an Unseen Hand.

Great musicians have listened and heard the music within; they wrote down what they heard inwardly. In meditation Lincoln listened to the principle of liberty; Beethoven heard the principle of harmony.

If you are intensely interested in the principle of mathematics, you love it; as you love it, it will reveal all its secrets to you.

Jesus heard the voice of the turtle dove when he said, "Peace, I leave with you; my peace I give unto you; not as the world giveth, give I unto you. Let not your heart be troubled; neither let it be afraid." How wonderful you will feel as you drink in these words and fill your mind with their therapeutic potency.

Job heard the voice of the turtle dove when he said, "Acquaint now you with Him, and be at peace." "Thou wilt keep him in perfect peace, whose mind is stayed *on* thee: because he trusted in thee." "For God is not the author of confusion, but of peace."

You can hear the voice of the turtledove by turning to the Infinite Intelligence within you, saying, "Father, this is what I want . . ." then state specifically and clearly the thing you desire. You are now turning your desire over to the God-Wisdom within you, which knows all, sees all, and has the "know how" of accomplishment. You always know whether you have really turned your request over or not. If you are at peace about it, you have turned it over. If anxious and worried, you have not subjectified your prayer; you do not fully trust the God-Wisdom within.

If you want guidance, claim Infinite Intelligence is guiding you now; it will differentiate itself as right action for you. You will know you have received the answer, for the dove of peace will whisper in your ear, "Peace is still." You will know the Divine answer, for you will be at peace, and your decision will be right.

A girl recently was wondering whether to accept a position in New York for considerable more money or remain in Los Angeles in her present position. At night as she went to sleep, she asked herself this question, "What would be my reaction if I had made the right decision now?" The answer came to her, "I would feel wonderful. I would feel happy having made the right decision." Then she said, "I will act as though I had made the right decision," and she began to say, "Isn't it wonderful! Isn't it wonderful! Over and over again, as a lullaby, and lulled herself to sleep in the feeling, "It is wonderful."

She had a dream that night, and the voice in the dream said, "Stand still! Stand still!" She awakened immediately, and knew of course that was the voice of the turtle dove—the voice of intuition.

The fourth dimensional-self within her can see ahead; it knows all and sees all; it can read the minds of the owners of the business in the east. She remained in her present position. Subsequent events proved the truth of her Inner Voice; the Eastern concern went into bankruptcy. "I the Lord will make myself known unto him in a vision, and will speak unto him in a dream."

"My beloved *is* mine, and I *am* his; he feedeth among the lilies." The lilies represent the poppies, which grow in the East. To see the poppy field sway in the breeze is a very beautiful sight. Here the inspired biblical writer is telling you to have a romance with God. As you turn to the God-Presence, It turns to you. You experience the mystic marriage, the wedded bliss, when you fall madly in love with truth for truth's sake; then you become full of the new wine, the new interpretation of life.

The lilies symbolize beauty, order, symmetry, and proportion. As you feed or feast on the great truth that God is Indescribable Beauty, Boundless Love, Absolute Bliss, Absolute Harmony, and Infinite Peace, you are truly feeding among the lilies. When you claim that what is true of God is true of you, miracles will happen in your life.

By realizing and knowing these qualities and attributes of God are being expressed through you, and that you are a channel for the Divine, every atom of your being begins to dance to the rhythm of the Eternal God. Beauty, order, harmony, and peace appear in your mind, body, and business world as you feed among the lilies; you feel your oneness with God, Life, and God's Infinite Riches. You are married to your Beloved, for you are now married to God; you are a bride of the Lord (I AM). From this moment forward you will bring forth children of your Beloved; they will bear the image and likeness of their Father and Mother.

The father is God's idea; the mother is the emotionalizing of the idea, and its subjective embodiment. From that union of idea and feeling come forth your health, abundance, the happiness, and inner peace.

Sit down and feed among the lilies by realizing that every night of the year when you go to sleep, you go before the King of Kings, the Lord of Lords, and the Prince of Peace. Be sure you are dressed properly as you enter into His Holy Presence. If you were going before the President, you would put on your best clothes. The clothes you wear as you enter into the heavens of your own mind every night represent the mood, or the tone you wear. Be sure it is always the wedding garment of love, peace, and good will to all.

Be absolutely sure that you can say, "Behold, thou art fair." There must be no resentment, ill-will, condemnation of self or others, and no criticism of any person. God's Love must really fill your heart for all men everywhere. You must sincerely wish for everyone what you wish for yourself; then you can say to your mood or feeling, "Behold, thou *art* fair." "And when ye stand praying, forgive, if ye have ought against any."

"My beloved is mine." That entire God is yours, for God is within you. All you can possibly desire is already yours. You need no help from the outside to feed among the lilies.

When you go to sleep tonight, forgive everyone, and imagine and feel your desire is fulfilled. Become absolutely and completely indifferent to all thought of failure, because you now know the law. As you accept the end, you have, as Troward so beautifully stated, willed the means to the realization of the end. As you are about to enter sleep, galvanize yourself into the feeling of being or having your desire. Your mental acceptance or your feeling as you go to sleep is the request you make of your Beloved; then She looks at your request (conviction in the subconscious mind), and being the Absolute Lover, she must give you what you asked.

"You feed among the lilies until the day breaks and the shadows flee away." The shadows are fear, doubt, worry, anxiety, and all the reasons why you cannot do something. The shadows of our five senses and race belief hover over the minds of all as we pray.

Prolonged worry robs you of vitality, enthusiasm, and energy and leaves you a physical and mental wreck. Psychosomatic physicians point out that chronic worry is behind numerous diseases such as asthma, allergies, cardiac trouble, high blood pressure, and a host of other illnesses too numerous to mention.

The worried mind is confused, divided, and is thinking aimlessly about a lot of things which are not true. Worry can be solved, however, by the application of the law of mind.

Your problem is in your mind. You have a desire, the realization of which would solve your problem. But when you look at conditions and circumstances as they are, a negative thought comes to your mind and your desire is in conflict with your fear. Your worry is your mind's acceptance of the negative conditions.

Realize that your desire is the gift of God, telling you to rise higher in life and that there is no power to challenge God, the Living Spirit Almighty within you. Then affirm to yourself: *God (Cosmic Wisdom) gave me this desire, and the Almighty Power is now backing me up, revealing to me the perfect plan for its unfoldment, and I rest in that conviction.* When fear or worry thoughts come to your mind, remind yourself that God is bringing your desire, ideal, plan, or purpose to pass in Divine order, and continue in this attitude of mind until the day breaks and the shadows flee away.

Chapter 17

SUGGESTING A QUIET MIND TO ACHIEVE THE RIGHT DECISIONS

When you have what you term a "difficult decision" to make, or when you fail to see the solution to your problem, begin at once to think constructively about it. If you are fearful and worried, you are not really thinking. True thinking is free from fear.

I suggest a simple technique you can use to receive guidance on any subject: Quiet the mind and still the body. Tell the body to relax; it has to obey you. It has no volition, initiative, or self-conscious intelligence. Your body is an emotional disk which records your beliefs and impressions. Mobilize your attention; focus your thought on the solution to your problem. Try to solve it with your conscious mind. Think how happy you would be about the perfect solution. Sense the feeling you would have if the perfect answer were yours now. Let your mind play with this mood in a relaxed way;

If your mind is to be stilled, it must be sheltered from the physical disturbances of noise and discomfort, from the winds and storms of the emotions, and from the anxieties and tensions of the day.

The ideal stillness achieved by holy men is a goal for most of us. But in some small measure, each time you withdraw into your prayer room, your mind, you can create a tranquil atmosphere sufficient to make your prayers effective.

Your prayers will never be effective until you cease to battle discords, grief, passion, anger, resentment, and the host of petty emotions that fill too many thoughts. The discipline is for you to release your attention from these disturbances and contemplate the Presence and Power of God within you.

Untroubled by distractions, you can begin to think about a clear understanding of such abstractions as beauty, love, peace, and harmony. When you begin to know the nature of harmony, you can begin to project that quality into the affairs and activities of your life.

If I offer you a gift of a book, in order to receive it, you must reach for it by stretching forth your hand. In like manner, since all the riches of God are within you, you must make some effort to claim them. God is the giver and the gift, but you are the receiver. Open your mind and heart and let in God's river of peace. Let it fill your mind and heart, for God is peace.

Contemplate the following verses of the Eighth Psalm and you will find a deep river of life, love, quiescence and equanimity steal over the barren areas of your mind bringing rest to the troubled soul:

When I consider thy heavens, the work of thy fingers, the moon and the stars, which thou hast ordained; what is man, that thou art mindful of him? And the son of man, that thou visit him? For thou hast made him a little lower than the angels, and hast crowned him with glory and honor. Thou maddest him to have dominion over the works of thy hands; thou hast put all things under his feet (Ps. 8:3, 4, 5,6)

Meditating on the eternal verities contained in this Psalm and on the immeasurable nature of the universe to which we belong, the Infinite Mind and Infinite Intelligence, which created us and which animates and supports us, and which moves rhythmically harmoniously, ceaselessly, changelessly and with mathematical precision, gives you faith, confidence, strength and security. Know that you have, as the Psalmist says, dominion over your thoughts, feelings, actions and reactions in life. This fills you with self-esteem and a sense of worthiness and power, which endows you with strength to do your work, live joyously, and walk the earth with the praise of God forever on your lips.

Some time ago I had a conversation with a businessman, who finally said to me, "How can I get a quiet mind in a troubled and confused world? I know that it is said: 'A quiet mind gets things done.' I'm confused and troubled, and the propaganda in the newspapers, radio and television is driving me half-crazy."

I said to him that I would attempt to throw some light on his problem; provide him with spiritual medicine, which would allay his fears and anxieties; and give him the quiet mind which gets things done. I pointed out that if his thoughts morning, noon and night revolved about war, crime, sickness, disease, accidents and misfortune, he would automatically bring on the mood of depression, anxiety and fear. But if, on the other hand, he gave some of his time and attention to the eternal laws and principles which govern the cosmos and all life, he would automatically be lifted up into the mental atmosphere of inner security and serenity.

As a result, three times a day this man autosuggested his mind with the following truths: "*The heavens declare the glory of God; and the firmament shewed his handiwork*" (Ps.19: 1). I know a Supreme Intelligence governs the planets in their courses and controls and directs the entire universe. I know there is Divine law and order operating with absolute certainty fashioning the entire world, causing the stars to come nightly to the sky, and regulating the galaxies in space; and God is ruling the universe. I move mentally into the stillness of my own mind and contemplate these eternal truths of God.

"*Thou wilt keep him in perfect peace, whose mind is stayed on thee: because he trusted in thee* (Isa. 26:3).

Peace I leave with you, my peace I give unto you: not as the world giveth, give I unto you. Let not your heart be troubled, neither let it be afraid (John 14:27).

"*For God is not the author of confusion, but of peace* . . . (I Cor. 14:33).

"*And let the peace of God rule in your heart* . . . (Col. 3:15)."

Maintaining a Serene Mind

In talking to many business and professional men of different religious persuasions, they have informed me that regularly and periodically they go to a church retreat where they listen to talks on God, prayer and the art of meditation, and then into a silent period. After a morning meditation, they are told to contemplate what they heard and remain silent for several days, even during mealtime. All this time they are suggested to dwell calmly and quietly on the instructions and meditations given each morning.

All of them have told me that they come back renewed, refreshed and replenished spiritually and mentally. Following their return to their offices, factories and professional lives, they continue to maintain quiet periods for fifteen to twenty minutes every day, morning and evening, and they have found that what the Bible says is true: The peace of God, which passeth all understanding, shall keep your hearts and minds . . . (Phil. 4:7).

Benefits of Recharging Mental and Spiritual Batteries

Having spiritually recharged their mental and spiritual batteries, these men are able to meet head on and, with faith, course and confidence, cope with the problems, strife, vexations and contentions of the day. These men know where to receive renewed spiritual power—by tuning in quietly, as Emerson says, with the Infinite, which lies stretched in smiling repose. Energy, power, inspiration, guidance and wisdom come out of the silence and the stillness of the mind when tuned in with God. These men have learned to relax and to give up their egoistic pride. They have recognized, honored and called upon a wisdom and power that created all things visible and invisible and that governs all things ceaselessly, timelessly and forever. They have decided to go the way of wisdom. *Her ways are ways of pleasantness, and all her paths are peace* (Prov. 3:17).

Inner Conflict Can Be Calmed

One day in Beverly Hills, a man who recognized me stopped me on the street and said that he was terribly disturbed. He asked, "Do you think I can get a quiet mind? I have been at war with myself for over two months." There was a conflict raging within him. He was full of fears, doubts, hates and religious bigotry. He was furious because his daughter had married into a different faith, and he said that he hated her husband. He was not on speaking terms with his own son because the son joined the armed forces and he (the father) belonged to a peace crusade. And to top things off, his wife was suing him for divorce.

I was not able to give him much time on the street corner, but I told him briefly that he should be delighted that his daughter had married the man of her dreams and that, if they loved each other, they certainly should marry, as love knows no creed, race, dogma or color. Love is God, and God is impersonal and no respecter of persons.

Regarding his son, I suggested that he write the young man and tell him how much he loves him and to pray for him. I said he should respect his son's decision and not interfere with him other than to wish for him all the blessings of life. I also told him that I gathered from his conversation that the bickering and quarrelling in their marriage was probably due to an unresolved childhood conflict with his mother and that he expected his wife to be a substitute for his mother.

I wrote down on a piece of paper these everlasting truths and gave them to him to read and digest: "Thou wilt keep him in perfect peace, whose mind is stayed on Thee, because he trusted in Thee." I urged him to keep his mind focused on God with trust, faith and certainty, and that he would then feel the river of life, love and inner quietude filling his heart. I added that whenever he thought of anyone in his family, he was to say, "God's peace fills my soul and God's peace fills his or her soul."

How His Healing Was Accomplished

A few days later I had a note from this man, which said, "Life was like hell for me. I hated to open my eyes in the morning. I took Phenobarbital every night in order to sleep. After I left you on the street, and as you suggested, I surrendered my family and myself to God and affirmed constantly: 'God will keep me in perfect peace, because my mind is stayed on Him.' The change that has come over me is unbelievable. Life has become full of joy and wonder. My wife cancelled divorce proceedings and we are back together again. I wrote letters to my daughter and son-in-law and to my son, and there are peace, harmony and understanding among us all."

All that this man did was get all the hatred and resentment out of his heart. As he surrendered to the golden river of peace within, it flowed in response to him, and all the pieces fell into place in Divine order.

Key to Praying Effectively

The Bible gives the perfect formula for making prayer more effective. Consider what it says; *Let the words of my mouth and the meditation of my heart, be acceptable in thy sight, O Lord, my strength, and my redeemer.* Psalms 19:14. Answers to your prayers will happen in your life when your inner thought and feeling agree with the words of your mouth.

Long Delayed Lawsuit

A friend of mine was involved in a legal battle which had cost him considerable time, legal fees, etc. He was exasperated, bitter, and hostile toward the opposition and his own attorneys. His inner speech which represents his inner, silent, unexpressed thoughts was more or less as follow: "It's hopeless! This has gone for five years; I am being sold down the river. It is useless to go on. I might as well give up." I explained to him that this inner speech was highly destructive and was undoubtedly playing a major role in prolonging the case. Job said, *for the thing which I greatly feared is come upon me.* Job 3:25.

He changed his inner and outer speech completely when he fully understood what he had been doing to himself. Actually he had been praying against himself. I asked him a single question as follows. "What would you say if I told you this minute that there had been a perfect, harmonious solution reached and the whole matter was concluded?"

He replied, "I would be delighted and eternally grateful. I would feel wonderful knowing that the whole thing was finished."

He agreed from that moment on to see to it that his inner speech would agree with his aim. Regularly and systematically he applied the following prayer, which I gave him: "I give thanks for the perfect, harmonious solution which came through the Wisdom of the All-Wise One." He auto suggested this frequently during the day, and when difficulties, delays, set-backs, arguments, doubt, and fear came to his mind, he would silently affirm the above truth. He ceased completely making all negative statements verbally and also watched his inner speech knowing that his inner speech would always be made manifest. It is what we feel on the inside that is expressed. We can say one thing with the mouth and feel another in our heart; it is what we feel that is reproduced on the screen of space. We must never affirm inwardly what we do not want to experience outwardly. The lips and the heart should agree; when they do, our prayer is answered.

We must watch our inner psychological state. Some people mutter to themselves, are envious, jealous, and seething with anger and hostility. Such a mental attitude is highly destructive and brings chaos, sickness, and lack in its train. You are familiar with the person who justifies himself; he tells himself that he has a perfect right to be angry, to seek revenge, and try to get even. He is playing an old subconscious record which recites all the alibis, excuses, and justification for his inner boiling state. In all probability he does not know that such a mental state causes him to lose psychic energy on a large scale, rendering him inefficient and confused. Man's negative inner speech is usually directed against some person.

Truth Made Him Whole

I talked to a man recently who told me that he had been treated shabbily; how he planned to get even and how hateful he was toward his former employer, etc. This man had ulcers of the stomach as a result of his inner turmoil and irritation. I explained to him that he had been making very destructive impressions of anger and resentment on his subconscious mind which always expresses what is impressed upon it. These destructive emotions must have an outlet and they came forth as ulcers and neurosis in his case.

He reversed his mental processes by releasing his former employer into the boundless ocean of God's Love and wishing for him all the blessings of heaven. At the same time he filled his mind with Truths of God by identifying himself with the Infinite Healing Presence, realizing that the harmony, Peace, and Perfection of the Infinite One were saturating his mind and body, making him every whit whole. These spiritual vibrations permeating his mind were transmitted throughout his entire system, and the cells of his body took on a new spiritual tone resulting in a healing of his discordant condition.

The Subconscious Recording Machine

The Bible says, *if two of you shall agree on earth as touching anything that they shall ask, it shall be done for them of my Father, which is in heaven.* Who are these two? It means you and your desire; i.e., if you accept your desire mentally, the subconscious mind will bring it to pass because your conscious and subconscious have agreed, are synchronized. The two agreeing represent your thought and feeling, your idea and emotion. If you succeed in emotionalizing the concept the male and female aspect of your mind have agreed and there will be an issue or mental offspring, namely the answered prayer.

It must be recalled that whatever we accept or feel as true is impregnated in our subconscious mind. The subconscious is the creative medium; its tendency, as Troward points out, is always life ward. The subconscious controls all your vital organs, is the seat of memory, and the healer of the body. The subconscious is fed by hidden springs and is one with Infinite Intelligence and Infinite Power.

It is very important to give the proper suggestion to the subconscious. For example, if a man dwells on obstacles, delays, difficulties, and obstructions to his program, the subconscious will take that as his request and proceed to bring difficulties and disappointments into his experience; hence, feed the subconscious with premises which are true.

What kind of autosuggestion goes on in you all the time, which is not being expressed audibly? It is your auto suggestion that the subconscious listens to and obeys. Your subconscious records your silent thought and feeling, and it is a very faithful recording machine. It records everything and plays the record to you in the form of experiences, conditions, and events. You do not have to travel psychologically with fear, doubt, anxiety, and anger. There is no law which says that you have to travel with gangsters, assassins, murderers, intruders, and such thieves and robbers in hour mind; they rob you of health, happiness, peace, and prosperity, and make you a physical and mental wreck.

Inner Speech is a Form of Auto Suggestion

A woman had a blood pressure of over two hundred accompanied by severe migraine attacks; the cause of all this was destructive. She felt that someone had not treated her right and she became very negative toward that other person. She justified herself in being hostile and antagonistic toward this other person, allowing this condition to go on for weeks and was in a deep emotional stew. This negative attitude drained force from her bringing about psychological changes in her blood stream. She was ready as she said, to explode with anger. This inner pressure, mounting tensions, and seething hostility was the cause of her high blood pressure or hypertension plus the migraine.

This woman began to practice the wonders of prayer therapy. She realized she had been poisoning herself and that the other woman was in no way responsible for the way she was thinking or feeling about her. She was the only thinker in her universe, and she had been thinking vicious, destructive, malicious thoughts which were poisoning her whole system.

She began to comprehend and see that no one could possibly touch her except through her own thought or the movement of her own mind. All she had to do in order to practice the wonders of true spiritual inner speech was to identify with her aim. Her aim was peace, health, happiness, joy, serenity, and tranquility. She began to identify with God's River of Peace and God's Love flowing through her like a golden yellow river soothing, healing, and restoring her mind and body.

She prayed for fifteen minutes three or four times a day. Her inner thoughts and feelings were as follows: "God is Love, and His Love fills my soul. God is Peace, and His Peace fills my mind and body. God is Perfect health, and His health is my Health. God is Joy, and His Joy is my Joy and I feel wonderful. This kind or prayer therapy which represented her inner thoughts of God and His qualities brought about a complete sense of balance, poise, and harmony to her mind and body. When the thoughts of the other woman came to her mind, she would immediately identify with her aim—God's peace. She discovered the wonders of real effective prayer where her lips and heart united in identifying with the Eternal Truths of God, thereby rendering her impermeable the impact of negative ideas and thoughts.

How do you meet people in your mind? That is the acid test for the Truth which sets you free. If you meet them and see the God in them, that is wonderful; then you are practicing the wonders of inner speech from a constructive standpoint because you are identifying with your aim which is God or the good. Ouspensky, author of New *Model of the Universe*, pointed out that your inner speech should always agree with your aim.

He Listened

A young man had an aim for perfect health; however his conscious mind reminded him that he had been sick with a blood disorder for years. He was full of anxiety, fear, and doubt. His relations kept reminding him that it would take a long time and that he might never be healed. His inner speech had to agree with his aim. In other words, the two phases of his mind had to synchronize and agree. This young man began to talk in a different tone to his subconscious. I told him as he listened carefully and avidly to affirm slow, quietly, lovingly, and feelingly several times daily as follows: "The Creative Intelligence made my body and is creating my blood now. The Healing Presence knows how to heal and is transforming every cell of my body to God's pattern now. I hear and I see the doctor telling me that I am whole. I have this picture now in my mind, I see him clearly, I hear his voice, and he is saying to me, "John, you are healed. It is a miracle!" I know this constructive imagery is going down into my subconscious mind where it is being developed and brought to pass. I know my subconscious mind is in touch with the Infinite One, and Its Wisdom and Power are bringing my request to pass in spite of all sensual evidence to the contrary. I feel this, I believe it, and I am now identifying with my aim—perfect health—this is my inner speech morning, noon, and night."

He repeated this prayer ten or fifteen minutes four or five times daily, particularly prior to sleep. Due to habit he found his mind running wild at times, fretting, fussing, worrying, recounting the verdict of others and his previous repeated failings in the healing process. When these thoughts came to his mind, he issued the order, "Stop! I am the master. All thoughts, imagery, and responses must obey me. From now on all my thoughts are on God and His Wonderful Healing Power. This is the way I feed my subconscious, I constantly identify with God, and my inner thought and feeling is 'Thank you, Father.' I do this hundred times a day or a thousand times, if necessary."

The young man had a healing of the blood condition in three months. His inner speech became the same as it would be if he had already been healed. Believe that you have it now and you shall receive. He succeeded by repetition, prayer, and meditation to get his subconscious mind to agree with his desire; then the Creative Power of God responded according to the agreement. Thy faith hath made thee whole.

Example of Wrong Auto-Suggestion

Here is an example of wrong auto suggestion: A member of our organization was trying to sell a home for three years. She would decree, "I release this beautiful home to Infinite Mind. I know it is sold in Divine Order to the right person at the right price, and I give thanks now that this is so." This was her prayer and there is nothing wrong with it, but she constantly neutralized it by silently saying to herself, "Times are slow, the price is too high, people don't have that kind of money. What's wrong with me? Why can't I sell it?" You can see that she was rendering her prayer null and void.

As a man thinketh in his heart so is he. Her inner speech was very negative and that was the way she really felt about the whole matter; therefore that mental state was manifested for three years. She reversed the procedure and every night and morning she would close her eyes for five or six minutes and imagine the writer congratulating her on her sale. During the day her inner speech was: "I give thanks for the sale of my home. The buyer is prospered and blessed because of this purchase." The repetition of these prayers were impressed on her subconscious mind and made manifest. A week later a man who sat next to her in church the following Sunday bought her home and was very satisfied. She realized you can't go in two directions at the same time.

Let the words of my mouth, and the meditation of my heart, be acceptable in thy sight, O Lord, my strength, and my redeemer. Psalms 19:14.

Chapter 18

SUGGESTIONS FOR HARMONIOUS RELATIONSHIPS

Sigmund Freud, the Austrian founder of psychoanalysis, said that unless the personality has love, it sickens and dies. Love includes understanding, good will, and respect for the divinity in the other person. The more love and good will you emanate and exude, the more comes back to you.

If you puncture the other fellow's ego and wound his estimate of himself, you cannot gain his good will. Recognize that every man wants to be loved and appreciated, and made to feel important in the world. Realize that the other man is conscious of his true worth, and that, like you, he feels the dignity of being an expression of the One Life-Principle animating all men. As you do this consciously and knowingly, you build the other person up, and he returns your love and good will.

The best time to prevent a divorce is before marriage. Ignorance of the powers within you is the cause of all of your marital trouble. Learn how to attract the right wife or husband. For instance, if you are a girl seeking a husband, do not begin to tell yourself all of the reasons why you cannot get married; rather tell yourself all of the reasons why you can be happily married. Eradicate the word *cannot* from your vocabulary. He can, who believes he can!

You are now acquainted with the way the subconscious mind works. You know that whatever you impress upon it shall be experienced in your world. Begin now to impress your subconscious mind with the qualities and characteristics you admire in a man.

This is one technique: Sit down at night in your armchair; close your eyes; let go; relax the body; become very quiet, passive, and receptive. Talk to your subconscious mind, and say to it, "I am now attracting a man into my experience who is honest, sincere, loyal, kind, faithful, and prosperous. He is peaceful and happy. These qualities are sinking down into my subconscious mind now. As I dwell upon these qualities, they become a part of me. I know there is an irresistible law of attraction, and that I attract to me a man according to my subconscious belief. I attract that which I feel as true in my subconscious mind. In other words I know that according to the law, I will attract a man in accordance with my feelings, beliefs, and impressions made on my subconscious mind regarding the type of man I seek."

Practice this process of impregnating your subconscious mind; then you will have the joy of attracting a man having the qualities and characteristics you mentally dwelt upon. The subconscious intelligence will open up a pathway whereby both of you will meet according to the irresistible and changeless law of your own subconscious mind. Have a keen desire to give the best that is in you of love, devotion, and cooperation. Be receptive to this gift of love which you have given to your subconscious mind

True marriage finds its bliss and happiness in an accord of ideals, a harmony, and purity of purpose. Let us stop blaming God for the abuses that go on under the name of marriage. The name to many people is like "sounding brass and tinkling cymbal"; it is to them a mockery of the word. Let us awake and discover the true, impersonal, universal love; then marriage will be a happy state or union, blessed by the fire of Divine Love.

Love seeketh not her own. Love is, and all there is, is Love. Love is the knot that binds man and woman (thought and feeling) in the endless cord of life, binding past and future in the eternal present. All that was, and all that shall be, now is; for in Love's eyes time is not. Love is the way of life. Take heed that ye despise not God in human form. He may be at your side in the person of your beloved one, through the working of God's grace.

The desire for freedom is oftentimes a desire to marry another. By example, a lady gets a divorce; she is bitter and resentful towards her former husband. If she remarries without forgiving, what does she find? The second is worse than the first! She tries a third, a fourth, and a fifth time; each is worse than the preceding one. All the while she does not know that her inner mood of resentment caused her to attract similar types of men based upon the laws of attraction.

The cure is to give herself a mood of love and peace for the mood of resentment; then she has forgiven (given for) herself. She has given the mood of love for the mood of hate; she is at peace. Living in the mood of resentment over supposed wrongs committed by a former husband caused her to attract lack and limitation, because she was living and moving in the attitude of lack.

Her ideas of love and marriage have to change as she seeks to find true harmony. She must lift love to a spiritual basis. Let us not limit love, bind it, or circumscribe it. Love, freedom, and respect are one, and the one is three. If any one of them is absent, there is no love present; the three are synonymous.

"But he said unto them, 'All men cannot receive this saying, save they to whom it is given.'" All men cannot see this truth. They believe in chance, coincidence, accidents, good luck, and bad luck. They cannot receive the saying: "All is Law, and all is Love." There is only Law, and there cannot be chance, coincidence, or bad luck in a world ruled by Law.

An unhappy marriage or divorce is a perfect out-picturing of a given state of consciousness. It is the external manifestation of the discord in the man and his wife. It is good and very good, therefore; it is a perfect working of a Law which never changes, or plays favorites. We see a part of the process and condemn it, but if we could see spiritually, we would see the perfect ending. "All men shall see the transcendent glory which I am." When we learn that the Law is really one of freedom, and cooperate with it, we find it is a Law of Love.

Marriage between man and woman should be an act of love. Honesty, sincerity, kindness, and integrity are forms of love. Each should be perfectly honest and sincere with the other. There is not a true marriage when the man marries a woman for her money, social position, or to lift his ego, because there is no sincerity or honesty there. The marriage is not of the heart. When a woman says, "I am tired working; I want to get married, because I want security;" her premise is false; she is not using the laws of mind correctly. Her security depends upon her knowledge of the interaction of the conscious and subconscious mind and its applications.

For example, a woman will never lack for wealth or health if she applies the technique outlined in the respective chapters of this book. Her wealth can come to her independent of her husband, father, or anyone else. A woman is not dependent on her husband for health, peace, joy, inspiration, guidance, love, wealth, security, happiness, or anything in the world. Her security and peace of mind come from her knowledge of the inner powers within her, and her constant use of the laws of her own mind in a constructive fashion. Marrying for money or to get even with someone is, of course, a farce and a masquerade.

A man and a woman must be subjectively united in the sense that a real love or sense of oneness prevails; in other words two hearts are united in love, freedom, and respect.

A number of people have said to me, "Oh, we love each other, why should we bother getting married?" The answer to this is extraordinarily simple: What we subconsciously feel and accept as true is always objectified or made manifest on the screen of space. Their reasoning, therefore, is false and insincere. The law of mind is, "As within, so without."

Let us take the case of a man or a woman who has made an honest mistake. She now finds herself married to a drug-addict; he refuses to work; she has to support him; he is ruthless and cruel. It is true that due to her state of mind, she attracted that man; yet she is not condemned to live in a world of misery brought about by her own mood or ignorance. Had she used her subconscious mind in the right way, this would not have happened. (I am sure that if you fell into the gutter, slipped perhaps on a banana peel, it would be silly to condemn yourself and stay in the gutter. The obvious thing to do would be to get up out of the gutter, washes yourself, and keep on going.) The woman herein referred to, packed her belongings, and left this man. She realized it was an intolerable situation. Surely this woman is not condemned to live with this man when their hearts and minds are miles apart. You can tie two people together with a rope; yet they can be as far apart as the poles in thought, feeling, and perspective.

Union of Two Hearts

You are divorced mentally when your mind and heart are elsewhere. To stay together in such circumstances is chaotic from all angles. Marriage is a union of two hearts; there is no marriage where the hearts are not bound together in love and peace. Adultery takes place in the heart first. The heart is the seat of the emotions. If you are resentful, hateful, and critical of your partner, you have already committed adultery in your heart.

To direct your mental and emotional operations along destructive and negative channels is to commit adultery. Always remember the adulterous state takes place in the mind. Bodily acts follow mental states; they do not proceed.

Perhaps as you read these pages, you are saying, "I know a young couple who got married recently. They both used the laws of mind; they seemed perfectly happy in every way. Now they are contemplating a divorce." The mental attitude which attracted and endeared them to each other must be maintained and strengthened, in order to preserve the marriage. If a disagreement arises or some slight argument occurs, and one of the partners engages the mind on a negative idea such as resentment or hostility, he is uniting with the error in his mind, and it is destructive to marital happiness.

The little arguments and quarrels which married people engage in will not hurt; it is the sustained grudge or ill feeling which does the damage. When the harsh words said are all forgotten and forgiven a few minutes later, no harm has been done. It is when the feeling of being hurt is prolonged, that the danger lies.

If a man begins to brood, grows morbid against his wife, because of the things she said or did, he is committing adultery, since he is mentally engaged in bitterness. This mood will endanger the marriage except he forgives and radiates love and goodwill to his partner. Let the man who is bitter and resentful swallow his sharp remarks; let him go to great length to be considerate, kind, and courteous. He can deftly skirt the difference. Through practice and mental effort, he can get out of the habit of antagonism; then he will be able to get along better not only with his wife, but with business associates also. Assume the harmonious state, and eventually you will find peace and harmony.

The Quickest Way to Get Rid of a Man

Let us have a few remarks about the nagging wife. Many times the reason she is a nagger is because she gets no attention; oftentimes it is a craving for love and affection. Give it to her. There is also the nagging type of woman who wants to make the man conform to her particular pattern. This is about the quickest way in the world to get rid of a man.

The wife and the husband must cease being scavengers—always looking at the petty faults or errors in each other. Let each give attention and praise to the positive and wonderful qualities in the other.

Suggested Do's and Don'ts

A great mistake is to discuss your marital problems or difficulties with neighbors and relatives. Suppose, for example, a wife says to the neighbor, "John never gives me any money; he treats my mother abominably; drinks to excess, and he is constantly abusive and insulting." Now this wife is degrading and belittling her husband in the eyes of all of the neighbors and relatives; he no longer appears as the ideal husband to them. Never discuss your marital problems with anyone except a trained counselor. Why have many people thinking negatively of your marriage? Moreover, as you discuss and dwell upon these shortcomings of your husband, you are actually creating these states within yourself. Who is thinking and feeling it? You are! As you think and feel, so are you.

Relatives will usually always give you the wrong advice; it is usually biased and prejudiced, because it is not given in an impersonal way. Any advice you receive which violates the golden rule—which is a cosmic law—is not good or sound. It is well to remember that no two human beings ever lived beneath the same roof without clashes of temperament, periods of hurts, and strain. Never display the unhappy side of your marriage to your friends. Keep your quarrels to yourself. Refrain from criticism and condemnation of your partner.

If there are children in the home, let the father praise their mother; let him call attention at times to her fine qualities and the happy aspects of the home.

A husband must not try to make his wife over into a second edition of himself. The tactless attempt to change her in may ways is so foreign to her nature; these attempts are always foolish; many times they result in a dissolution of the marriage. These attempts to alter her destroy her pride and self-esteem, and arouse a spirit of contrariness and resentment that proves fatal to the marriage bond.

Adjustments are needed, of course, but if you have a good look inside of your own mind, and study your character and behavior, you will find so many shortcomings there to keep you busy the rest of your life. If you say, "I will make him over into what I want," you are looking for trouble and the divorce court. You are asking for misery. You will have to learn the hard way that there is no one to change but yourself.

If you have a marital problem, ask yourself what it is you want; then realize that you can achieve that goal. You would solve your marital problem in the same way as any other problem. Define clearly what you want; then realize that what the mind engages in, it creates.

A woman told me one time that after thirty years her husband to drink heavily, neglecting his home and children. She began to claim peace and harmony in her home and heart. She paid no attention to the circumstances or conditions. She quietly engaged her mind on her goal, knowing that his subconscious mind would bring about and magnify what she gave her attention to. Harmony and peace were again restored after a few months devotion to her true goal. This is an illustration of the miracles of the subconscious mind.

By resenting and fighting the situation, this woman would only make matters worse. If there is quarrelling and bickering in the home, turn your attention on your ideal, which is love, peace, and harmony. As you feed your mind upon these ideas, the subconscious mind will respond and bring about harmony.

I am often asked this question, "If one of the partners has an intense desire to terminate the marriage, and the other has an equally intense desire to remain united in marriage, and they are both sincere, what will happen?" In such case there is a mental tug of war; this is a house divided again itself; sooner or later it will dissolve; however, their attitude of mind may prolong the situation.

The proper and correct way to solve this marital problem is to lift the thought above personalities and conditions, and begin to direct your thought to your true desire, trusting the infinite intelligence within you to bring about the perfect solution. Through the right application of the law of your subconscious mind, you can bring harmony where discord is, and resurrect peace where confusion reigns; moreover, the right application of your subconscious mind can dissolve a bad marriage.

Do not let foolish pride, anger, and a desire to get even take you to the divorce court, when all of the while your heart is one with the husband you left. Let love, goodwill and kindness lead you back to the one you love in your heart. You can heal any problem through the right application and direction of your subconscious mind. Listening to the intuition or guidance which comes from the subjective wisdom within you would have perhaps prevented you from contracting the present marriage. You did not know how to use it; now you do. If you had a bad start, you can adjust it now by using the procedure and techniques outlined in this chapter. By exalting, and lifting up your partner in thought and feeling, and always cherishing the lovely qualities which brought you together, you can make your marriage a beautiful experience and a joy forever.

Chapter 19

THE LAW OF LIFE IS THE LAW OF BELIEF

Whatever thoughts, beliefs, opinions, theories, or dogmas you write, engrave, or impress on your subconscious mind, you shall experience them as the objective manifestation of circumstances, conditions, and events. What you write on the inside, you will experience on the outside. You have two sides to your life, objective and subjective, visible and invisible thought and its manifestation.

Your thought is received by your brain, which is the organ of your conscious reasoning mind. When your conscious or objective mind accepts the thought completely, it is sent to the solar plexus, called the brain of your mind, where it becomes flesh and is made manifest in your experience.

As previously outlined, your subconscious cannot argue. It acts only from what you write on it. It accepts your verdict or the conclusions of your conscious mind as final. This is why you are always writing on the book of life, because your thoughts become your experiences. The American essayist, Ralph Waldo Emerson said, "Man is what he thinks all day long." Further, Emerson said: "All successful men have agreed in being causations." They believed that things were not by luck but by law, and that there was not a weak or cracked link in the chain that joins the first and the last of things—the cause and the effect. Shallow men believe in luck; wise and strong men believe in cause and effect.

The law of life is the law of belief. Whatever you mentally accept and feel to be true will come to pass. Learn to believe in the workings of your subconscious mind, knowing that whatever you impress on your subconscious will be expressed subsequently in your experience. The way you really think and feel deep down in your heart governs all phases of your life.

Believe in good fortune, and you shall have it. I believe that "luck" is a very good word if you put a "p" before it. The man who believes that luck controls his destiny is ever waiting for something to turn up. He lies in bed, hoping that the postman will bring him news of a legacy or that he has won the Irish Sweepstakes. The other man fashions, molds, and shapes his future by his attitude of mind. He knows that he is born to succeed and that he is equipped to be a winner, and with a busy pen or ringing hammer he lays the foundation of a competence. He is industrious, zealous, and diligent in his work, and he whistles while he labors. The man who thinks about luck usually whines, whimpers, and complains. Luck relies on chance. Successful men rely on character, for character is destiny.

Mark Twain said, "Fortune knocks at every man's door, but in a good many cases the man is in a neighborhood saloon and does not hear her." Man must be alert, alive, and on the *qui vive*. He must take advantage of the opportunities all around him. Man must not expect to be rewarded for indolence, apathy, or slothfulness.

Man is what he thinks all day long, and his character is the totality of his thinking. Cause and effect are as absolute and undeviating in the hidden realm of thought as in the world of visible and material things. Man's joy and suffering are the reflections of his habitual thinking. Thus does a man garner the sweet and bitter experiences in his life?

In order to experience good luck or good fortune, realize that you are the master of your thoughts, emotions, and reactions to life. You are the maker and shaper of your conditions, experiences, and events. Every thought felt as true, or allowed to be accepted as true by your conscious mind, takes root in your subconscious mind, blossoms sooner or later into act, and bears its own fruit of opportunity and experience. Good thoughts bring forth good fruit; bad thoughts harvest bad fruit.

It is not cruel fate that sends a man to jail or to the poorhouse, but it is the pathway of vicious, destructive, or criminal thinking which he had been secretly fostering in his heart. When these reached a point of saturation in his subconscious mind, they were precipitated into external experiences, fashioned after the image and likeness of his negative thinking.

The Wonders of the Subconscious Mind

Many scientists realize the true importance of the subconscious mind. Edison, Marconi, Kettering, Poincare, Einstein, and many others have used the subconscious mind. It has given them the insight and the "know-how" for all their great achievements in modern science and industry. Research has shown that the ability to bring into action the subconscious power has determined the success of all the great scientific and research workers.

An instance of how a famous chemist, Friedrich von Stradonitz, used his subconscious mind to solve his problem as follows: He had been working laboriously for a long time trying to rearrange the six carbon and the six hydrogen atoms of the benzene formula, and he was constantly perplexed and unable to solve the matter. Tired and exhausted, he turned the request over completely to his subconscious mind. Shortly afterward, as he was about to board a London bus, his subconscious presented his conscious mind with a sudden flash of a snake biting its own tail and turning around like a pin wheel. This answer, from his subconscious mind, gave him the long-sought answer of the circular arrangement of the atoms that is known as the benzene ring.

How a Distinguished Scientist Brought Forth His Inventions

Nicola Tesla was a brilliant electrical scientist who brought forth the most amazing innovations. When an idea for a new invention came into his mind, he would build it up in his imagination, knowing that his subconscious mind would reconstruct and reveal t his conscious mind all the parts needed for its manufacture in concrete form. Through quietly contemplating every possible improvement, he spent no time in correcting defects, and was able to give the technicians the perfect product of his mind.

He said, "Invariably, my device works as I imagined it should. In twenty years there has not been a single exception."

The Secret of Guidance

The secret of guidance or right action is to mentally devote yourself to the right answer, until you find its response in you. The response is a feeling, an inner awareness, an overpowering hunch whereby you know that you know. You cannot possibly fail or make one false step while operating under the subjective wisdom within you. You will find that all your ways are pleasantness and all your paths are peace.

Predicting My Future

Thou maddest him to have dominion over the works of thy hands . . . (Psalm 8:6). I know that my faith in God determines my future. My faith in God means my faith in all things good. I unite myself now with true ideas and I know the future will be in the image and likeness of my habitual thinking. "As a man thinketh in his heart, so is he." "Whatsoever things are true, whatsoever things are honest, whatsoever things are just, whatsoever are lovely, and of good report," day and night I meditate on these things, and I know that these seeds (thoughts) which I habitually dwell upon will become a rich harvest for me. I am the captain of my own soul; I am the master of my fate; for my thought and feeling are my destiny.

Remember that the future, the result of your habitual thinking, is already in your mind except when you change it through prayer. The future of a country, likewise, is in the collective subconscious of the people of that nation. There is nothing strange in the dream I had wherein I saw the headlines of the New York newspapers long before the war began. The war had already taken place in mind, and all the plans of attack were already engraved on that great recording instrument, the subconscious mind or collective unconscious of the universal mind. Tomorrow's events are in your subconscious mind, so are next week's and next month's, and they may be seen by a highly psychic or clairvoyant person.

No disaster or tragedy can happen to you if you decide to pray. Nothing is predetermined or foreordained. Your mental attitude, i.e., the way you think, feel, and believe determines your destiny. You can, through scientific prayer, which is explained in a previous chapter, mold, fashion, and create your own future. *Whatsoever a man soweth, that shall he also reap.*

Suggested Highlights to Recall

1. Remember that the subconscious mind has determined the success and wonderful achievements of all great scientific workers.
2. By giving your conscious attention and devotion to the solution of a perplexing problem, your subconscious mind gathers all the necessary information and presents it full blown to the conscious mind.
3. If you are wondering about the answer to a problem, try to solve it objectively. Get all the information you can from research and also from others. If no answer comes, turn it over to your subconscious mind prior to sleep, and the answer always comes. It never fails.
4. You do not always get the answer overnight. Keep on turning your request over t your subconscious until the day breaks and the shadows flee away.
5. You delay the answer by thinking it will take a long time or that it is a major problem. Your subconscious has no problem, it knows only the answer.
6. Believe that you have the answer now. Feel the joy of the answer and the way you would feel if you had the perfect answer. Your subconscious will respond to your feeling.
7. Any mental picture, backed by faith and perseverance, will come to pass through the miracle-working power of your subconscious. Trust it, believe in its power, and wonders will happen as you pray.

8. Your subconscious is the storehouse of memory, and within your subconscious are recorded all your experiences since childhood.
9. Turn over your request for a solution to your subconscious prior to sleep. Trust it and believe in it, and the answer will come. It knows all and sees all, but you must not doubt or question its powers.
10. The action is your thought, and the reaction is the response of your subconscious mind. If your thoughts are wise, your actions and decisions will be wise.
11. Guidance comes as a feeling, an inner awareness, and an overpowering hunch whereby you know that you know. It is an inner sense of touch. Follow it.

CHAPTER 20

THE POWER OF SUGGESTION TO SUCCESS

Every person in the world wants to succeed. You are born to win, to conquer and to lead the triumphant life. You should be a wonderful success in your prayer life, your chosen work, and your relationship with people and in all other phases of your life.

Success itself is a powerful incentive, for the Life Principle in you are always seeking expression through you at higher levels. You are successful when you lead a full and happy life, when you are expressing yourself at your highest level and contributing your talents to the world. In a successful undertaking you rise as high as you can, and your enterprise is of benefit to humanity. It brings you material reward and its production is a pleasure to you. Success is many-sided, however, and what is deemed success by one may be regarded as failure by another.

He Said, "I Am Not a Success"

Recently I talked with a man who said that he had subordinated all ends to money-making, and he had accumulated a vast amount of money and real estate holdings. He added that in the business world he is called a great success. He admitted to me, though, that he was not a success; he had used questionable means to take advantage of others and had won his fortune through cheating and deceiving others who had trusted him. He was presently suffering from bleeding ulcers and extremely high blood pressure. Furthermore, he had a guilt complex, which meant to him that he had to suffer and be punished.

His bleeding ulcer, as I explained to him, was due to ulcerated thoughts. Further, if he would reverse his thought pattern a healing would follow. He was suffering from the side effects of the drugs he was taking. He consequently reversed his thought patterns by reiterating the following truths out loud night and morning:

"The Lord is my shepherd. I sing the song of the jubilant soul for I have chosen God as my shepherd. Divine Intelligence rules and guides me in all my ways. I shall not want for peace, harmony, or guidance because God's wisdom governs me. I lie down in green pastures always, since God is prospering me beyond my wildest dreams. I find myself beside the still waters as I claim the Infinite peace of God floods my mind and heart. My emotions (waters) are stilled and calm. My mind is now serene and it reflects God's heavenly truths and light (my soul is restored). I think of God's Holy Presence within me all day long. I walk the path of righteousness through my devotion and attention to God's eternal verities. I know there is no death and I fear no evil. I know 'God has not given us the spirit of fear, but of love and power, and a sound mind.' God's rod (love) and staff (truth comfort, sustain and nourish me. The banquet table of God is always set before me; it is the secret place of the Most High, where in my thoughts I walk and talk with God. I eat the nourishing truths of God whenever fear and worry (my enemies) trouble me. The bread I eat is God's idea of peace, love and faith in all things good. The meat I eat is the omnipotence of God; the wine I drink is the essence of joy. The wisdom of God anoints my intellect; it is a lamp unto my feet and a light on my path. My cup (heart) is truly the chamber of God's Holy Presence; it runneth over with love and joy. I mentally dwell on goodness, truth and beauty; this is my house of God."

As he saturated his mind with the interpretation of the 23rd Psalm over a period of time, he noticed a distinct change in his whole demeanor and outlook on life. He became more kindly, considerate and more loving in all ways. Drugs were no longer necessary. He discovered that a changed attitude changed everything.

He ceased condemning himself. The Life Principle never condemns, and when you begin to use your mind in the right way, right results follow. Your mind is a principle, and if you think good, good follows; if you think lack, lack follows. The Life Principle holds no grudges, no more so than the principles of mathematics or chemistry hold grudges.

You may have been fired by companies you worked for because you could not add or subtract correctly, but by following proper instruction you don't make these mistakes any more. The principle of mathematics has no grudge against you. The same is true of your mind. Begin to use the law of mind in the right way according to the Golden Rule and the law of love. The Mind Principle has no Grudge against you. The past is forgotten and remembered no more.

The Law of Reversibility

Edison knew that speech produced adulatory waves and theorized that these vibrations could reproduce the speech or song. In other words, he conceived of inverse transformation, the reproduction of speech or song by mechanical motion, namely the phonograph.

Students of scientific laws know that all transformations of force are reversible. Heat produces mechanical motion. Reverse it and you discover that mechanical motion can produce heat. Science says electricity produces magnetism; likewise, magnetism can produce electric currents. Cause and effect, energy and matter, action and reaction are the same and are inter-convertible.

Therefore, I say unto you. What things sever ye desire, when ye pray, believe that ye receive them, and ye shall have them (Mark 11:24). Here you are told to pray, believing that you already possess what you pray for. This is based on the law of inverse transformation.

Achieving Success Through Prayer

A mother wished to visit her son in London, who was graduating from college. However, she did not have the necessary funds. I asked her what her attitude would be if she were over there now, embracing him and witnessing the graduation exercises. She said, "Oh! I would be so happy! I would be delighted."

I suggested that she experiment at night prior to sleep, making there here and the future now and to feel herself embracing her son, making the whole scene vivid and realistic—so much so that when she opened her eyes she would be amazed that she was not in London with her son.

Experimenting along these lines, the third night she subjectified the state. When she opened her eyes she was really amazed that she was not physically there. The answer to her prayer came with the repayment of a loan she had given to a woman ten years previously. With the interest added to it, it was more than the amount necessary for her trip.

She assumed that she was already witnessing the ceremony and conversing with her son, and that joyous feeling and assumption brought about the joy of the answered prayer. She contemplated her objective as an accomplished fact. She understood that all transformations of force are reversible. She knew that her physical presence in London would bring her great joy and satisfaction. Capturing in her mind the joy that would be hers in being there, this mood, she knew, must produce the answer to her prayer.

. . . . He . . . . Falleth those things, which be not as though they were (Romans 4:17). Success in your prayer life is based on laws of mind. Realize that if a physical fact can produce a joyous mental state in you, the joyous mental state can produce the physical fact.

The Successful Man

When a man uses unscrupulous financial or business methods, he may not suffer financial, loss, but loss can come to him in many ways, such as loss of health, loss of promotion, loss of prestige, loss of self-respect, loss of love, etc., for the ways of the subconscious are past finding out. All misdeeds or misuse of the law of mind must be accounted for sooner or later.

The only success that permits a man to rest peacefully and harmoniously is that which conforms to the Golden Rule, i.e., to think, speak and act toward others as he would wish others to think, speak, feel and act toward him. Success is primarily moral and spiritual, governed by honesty, integrity and justice and tempered by goodwill to all men everywhere.

All of us are interdependent, and it is reasonable to assume that the welfare of others is essential to the success of every man. It is undoubtedly true that the more man cares for and appreciates the spiritual life, the more he will use his material wealth wisely, judiciously and constructively.

A spiritually-minded person should be comfortably housed, clothed and fed. In other words, he realizes that all things are here for his use and enjoyment . . . *God, who giveth us richly all things to enjoy* (I Timothy 6:17).

It is true that no one possesses anything in the absolute sense. God possesses all, but we have the use of God's treasures in the earth, including the sea and the air. A spiritual-minded person should have all the money he needs to do what he wants to do, and when he wants to do it. Money is simply a medium of exchange, and it has taken many forms down through the ages. It is God's way of maintaining the economic health of a nation.

You must realize that a spiritual work or a spiritual organization is not a success if it is constantly begging for more money. This practice is evidence of downright failure. This could be called spurious spirituality. If the spiritual approach to life is successful, it is needed by the world and will be supported.

The successful man is not a mere partisan, but a real truth seeker. The spiritual-minded person is not a proselyte, but a co-worker on the way. The secret of the truth seeker is his fidelity to the inner promptings of his Higher Self. The Infinite Presence in each of us grants us the potentialities of success, and we are here to go forth conquering and to conquer.

She Ceased Blocking the Answer

A woman wrote me saying, "I don't know what to do. I am full of fear. Shall I accept the new position offered me or stay where I am? Shall I keep or sell my home? Shall I marry the man with whom I am going? I must have answers right away; what decisions shall I make?"

Her fear of doing the wrong thing was blocking the answers to these perplexing questions. Furthermore, her fear was really based on ignorance and failure to understand the workings of her subconscious mind.

I explained to her that whenever her subconscious accepts an idea, immediately it begins to execute it. It uses all its mighty resources to that end and mobilizes all the unlimited mental and spiritual powers in our depths. This law is true for good or bad ideas.

The young lady ceased blocking her answer by such statements as, "I will never get an answer. I don't know what to do. I'm all mixed up." She came to a clear-cut conclusion in her conscious mind, knowing that Infinite Intelligence within her subconscious knows only the answer.

She prayed frequently as follows: "Infinite Intelligence is all-wise. The wisdom of my subconscious mind reveals to me the right answers. I am Divinely guided regarding my home and my selection of a husband, and I am confident Infinite Intelligence knows my hidden talents and guides me to my true place in life where I am doing what I love to do, divinely happy and Divinely prospered."

This woman accepted a position in a legal office, married her employer, and both of them live in her home. There was a perfect solution and an ideal answer to all her requests. The wisdom of the subconscious is past finding out.

Not Successful in the Art of Living

Recently I gave some spiritual advice to a president of a very large corporation. He was very successful, had all the money he needed, lived in a million dollar home and had all the comforts and luxuries of life. Of course, there is nothing wrong with that. He came to this country penniless and had reached the top in his field, all of which is good.

However, he was not successful in the art of living. He had very high blood pressure, and suffered from migraine headaches and colitis. He said to me, "I am a nervous wreck. I have tried tranquilizers, sedatives, antispasmodic tablets and nothing seems to help."

I suggested that all he really needed was peace of mind and that no one could give him that but himself. I pointed out to him the direction where he could find it. I suggested that he read and meditate on the inner meaning of the 23rd Psalm two or three times a day and affirm frequently during the day, "God's peace fills my soul." I emphasized that if he began to think constructively and about the eternal verities in the 23rd Psalm is given. He had an open mind and began to meditate on the Psalm and other chapters of the book. He found that inner quietude and peace which he had been seeking. Turning back to the God Presence within and communing with Divine love and Divine peace, his soul was restored.

He Opened His Mind

A full cup cannot receive any more. There are some minds so full of false beliefs, opinions, and weird and grotesque concepts of God that it is impossible to insert anything new, vital and constructive. I recently said to an alcoholic, "Admit that you are an alcoholic. Open your mind to new ideas and suggestions. A closed mind can receive no suggestions, no more so than your closed hand can receive a proffered gift of a book from me."

He said that his excessive drinking was all due to pressure and tension at work. He made a great deal of money, but most of it went to the bar. He was hungry and thirsty for a healing. At his point he came to a decision that he wanted to be healed, which in itself is seventy-five percent of the healing process.

I explained to him that his subconscious mind would accept suggestions and that his sincerity was essential. At night prior to sleep, he affirmed feelingly, knowingly and lovingly: "God gives me freedom, sobriety and peace of mind. Thank you, Father." That was his prayer for five or six minutes every night. Actually, he was writing with his conscious mind freedom, peace and sobriety in his subconscious mind. In less than a week he succeeded in impregnating his subconscious mind and he lost all desire for alcohol.

The True Lord

The Bible says: Come unto me, all ye that labor and are heavy laden, and I will give you rest (Matthew 11:28). The Bible is a psychological and spiritual textbook and is not referring to a particular man. The characters in the Bible are personifications of truth. You do not go to any person for rest, security or peace of mind. You go to the God of peace within you and boldly claim: "God's river of peace, love and joy is now flowing through me vitalizing, healing and restoring my soul."

The Divine Presence is within you. As you contemplate God's love, light, truth and beauty in your own heart, you are enfranchised and lifted up because you have found God in your own heart. The Divine Center is within you.

The Psalmist says,* *Rest in the Lord, and wait patiently for him* .... (Psalm 37:7). The word "Lord" represents spiritually the Lordly power, which is God; but to "rest in the Lord" means to rest and trust that Infinite Spirit in you which created you, governs all your vital organs as you sleep and is in complete control of all externals. In other words, it is your Higher Self.

In ancient times there were feudal barons who had the power of life and death over the serfs, slaves and peasants under their control. The lords in England today represent titled nobility and have no such power. Look at the whole thing this way: The Lord in you is really your dominant conviction, your master thought or belief, which controls and dominates all lesser thoughts, ideas, opinions, actions and reactions. For example, your Lord could be fear, i.e., if you are dominated by fear. If fear predominates, then fear governs and controls all your thoughts, feelings, actions and reactions.

A wonderful Lord to enthrone in your mind would be a God of love ruling, guiding, and directing you along all lines. This dominant conviction would work wonders in your life, and your whole world would magically melt in the image and likeness of your dominant conviction. When Divine love and Divine right action govern you, the true Lord is ruling in you and will keep you in peace. You will be successful in your work and in your relationships with people. You will have good health and be free from despondency and melancholia.

Your dominant belief rules your world and determines your future, where you shall go and what your experiences will be, whether good or bad. Quimby said in 1847: "Man is belief expressed." You will be assured of success, true expression and harmonious relations with others when you make it a habit to tune in to the Divine Center within you and look upon the Divine Presence within you as a guide, counselor, way shower and source of your promotion and welfare. Then all the petty, fearful, annoying worries, jealousies and envies will fall away. There is no room for them in your mind anymore.

All of us suffer until we get the sight to look within. The Bible says: ... *In returning and rest shall ye be saved*. (Isaiah 30:15).

Successful Living

There is a man of over ninety years, chronologically speaking, who comes to hear me occasionally on Sunday mornings. Recently he said to me that about thirty years ago he had had the same concept of God as he had had when a little boy. His concept was that of an angry, spiteful God, a sort of Oriental sultan who ruled tyrannically. He lived in fear and thought that the will of God was

---

* See *Songs of God. An Interpretation of My Favorite Psalms*. By Dr. Joseph Murphy. De Vorss & Co., Marina del Rye. 1979.

IC020915W
398

Dispatch Note

Order Number 106-0663539-0803427   Supplied by PBShop

106-0663539-0803427

Catalogue Number   Title and Artist   Qty

= 9781450004213   The Unbelievable Power of Suggestion [Paperback] [1

Thanks for shopping with us. Please note that if you ordered more than one item we may ship them in separate packets. If you have a query about your order please email us at:

Returns: Please enclose this slip with your items and return to the address on the front of the packet.
Why are you returning the item? _____
Would you prefer a refund or a replacement? _____

Please note, with some items a replacement is not possible.

that he should suffer. He became very ill and the doctor said, "You have about two months to live. Get your affairs in order."

A young woman visiting another patient in his hospital room gave him a pamphlet on how to use the Healing Power, which he read avidly. All of a sudden, he had a great thirst and hunger to live. He got up out of bed, insisted on going home, and invited all of his friends to a restaurant for dinner and refreshments. He said, "I am celebrating my resurrection." His belief and new insight into the Infinite Healing Presence within him responded, and his spiritual transfusion transformed his whole life.

He said that he has accomplished far more in the last thirty years than he had in all the previous sixty years. He broke away from all of the old, moth-eaten patterns, the old ruts and false concepts, and entered into a new life wherein he contributed to the success of all those he supervised and befriended.

Emerson said, "Nothing will give you peace but the triumph of principles." You would not wire your house unless you understood and applied the principles of electricity. You would not manufacture chemicals unless you understood the principles of chemistry. In building a house, you must be initiated into the principles of construction. If you decide to become a musician, you must study music and practice, and as time goes on, perhaps you can play a classical piece of music even though blindfolded. You will have established the equivalent in your subconscious mind, which enables you to play automatically.

Your mind is a principle. Think good and good follows; think of lack and limitation and you experience lack and impoverishment. You are what you think all day long. Learn the laws of your mind and practice them. For example, any idea you have which is emotionalized and felt as true enters into your subconscious mind and comes to pass. Knowing that, you are careful how you impress your subconscious mind.

Why They Did Not Pay

During a conversation I had with a practitioner, she mentioned that she gives people a lot of time and good advice but many never pay her. I suggested to her that she could overcome that by affirming that all those who come to her are blessed, healed and prospered and that they gladly pay in Divine order.

She changed her attitude and her subconscious responded. The reason many clients had not paid her was because in the daytime she was a social worker and her subjective thinking was about poor people and poverty. She became very successful following her new insight into the way the mind works.

Some Common Superstitions

Many people say, "If it's the will of God, I want it." If your prayer is preceded by "if," your manifestation will be very "iffy" and probably will never come to pass. A woman seeking companionship said, "I'm too old. I'm homely." She recited all the reasons why she could not get married instead of all the reasons why she could.

I said to the woman who had these defeatist ideas, "The man you are seeking is seeking you. The last time he got married his wife was so beautiful she ran around and slept with all the boys. He does not want that now; he wants you."

I continued by saying that she should read the newspapers and see all the names and ages of people sixty, seventy and eighty years of age getting married. Infinite Spirit will attract to you the right companion in Divine order, but you must claim it. Think of all your good qualities and what you have to give a man. Let that be your broadcast, and by the law of reciprocal relationship, you will attract the right man into your life. Your sincerity will make it real.

She followed these simple suggestions and in due course received an answer to her prayer.

Another superstition is, "If it's God's will." That is too absurd for words. The will of God is a greater measure of life, freedom, expression and growth. Any idea or desire that you have for growth, wealth, success or healing is the will of God for you. Focus on your desire. Bring your conscious and subconscious together at one point—then you will bring your desire to pass.

Another superstition is, "If it's right for me." What is not right for you? It is right for you to lead the abundant life. It is right for you to lead the abundant life. It is right for you to have perfect health, peace, harmony, joy, abundance, security, true place and all the blessings of life. God gave you richly all things to enjoy.

The Law of Mind is Impersonal

Take a weaver's loom. All threads are on it—black, brown, yellow, etc. The loom takes all the threads and cares not. Supposing you look at a carpet and say that it is awful, an eyesore. Change the thread and the loom is mechanical and responds accordingly. Your conscious mind is the weaver; your subconscious is the loom.

A man opens up a brothel and makes a lot of money. The subconscious does not care; it has no morals. It expresses what is suggested upon it, whether good or bad. For example, a man may inherit a lot of money. Perhaps he will spend it badly. Perhaps he will gamble and lose it all, or perhaps, if he is of a religious persuasion, he will teach limitation and suggest fear into the minds of people.

Remember, the law is impersonal. If you misuse the law by hurting others or by robbing or depriving them in any way, the law of your mind responds in its own way . . . *Vengeance is mine; I will repay, saith the Lord* (Romans 12:19). Live according to your highest ideals.

A man asked me why it was the sexual perverts and dope fiends write good poetry, music and wonderful plays. The answer is simple: God, or Infinite Intelligence, is no respecter of persons and will respond to the altruist, pervert or murderer, providing he believes; and according to his belief is it done unto him.

Another superstition that some people have is that God is testing them. They have a sort of Messianic complex that God is up there in the clouds somewhere and is going to drop a great challenge to them to see how they are going to handle it. God does not punish or test anyone. Man punishes himself because of ignorance and misuse of the laws of mind. The only sin is ignorance, and all the suffering in the world is the consequence.

You Are Unique

The poet said: "We are all parts of one stupendous whole whose body nature is and God the soul." There must be joy in our work. In olden days when they made a table, a statue or a chair, there was a song in their heart. They took pride in their work. The larger piece in the table or the building needs the small. All the component parts go to make up the unit. You are needed. There is no misfit in the universe. All notes are necessary for the symphony.

There is no one in the entire world that can do something just like you because only you are you. You are unique. If you are a cook you are essential to the General of the Army. There is nothing useless but your belief and concept that you are. Your subconscious accepts what you really believe, and you experience accordingly.

Putting God First

Recently I conducted a memorial service for a man who was 104 years old. His widow said that as far as she could recall, he had never been sick, but the night prior to his transition, though, he had told her that he was going on to meet his loved ones. He then passed on in his sleep. His widow said that every morning of his life he had read out loud the 91st Psalm, emphasizing the phrase; *with long life will I satisfy him . . .* (Psalm 91:16). He emphasized the following statement also: *Thou wilt show me the path of life . . .* (Psalm 16:11). *Keep thy heart with all diligence; for out of it are the issues of life* (Proverbs 4:23).

Life to this man meant a life of happiness, achievement and usefulness. He enjoyed life and gave of his talents in a wonderful way. The long life spoken of in the Bible is a long period of joy, freedom, peace and accomplishment. The abundant life comes to all when they keep and practice the Golden Rule and put God first in their lives.

Suggested Prayer for Business Success

"*'Wits ye not that I be about my Father's business?'* . . . Luke 2:49. I know that my business, profession or activity is God's business. God's business is always basically successful. I am growing in wisdom and understanding every day. I know, believe and accept the fact that God's law of abundance is always working for me, through me and all around me.

"My business or profession is full of right action and right expression. The ideas, money, merchandise and contacts that I need are mine now and at all times. All these things are irresistibly attracted to me by the law of universal attraction. God is the life of my business; I am Divinely guided and inspired in all ways. Every day I am presented with wonderful opportunities to grow, expand and progress. I am building up goodwill. I am a great success because I do business with others as I would have them do it with me.

Take a Personal Inventory

Are you experiencing friction, and resentment in your relationships with others? These unsatisfactory personal adjustments are due to the bad company you are keeping in your mind. When you were young, your mother warned you to keep away from bad company, and if you disobeyed you were soundly spanked. In a somewhat similar manner, you must not walk down the dark alleys of your mind and keep the company of resentment, fear, worry, ill will, and hostility; these are the thieves of your mind which rob you of poise, balance, harmony, and health.

You must positively and definitely refuse to walk and talk with them in the galleries of your mind. On the contrary, you must make it a practice to walk the sunlit streets of your mind, associating with lovely, spiritual companions called confidence, peace, faith, love, joy, good will, health, happiness, guidance, inspiration, and abundance. You can choose your companions in the objective world, and I feel sure that when you do you will select them according to the criteria of honesty and integrity.

You select your clothes, work, friends, teachers, books, home, and food. You are a choosing, volitional being. When you choose something, you portray a preference for one thing over another; it may be a hat or a pair of shoes.

Having taken a personal inventory of the contents of your mind, choose health, happiness, peace and abundance, and you will reap fabulous dividends.

Understanding Banishes Needless Suffering

You must give up your false beliefs, opinions, and theories and exchange them for the truth which sets you free. You are not a victim of your five senses; neither are you controlled by external conditions or environment. You can change conditions by changing your mental attitude. Your thought and feeling create your destiny and determine your experience. Therefore, you can no longer blame others for your misery, pain, or failure.

When you see clearly that what you think, feel, believe, and give mental consent to, consciously or unconsciously, determines all happenings, events, and circumstances of your life, you will cease to fear, resent, condemn, and blame others, you will discover there is no one to change but yourself.

CHAPTER 21

THE POWER OF SUGGESTION TOWARDS WHOLENESS

Recently I talked with a woman in Munich, Germany, who is 80 years of age, chronologically speaking. She said that her physical condition at one time had been considered hopeless and incurable, but that she had been saved from the abyss of death by spiritual means when all material help had failed.

Someone had told her about a spiritual healer. He did not give medicines or drugs. He had no system of physical treatment. He asked her no questions about her symptoms, aches or pains, but sat meditatively by her and said, "Let us think about God and His wonders." Then he affirmed out loud: "God is a loving, guiding Father, immediate and accessible, an intimate healing power. God is present as Living Spirit and His Holy Presence is flowing into all parts of your being."

A remarkable change had taken place as she opened her mind and heart to the influx of the Holy Spirit. Her realization of the Infinite Healing Presence and her receptivity had caused a resurrection of wholeness, vitality and perfection, and a wonderful healing had followed. This is the power of the Spirit, or God. The turning point had come when she had realized that infinite resources of Divine love and wisdom were ready at hand within her.

A Simple Truth

The power of the Spirit (God) is not a half-way measure. We must carry the spiritual life into every sphere of our natural and social interests. We are here to live by the Spirit. God is Spirit, and this Spirit has become manifest in this beautiful world of time and space. This Spirit in us gives us the power to be victorious. There is in a Divine Presence enabling us to lift our problems into heavenly light and see them transfigured by the guidance we claim and receive. There is guidance for every need; there is love for each heart. Love is the greatest healing power, touching the subconscious, quickening, strengthening and transforming us into radiating centers which bless mankind.

Divine Love Heals

After speaking in London a few months ago, I had a conference with a woman who told me that all of a sudden she had suffered from glandular inflammation and her tissues had swollen badly. She was taking medicine and stated that the inflammation would subside for a few weeks, and then the condition would recur.

I asked her about her emotional life, pointing out that glands secrete hormones, and the word hormones means harmony. This woman revealed that she hated her sister, who had cheated her out of a large sum of money, and this hatred and hostility had caused the inflammation of her glands and other organs. In other words, she was imbibing poison.

Accordingly, she decided to release her sister and heal herself. I explained to her that she did not have to mentally coerce or force herself to love her sister, as that procedure would bring about the laws of reversed effort. All she had to do was to fill her soul, or subconscious, with Divine love.

Her prayer was: "God's healing love fills my whole being. God loves me and cares for me. God's river of peace saturates my whole being." She affirmed these truths for 20 minutes at a time, three times a day. She also followed my suggestion, which was that whenever the thought of her sister crossed her mind, she was to affirm: "God's love fills my soul."

I had a wonderful letter from her a week ago, saying: "I am at peace. I no longer need medicine. When my sister comes to my mind, I am at peace. There is no sting there any more. I wish her well." This is the power of love. It dissolves everything unlike itself. If you are at peace and full of goodwill to all, your organs or nerves do not cry out in pain, nor will your stomach give you acute indigestion or ulcers.

He Learned the Value of Blessing Others

During a recent lecture tour in Europe, where I gave seminars in Munich, Frankfurt, Hanover, Zurich, Vienna and London, I met many interesting and outstanding people in the fields of science, medicine, business and politics. A highly placed government official visited me at my hotel in Munich, Germany, saying that he owed his success and advancement to practicing what he had read in *The Power of Your Subconscious Mind*,* which has been published in German for many years.

He said that he had had a rather low position and had been inadequately paid. He realized after reading my book that he had been given to criticizing, condemning and belittling others who had been promoted into higher echelons. In so doing, he realized that he was also demoting himself. He said that he had stopped doing it and had learned to bless them, understand them, appreciate them for what they had accomplished, and decided from that point on to cooperate and get along with them as they were. He continued, saying that he had found that in blessing others and rejoicing in their promotion and advancement, he was also blessing himself. He then told me that he was here to thank me for writing the book.

This was one of the nicest tributes I received on my journey. Love is the universal solvent, and when you ask yourself honestly: Would I like to live with what I am thinking and wishing for the other person? And if the answer is yes, you are building health, happiness, prosperity and success into your own mentality. The reason is very simple: You are the only thinker in your world, and your thought is creative. Whatever you think about the other person, you are also creating in your own life.

The Inner Meaning of the Golden Rule is Important

The Golden Rule is known to almost everyone, but how many understand what it really means? To put it in simple, everyday language, all it means is that whatever you think about another person you are creating in your own life, because your thought is creative. Knowing this to be true, you will be careful to think only God-like thoughts about the other. Every thought tends to manifest itself.

What a different world it would be if all of us practiced the Golden Rule and the law of love. We would create heaven on earth. The average man can quote the Golden Rule by heart, but he does not really understand the inner meaning of it. Therefore, he does not obey it.

And as ye would that men should do to you, do ye also to them likewise (Luke 6:31). This is a directive from within your own soul, which, when followed, brings harmony, health and peace into the lives of all who practice it. If people practiced the Golden Rule there would be no war, no crime, no cruelty, no rape, no suffering and no inhumanity. There would be no need for armies, navies,

---

*   See the Power of Your Subconscious Mind by Dr. Joseph Murphy, Prentice-Hall. Inc., Englewood Cliffs, N.J., 1963.

air forces, police, or atomic or other nuclear weapons. When your thought is right, your action will be right. It is impossible to produce right action out of a negative thought, in the same way that you cannot get an apple tree from a non-viable seed.

She Learned the Secret

A few months ago I gave a seminar in Vienna, Austria. During a conversation with an outstanding golfer, she disclosed that after learning all the rules and the techniques of playing she said to herself every night: "I am relaxed, I am poised, I am serene, and I am calm before every game, and the Almighty Power within me takes over. I play majestically and gloriously. I play for Him."

She had studied the game from all angles, practiced regularly and disciplined her mind and body; but she was smart enough to let her Higher Self govern her hands, stance and direction in its own superior and inimitable way. She saturated her subconscious every night with the right words.

After a certain amount of repetition, she succeeded in impregnating her subconscious and she was compelled to be the great and outstanding golfer. The law of the subconscious is compulsive.

Affirm the Good Constantly

The inside governs the outside. You can't love others unless you have loving and harmonious thoughts in your mind. The people who inhabit your mind are thoughts, ideas, beliefs, opinions and your reactions to everyday events. Be sure they conform to whatsoever things are true, lovely, noble and Godlike.

Your disciples and the disciples mentioned in your Bible represent the disciplined qualities of your mind. Are you disciplining your vision? Your vision is what you are focused on, what you are looking at in your own mind. And you go where your vision is. Your faith is disciplined when you adhere to and give allegiance to the creative laws of your mind and when you believe implicitly in the goodness of God in the land of the living. Your faith is not in creeds, dogmas, traditions, men or institutions, but in the eternal principles, which are the same yesterday, today and forever.

You discipline your imagination when you imagine what is lovely and of good report. Your judgment, when disciplined, means you decide upon the truth or falsity of any thought. When you affirm the good constantly, that is called righteous judgment and brings harmony and peace into your life. Whatever you make real you will demonstrate on the screen of space.

Remember, if your mind is full of fear, worry, resentment, prejudices, anger, jealousy or religious bias, then you cannot really love because the occupants of your mind are the opposite of love. You project your mental attitude upon others and you will blame them and criticize them.

He Said the Explanation Changed His Life

In the month of August, 1979, I spoke in Caxton Hall, London, and said suggested to a troubled man, "You must preach the gospel to yourself. The moneychangers and thieves that you are talking about are in your own mind. You are the temple of consciousness, and the thieves and moneychangers which rob you are fear, ignorance, superstition, self-condemnation, self-criticism and ill will. The spiritually minded man casts all of these thieves and robbers out of his mind by filling his subconscious mind with life-giving patterns and the eternal truths of God. Then he will experience peace and harmony within and confidently express it without, in his body, his business, and in his relationships with all people."

This man had been thinking of a temple which existed 2000 years ago and believed the thieves and moneychangers to be outside of his own mind. Realizing that he was robbing himself of vitality, peace, harmony, wealth and success, he stopped doing it. A light seemed to come into his mind, penetrating the fog. The explanation was the cure.

He Was a Workaholic

Recently, I talked with a man who had said he felt guilty if he did not keep going. He had a sort of compulsion to keep on working even after a full day in the office. He was a "workaholic." He would bring home material and work until midnight on figures, plans and business projects. He had had two heart attacks as well as bleeding ulcers, all due to ulcerated thoughts and emotional upheavals.

He had forgotten that God had ordained the Sabbath—not as a day of the week, but as a time of mental rest where you may tune in with the Infinite, claiming frequently: "Infinite Spirit leads and guides me in all my ways. God's river of peace saturates my mind and heart."

I suggested to him that every evening he set aside some time for prayer and meditation, such as reading and meditating on the 91st, 23rd, 27th, 46th and 42nd Psalms, alternating from time to time. He realized that he should turn regularly to the Source of strength, inspiration and quiet moments in the contemplation of God and His love, which would work wonders in his life.

He began meditating during his lunch hour, as well as every morning, on the great truths of *Quiet Moments with God** and discovered that he was completely

---

* See Quiet Moments with God by Dr. Joseph Murphy. De Vorss and Company, Inc., Marina del Rye, Ca., 1958 (Twelfth Printing.1978).

released from the tension-making activities and anxieties of the day. Don't forget to call regularly and systematically on the wisdom of God to anoint your intellect and the power of the Almighty to strengthen you. Take five or ten minutes two or three times a day to dwell on the great truths of God; then you are practicing the Sabbath, which is to surrender to God and let an influx of the Holy Spirit invade and nourish your mind and body.

This man started to invite the Infinite Spirit within him to participate in all of his undertakings, and he discovered that his Senior Partner—his Higher Self—revealed to him better ways to do all things.

Millions celebrate the Sabbath on the outside, thinking it is a sin to drive a nail in a piece of wood, etc.—all of which is absurd. They do not know that the Sabbath is on the inside. They fail to realize that it is celebrated every day, when man abides in the consciousness of the ever-availability of goodness, truth, beauty and abundance during the whole course of his life.

Reap a Rich Harvest

Many people have said to me that they wished for prosperity, success and the good things of life, and they prayed for a quiet and relaxed life, but nothing happened. Oftentimes they are so restless, fearful and habitually anxious that their routine thinking has become their master.

The way to overcome this is to think quietly about your desire for promotion, expansion, prosperity and success, realizing that your desire for growth and expansion is from God and that the power of the Almighty is bringing your desire to pass in Divine law and order. Gradually, as you think along these lines, you will succeed integrating your desire in your subconscious mind, which will bring it to pass.

Many people in offices, factories and business establishments are more or less mechanical men and women, merely responding to the pressures and suggestions all around them, in this way, they tend to become automatons by responding to every wind that blows. Many are repeating the wrong thing, both in thought and action. Be sure to repeat to yourself the eternal verities. By repetition, faith and expectancy, you will reap a rich harvest.

True Faith

True faith consists in knowing that the Infinite Presence which crated you from a cell knows all the processes and functions of your body and certainly knows how to heal you. When you consciously tune in on the healing power of your subconscious, knowing and believing it will respond to you, you will get results. In other words, true faith is the combined use of your conscious and subconscious mind scientifically directed for a specific purpose

Blind faith consists of belief in amulets, charms, talismans, bones of saints, certain shrines and waters to heal, etc. In other words, it is faith without any understanding and is often only temporary in its therapeutic value.

I suggest to people who are sick to make use of the services of a physician and to keep on praying not only for themselves but also for the physician.

The following are the reasons why:

> *Honor a physician with the honor due unto him for the uses, which ye may have of him; for the Lord hath created him. For of the highest cometh healing, and he shall receive honor of the king. The Lord Hath created medicines out of the earth; and he that is wise will not abhor them . . . and he hath given men skill, that he might be honored in his marvelous works.*
>
> *"My son, in thy sickness be not negligent, but pray unto the Lord, and he will make thee whole . . . Then give place to the physician, for the Lord hath created him; let him not go from thee, for thou hast need of him. There is a time when in their hands there is good success. For they shall also pray unto the Lord, that he prosper that which they give for ease and remedy to prolong life . . ."* Ecclesiastics, Chapter 38: Paragraphs 1 and 2).

On the Road to Recovery

My friend began to see that he had not reached the cause of his condition. He began to understand that true, permanent healing comes with forgiveness, love and goodwill to all, and spiritual insight—all these are real healing forces. He admitted he was seething with hostility, guilt, resentment and hatred toward many people. He began to realize that his destructive emotions contributed to his condition. I suggested that he cooperate with his doctor and pray for him and also bless him, which he promised to do.

Suggested Technique

In counseling a young man whose basic problem was that he was chronically ill, it became apparent that as soon as he recovered from one ailment he acquired another sickness. He had had six operations in six years. He maintained an image of himself as being sick. He had been told when he was young that he was sickly and would always be weak. He accepted this and, as a result, learned to be unhealthy. His belief that he was always destined to be sickly was in his subconscious mind, and whatever he believed came to pass.

Under my direction, he reversed this image and practiced the mirror treatment every morning for about five or ten minutes. He looked in the mirror and affirmed out loud: "I AM all health. God is my health." Gradually, the idea of wholeness entered into his subconscious mind, and he is now free from a false belief. He practiced the technique I gave him diligently and faithfully until it manifested in his life.

Healthy Vision

A young woman 22 years of age said to me, "I am hounded by all kinds of fear." She was afraid of God, of the future, of the after life, of evil entities, of a devil and of voodoo. The Bible says: *For God hath not given us the spirit of fear; but of power and of love, and of a sound mind* (II Timothy 1:7).

I explained to her that when young, we are all highly impressionable and malleable and that her parents and those around her had conditioned her mind with falsehoods about God, life and the universe. She began to realize that she was not born with any fears, sense of guilt or self-condemnation, and that all these had been given to her. She possessed weird ideas about evil entities and beliefs that the woods were full of goblins and sprites. Danger seemed to lurk everywhere.

She began to read and meditate on the 27th Psalm* night and morning and began to affirm many times a day: "God loves me and cares for me. I am a daughter of God and a child of Eternity." She practiced this simple affirmation doggedly and faithfully, and she found a new estimate of herself, a new blueprint of herself. With this healthy vision of herself, she is blossoming forth in Divine order.

The Road to Success

A young musician in Vienna told me of his struggle to reach what he called the top echelons of music. He said the opposition to his advancement, his poverty and lack of connections were a great handicap to him in the beginning. He had heard a lecture on the mind, however, and had begun to realize that the challenges, difficulties, impediments and delays which he had encountered had helped him to discover the powers within him. He had called on the Unseen Power, God, within him.

The odds were great against his rise, but he had kept on, repeating to himself that Infinite Intelligence opened up the way and that his sense of oneness with the Infinite would overcome all obstacles. All the challenges and setbacks had sharpened his mental and spiritual tools. His mother had had him read about

---

* See *Songs of God, An Interpretation of My Favorite Psalms*, by Dr. Joseph Murphy, De Vorss & Co., Marina del Rye, Ca., 1979.

Chopin, saying to him that his biography would give him strength. Apparently, it had given him the courage to keep on keeping on.

Chopin had been very ill and very poor, but he had had faith and confidence that there was a Power which would enable him to put the urges and dreams of his heart into manifestation. He had succeeded in composing 54 mazurkas and a great number of polonaise and many Polish songs. Infinite Spirit within him revealed the way. Though he was slowly passing on to the next dimension of life, he nevertheless fulfilled his heart's desire.

The old aphorism is still true: *"Things live by moving, and they gain strength as they go."* Paul says: *For when I am weak, then am I Strong* (II Corinthians 12:10). Give yourself wholly up to God; then nothing hinders his Power from being made perfect in you. *You are then strong . . . The Lord stood with me, and strengthened me* (II Timothy 4:17).

CHAPTER 22

HOW DOMINANT SUGGESTIONS CONTROL LESSER THOUGHTS

A woman who frequently studied astrology magazines read that the signs indicated she might have an accident. She became full of fear and in rapid succession had three accidents with her automobile in one day. The next day she fell down and cut herself severely. She burned her hand cooking.

I explained to her that the dominant idea in her mind controlled all lesser thoughts, ideas, suggestions, actions and reactions. Her dominant idea was that she would have an accident, and according to her belief it occurred.

She reversed her attitude of mind and decided to experience good fortune and Divine protection by affirming these great truths several times a day. The dominating thought of God's love watching over her and the whole armor of God enfolding her brings good fortune and determines her future.

Her belief determines her experience . . . . *Go thy way; and as thou hast believed, so be it done unto thee* . . . . (Matthew 8:13). Since it is done unto all of us according to our belief, it has nothing to do with the configuration of the stars or planets, or circumstances, conditions or events, or our genes, or any other thing on the surface of the globe. Your belief is your state of mind. Accept the truth in your mind and gain strength and confidence.

This is the prayer the "accident prone" woman used, which reversed her state of mind and brought peace to her soul: "God is all there is. One with God is a majority. *If God be for me who can be against me?* (Romans: 31). I know and believe that God is the Living Spirit Almighty—the Ever-Living One, the All-Wise One—and there is no power to challenge God. I know and accept completely that when my thoughts are God's thoughts, God's power is with my thoughts of good. I know I cannot receive what I cannot give, and I give out thoughts of love, peace, light and goodwill to this person or persons (mention name or names) and to everyone else. I am immunized and God-intoxicated, and I am always surrounded by the sacred circle of God's love. The whole Armor of God surrounds me and enfolds me. I am Divinely guided and directed, and I enter into the joy of living. . . . . *In thy presence is fullness of joy; at thy right hand there are pleasures for evermore* (Psalm 16:11)."

Mental Attitude

You have heard the Biblical expression; . . . *Thy faith hath made thee whole*. (Mark 5:34). The obvious meaning is that the power which effects the healing is resident within the individual and not in any extraneous form. Jesus proclaimed faith as the one proponent agency in the healing process. Faith is the mental attitude of the individual which releases the spiritual agencies within all of us. Many methods of healing prevail in the world today. They are varied in the many countries of the world. The only prerequisite to all of these methods is the requisite confidence on the part of the patient, and then results follow.

The Bible tells us that Jesus could not do many wonderful works among the people of his village because of their unbelief. In order for you to get positive results, it is necessary that you understand the principles involved.

Five Positions in Five Months

I gave advice to a young man one time that was afraid of life, of the future, and of people. He was fearful that no matter what position he got, the boss and the other workers would not like him and he would be fired. He suffered from insomnia, alcoholism, and melancholia. He was also irresponsible, shiftless, lazy, crude, and lacking in zeal, understanding, and application.

I explained to him that his dominant attitude of fear colored everything and that his gloomy outlook caused him to look at life from the dark or negative side. The good news he received from his family from time to time brought about only an occasional mood of cheerfulness which was drowned out in a few minutes by his dominant gloomy and depressed attitude.

At my suggestion, thing young man took a course in public speaking and another course at night school on the fundamentals of business where, with diligence, personal initiative, and application, he learned the rudiments of the commercial world. He began to pray for guidance and prosperity, claiming regularly that God was guiding him in all his ways and that he was prospered beyond his fondest dreams.

Gradually he commenced to die to the "old man" and "put on the new man." He developed enthusiasm, perseverance, stick-to-it-ive-ness, and eventually became the foreman of the shop where he worked. He became happy and joyous and began to express health, harmony and true living.

This man learned that practically all teaching, whether institutional, religious, or secular, has for its real purpose the inducement of a changed mental attitude toward life, people, and events. The first step in banishing his abnormal fear and in his onward march was correcting his attitude towards life.

God Watches

A girl who was attacked by a purse snatcher said, "God watches over me. He cares for me." Her attacker ran off. She called on her reserves and there was a response. This is a reciprocal universe; action and reaction are always and everywhere equal. In her emergency she called on the Almighty One and there was a response which set her free from the mugger.

Your whole body is made up of a confederation of intelligent cells, each of which performs its functions with an amazing intelligence according to its special duties. Your body is composed of billions of cells, and your body does not rest when you are asleep—that is an illusion. Your heart beats, you breathe regularly, digestion and assimilation go on ceaselessly, circulation of blood continues, the body perspires, hair grows, finger nails grow, etc. You might say that your body slows down, but, actually, it does not rest.

Begin every day with your thought of God and His love for you. Remember also a simple truth: The beginning of all manifestation or phenomena in this material universe is a thought or a word; and a word is a thought expressed. Your thought is first cause. God is the Creative Power in you, and the only immaterial power you know is your thought. Your thought is creative, and you are what you suggest to yourself all day long.

Control of Animals

Were it not for the law of suggestion it would be impossible for man to tame a tiger, subdue an elephant or tame a wild horse. The horse is subjective and subject to the conscious control of man. In order to be subject to man, the horse must be made to believe that man is much stronger than a horse. The horse trainer usually accomplishes this feat by the throwing the animal and holding him down until he ceases to struggle. Man can bind his legs with a rope. When man has successfully accomplished his superiority, the rest is easy, for man's suggestion of superior strength has been communicated to the subjective mind of the horse that it is useless to struggle against such power.

The subconscious mind of the horse is amenable to suggestion and control by the conscious mind of man.

The principle prevails in all encounters between man and the lower animals. Just in proportion to man's success in imparting suggestions to the animal he seeks to subdue will he succeed in rendering the animal permanently obedient and docile. Man is enabled to assert and maintain his dominion over the animal creation by virtue of the law of suggestion.

Self Preservation is the First Law of All Nature

While Speaking in Atlanta, Georgia, some months ago, a woman came to see me. During the course of the conversation, she said that a year previously two bandits had come into her store and had told her to open the safe and to hurry up. She was on crutches and she protested, pointing out that her husband would be there in a few minutes and that he usually opened the safe, because she had great difficulty bending down. One of the bandits then pointed a gun at her head and said, "I will give you thirty seconds to open the safe; if not, I will blow your head off." She threw away her crutches and opened the safe. She never used the crutches after that.

Self preservation is the first law of nature—the idea to save her life at all costs seized her mind and all the power of the Infinite flowed to that focal point of attention, bringing forth a remarkable healing. The power of God, or the Infinite Healing Presence, was within her all the time, but she had never called upon it, so it remained dormant. The Living Spirit Almighty was within her, as it is within all people. It cannot be paralyzed or crippled; and in the presence of that great shock she forgot she was crippled and released the power that moves the world.

Do Not Suggest What You Do Not Want to Happen

What Isaiah or the prophet of God says is only too true, "*Thou art wearied in the multitude of thy counsels.*" (Isaiah 47:13). He is looking for a God outside of himself; he is worshipping constantly at the shrine of the false gods. Whatever man accepts as true becomes a subjective reality. The subconscious mind of man, being absolutely impersonal, no respecter of persons and non-selective, accepts whatever man believes to be true and gives it form. The latter becomes an embodiment, an experience or condition in that man's world.

He is impressed by a suggestion that he will have an accident on the 15th of next month, and that he should avoid auto travel or train travel. This man lives in fear until the 15th; then he decides to lock himself in a room. Having impressed his subconscious with the belief in an accident, and having actuated it by fear, he knows it now must come to pass. He cannot escape. Something happens—he slips in the bathroom and hurts himself or he cuts his hand with a knife—perhaps a fire breaks out; something *must* happen.

Now, if man knows the Law of life and the Truth of Being—that *"I and the Father are one"* and that *"whatsoever ye shall ask in prayer, believing, ye shall receive,"* (Matthew 21:22)—this man will shape and mould his own destiny. He will laugh at all dire predictions because he knows his consciousness to be God. What he feels as true of himself must come to pass. Not liking what he has heard, he says to him, "How would I feel were the opposite true?" Then he enters into the spirit of it—gets into the mood that all things are possible to him who believes—enters into the conviction that it is so, and thrills to it. This man has actualized a new state subjectively and this must come to pass.

If a man believes that he must get hay fever this year, as he always has in the past, let him dispel all such beliefs in powers apart form himself. Let him turn his attention to the God within—yes, turn inward, towards the Real. *This is the internalization of consciousness.* In this state let him dwell in the feeling of perfect health—enter into the spirit or mood of being healed—and he will express health.

Your Assumptions Become Facts

During a recent conversation with an English army officer, he pointed out Adolf Hitler, at the time of armistice at the close of the First World War, was a prisoner. He refused to accept the fact that Germany was beaten, however. He went blind for a period of six weeks or longer, but it was a psychological blindness—no organic reasons could be found.

In the dark silence in which he existed he embodied the ideal of the German people at that time, which has a desire for vengeance or to get even, because of the wrongs they felt had been inflicted on them due to the Versailles Treaty. His assumption of that attitude made an impression on his subconscious mind, which responded accordingly. His name was Schickelgruber while a prisoner. When released, he became Hitler, and he no longer responded to Schickelgruber. He awoke a different man, having a new concept of him.

You also can use your subconscious for good or ill. It is all things to all men. Assume that you are illumined, noble and Godlike. As you keep up that attitude of mind, it will gel within you and your assumption will crystallize into a fact ... *When deep sleep falleth upon men, in slumbering upon the bed; then he opened the ears of men and healeth their instruction* (Job 33:15-16). Ofttimes man is instructed what to do during sleep time. For example, suppose you are seeking an answer to a perplexing problem. You could say to your deeper mind prior to sleep: "I seek the answers or solution to this problem." Then condense the sentence down to one word, "Answer," and repeat slowly. In other words, lull yourself to sleep with one word, "answer," and you will receive the solution wither in a dream vision of the night, or as a flash of illumination as you awaken in the morning.

It is said that the Russian General Cynarsky during the Napoleonic Wars paid no attention to the advice of his associates on the General Staff, who were mapping a strategy. He went to sleep contemplating only one thing—victory. He saw the end and snored while his associates discussed plans. He had his plan, and impregnated his subconscious mind with the idea of victory. He did not want to be swayed. Cynarsky undoubtedly knew that the conscious mind is inductive, i.e., it reasons from premise such as $2 + 2 = 4$, and it deuced the results from this. It bases its findings on factual evidence and reason, regarding the future or the probable. The subconscious mind is deductive only. It takes all impression given it as facts. It is wholly impersonal. It accepts the idea as existing now and acts accordingly, his conviction of victory impressed his subconscious mind and consequently it came to pass.

Your conscious mind is sometimes called the father; the subconscious the mother.

Upon this I awakened, and behold; and my sleep was sweet unto me. (Jeremiah 31:26).

Relaxed

A young woman with a wonderful voice tried to get a position singing on the radio or television but failed. She tried too hard and was overly anxious, tense and worried, which blocked her good. At my suggestion, prior to sleep she began to relax her entire body by closing her eyes and talking to herself this way: "My feet are relaxed, my ankles are relaxed, my toes are relaxed, my abdominal muscles are relaxed, my heart and lungs are relaxed, my spine is relaxed, my neck is relaxed, my face is relaxed. I am completely relaxed and at peace."

She repeated these suggestions four or five times, while knowing that the body and mind had to obey her. She said, "I felt very sleepy, completely relaxed and non-resistant., I heard the clock tick, the baby snoring, but I had no desire to move or do anything. In that sleepy state I affirmed: "I am a singer on TV now. It's wonderful!' having framed the sentence, I shortened it to one word, 'TV,' over and over again and lulled myself to sleep with one word, 'TV.' The next morning my agent called me saying he had a spot for me. My prayer was answered."

The above illustration is a very simple way of conveying the idea of desire of your heart to your subconscious mind.

Chapter 23

EXPERIENCE GOOD FORTUNE AND PEACE OF MIND THROUGH THE POWER OF SUGGESTION

It is very strange how people expect to get ahead in life, be happy and healthy, without organizing their mental faculties or even knowing anything about them. You would not operate an automobile if you had no experience, neither would you operate a chemical laboratory if you knew nothing about chemistry. Thinking is a process as real and as definite as the making of sodium hydroxide or bicarbonate of soda. You think with your own mind, and you can make wonderful mental combinations which will transform your life. Thoughts are things, and *as a man thinketh in his heart, so is he.*

Whatever you focus on and give your attention to, your subconscious magnifies and multiplies. Focus your mental lens on Divine right action, Divine law and order, Divine Beauty and Divine love. Then you will discover all these qualities of God are manifested in your life. As you continue along these lines you will be actively turning your eyes to the hills from whence cometh your help.

Thou wilt keep him in perfect peace, whose mind is stayed on thee . . . (Isaiah 26:3). *I will both lay me down in peace, and sleep: for thou, Lord, only makest me dwell in safety* (Psalm 4:8). Remember, it is not pills or capsules or other people that give you peace and tranquility, but rather, your contemplation of the truths of God from the highest standpoint. You become what you contemplate, and as you contemplate the eternal verities, you will find rest in mind and body. Peace of mind and good fortune will follow you all the days of your life.

Invest Wisely

Do not waste your energy. Watch the expenditure of your thought by seeing to it that all your thoughts are invested wisely. Remember that the law of parsimony must prevail in your mind, and you must economize in your mental assumptions. You must assume that God is and that He answers you.

Recently I talked with a man who had been experiencing an acute business problem. He needed a loan from the bank to tide him over for some moths, but due to recent restrictions he was turned down. He was very tense and anxious. He also understood that these negative emotions would generate the reverse of what he was praying for.

I suggested that he go to the Source of all blessings—namely, the Infinite spirit within him—and affirm the great eternal truths to bring his mind to a state of peace and rest. I suggested that he detach his mind from the problem and assume an attitude of Divine indifference, which means that it is impossible for your prayer to fail. Infinite Intelligence knows only the answer.

I suggested also that he reiterate the following age-old truths, realizing that when his mind was at peace, the answer would come. Accordingly, he meditated on the following scriptural verses several times a day, and when fear thoughts came to him, he would immediately quote one of the verses to himself:

— *In quietness and in confidence shall be your strength* . . . (Isaiah 30:15).
— *. . . Before they call, I will answer; and while they are yet speaking, I will hear* (Isaiah 65:24).
— *. . . According to your faith be it unto you* (Matthew 9:29).
— *. . . If thou canst believe, all things are possible to him that believeth* (Mark 9:23).
— *He shall call upon me, and I will answer him: I will be with him in trouble; I will deliver him, and honor him* (Psalm 91:15).
— *All things are ready if the mind were so* (Shakespeare).
— *The Lord is my light and my salvation; whom shall I fear?* . . . (Psalm 27:1).

He remained faithful to his meditation, and one of his customers, to whom he had previously mentioned his predicament, suddenly came to him and generously advanced him far more money than he needed and his problem was solved. When he established a Divine indifference to results, the answer came. Contemplating these statements of the Law of Life frequently, he succeeded in building into his mentality a state of peace and equilibrium.

The Psalmist expressed it this way: *But his delight is in the law of the Lord; and in his law doth he meditate day and night* (Psalm 1:2). You induce a quiet, receptive mind as you reflect on the great truths, and you then will dramatize the answer more quickly.

Positive Suggestion

A young college student came to see me and told me that the girl to whom he had been engaged and was about to marry had been killed in one of the recent air crashes. He was failing in his studies and was depressed, dejected and suffering from melancholia. At the same time he was taking tranquilizers, but when the effect wore off, he was right back where he started.

I suggested to him that he must not let these negative emotions gel and crystallize in his subconscious mind, which would cause a very negative subconscious complex with harmful results. I explained to him that an expert motorist here in Leisure World had had a crackup while going 90 miles an hour. He had not been seriously injured, and while the Automobile Club truck was towing his car to the repair shop, he immediately called a taxi and drove around for about an hour or more, the reason being that he wanted to prevent that experience from forming a negative pattern in his subconscious. He did not want to develop a fear complex.

This young man began to realize that everyone eventually passes on to the next dimension and that his gloom and despondency were not helping his sweetheart in the next dimension of life, but were actually holding her back. He decided to loose her and let her go, affirming whenever he thought of her, "God gives you peace and harmony."

He then redirected his mind to his studies and began to keep his mind tuned in to the Infinite Presence and Power, reflecting frequently on Divine guidance, peace and harmony. Following this procedure, his negative emotions were dissolved in the light of Divine love.

Their Negative Thoughts Boomeranged

. . . For the prince of this world cometh, and hath nothing in me (John 14:30). A young college girl in a nearby university, who has read several of my books, including Songs of God, said to me that she had belonged to a certain cult and had since dropped the association when she realized that it was all balderdash. The other three members had told her that they would pour imprecations upon her and that she would suffer.

She new that the prince of the world is fear and that there intention was to instill fear and terror into her mind, a sort of hypnotic suggestion. She read the inner meaning of the 91st Psalm and reiterated many passages during the day. Whenever the memory of their threat came into her mind, she would immediately affirm, "God loves me and cares for me."

She knew that if she could not give hate, she could not receive it. All she did was blessing them and walk on, laughing at their dire predictions, knowing full well that they were negative suggestions, which she refused to accept. Of course, the negative thoughts of her former friends boomeranged and were returned to them. All three, she told me, were subsequently killed in an auto crash.

The prince of this world (fear) had come to her and had found nothing in her to correspond to that fear. She knew the Law of Life. She had enthroned in her mind peace, harmony, right action and Divine love. The truths of the 91st Psalm had penetrated her subconscious and she walked with God, finding ways of pleasantness and paths of peace.

The Psalm of Protection (Psalm 91)

He that dwelleth in the secret place of the most high shall abide under the shadow of the Almighty.

I will say of the Lord, He is my refuge and my fortes: my God; in him will I trust.

Surely he shall deliver thee from the snare of the fowler, and from the noisome pestilence.

He shall cover thee with his feathers, and under his wings shalt thou trust: his truth shall be thy shield and buckler.

Thou shalt not be afraid for the terror by night; or for the arrow that flieth by day;

Nor for the pestilence that walked in darkness; nor for the destruction that wasted at noonday.

A thousand shall fall at thy side, and ten thousand at thy right hand; but it shall not come nigh thee.

Only with thine eyes shalt thou behold and see the reward of the wicked.

Because thou hast made the Lord, which is my refuge, even the most High, thy habitation;

There shall no evil befall thee, neither shall any plague come nigh thy dwelling.

For he shall give his angels charge over thee, to keep thee in all thy ways.

They shall bear thee up in their hands, lest thou dash thy foot against a stone.

Thou shalt tread upon the lion and adder: the young lion and the dragon shalt thou trample under feet.

Because he hath set his love upon me, therefore will I deliver him: I will set him on high, because he hath known my name.

He shall call upon me, and I will answer him: I will be with him in trouble; I will deliver him, and honor him.
With long life will I satisfy him, and show him my salvation.

She Rejected Their Suggestion

It might be true to say that fear comes to everyone at some time, somewhere, in some way. The writer remembers that many years ago, while flying over the North Pole on the way to Norway and Sweden, a great storm had taken place. All of the passengers had been terrified. A few of us had begun to recite the 91st Psalm out loud, which had quieted them to some degree. They were afraid of death and destruction that had been the only way to handle that group fear that had seized all of us.

Fear is contagious. Love is contagious, also. All of us must understand that no influence or suggestion from the external world can ever affect us unless it finds kinship with something inside of us. The girl previously referred to who had been threatened with a voodoo curse had rejected their suggestion because she knew it could not affect her unless she accepted it; and then it would be simply a movement of her own mind. This suggestion had found no home, no acceptance; therefore, it could not function and its force was dissipated.

As you continue to grow spiritually by absorbing and imbibing the great truths of life, you will be convinced that what the Psalmist said is true: *A thousand shall fall at thy side, and ten thousand at thy right hand; but it shall not come nigh thee* (Psalm (91:7). In verses 9 and 10 of the same Psalm, we read: *Because thou has made the Lord, which is my refuge, even the most high, thy habitation; there shall no evil befall thee, neither shall any plague come nigh thy dwelling.* This is a very beautiful and definite promise. It points out that you will always be protected, directed and watched over by the spell of God's love. By pondering frequently the fact that God loves you and cares for you, guides you and directs you, you are making the most High your habitation. Because you constantly remind yourself that God's love surrounds you, enfolds you and enwraps you, you are always immersed in the Holy Omnipresence and no trouble can touch you.

What You Wish For Others Comes Into Your Own Experiences

In the fifth chapter of Matthew, verse 5, we read: Blessed are the meek: for they shall inherit the earth. This does not mean that you should feel that you are a worm in the dust. If you do, everybody is going to step on you. Earth means manifestation, your body, home, business, social status and all phases of your life. To inherit the earth means you have dominion over all your external conditions.

In Biblical language the word "meek" refers to teach ability and open mindedness, faith in God and all things good. This is the key to success. Free your mind from stubbornness and the stiff-necked attitude of mind and let in the sunshine of God's love. When you pray, relax, let go and free your mind of resentment, pugnacity and ill will and wish for everyone all the blessings of life. What you wish for others comes into your own experiences.

Building a Glorious Future

Go to work in your thoughts, tune in on the Infinite One, and affirm boldly, "I am compassed about with songs of deliverance." Almighty God is within you. You are equipped to lead a glorious and wonderful life, for all the power of God is available to you. You should release His wisdom, power, and glory in your life.

If you don't use your muscles, they will inevitably atrophy. You have mental and spiritual "muscles" which must be exercised, also. If your thoughts, attitudes, motivations, and reactions are not God-like your contact with God is broken, and you become depressed, rejected, fearful, morose, and morbid.

Look within. *"The kingdom of God is within you."* God's power, wisdom, and strength to meet any and all challenges are within you. In the Book of Daniel (Ch. 11 v.32), you will read, *"The people that do know their God shall be strong, and do exploits."*

"Behold, I am the Lord, the God of all flesh: Is there any thing too hard for me?"

Jeremiah 32:27

The Greatest Formula of All

> *I know that the God in the other is the same God in me, and therefore if I hurt the other I would be hurting myself and that would be foolish. Knowing this I practice the greatest formula of all. I bless and exalt the good in the other. I make it a point to advance his interests and I know as I do I am advancing my own. I know that the ship which comes home to my brother comes home to me.*

Practice the above formula and you will like yourself more. You will see sermons in stones, tongues in trees, songs in running brooks, and God in everything, including your fellow men.